In Full Swing 1re

B1 ▸ B2

Annie Coghlan
Professeur
Université Paris Nanterre

Bernard Moro
Professeur
Académie de Grenoble

Mélanie Herment
Professeur, formatrice
Académie de Paris

Jérémy Corbé
Professeur
Académie de Rennes

Cindy Mathieu
Professeur
Académie de Versailles

Mark Wallace
Professeur
Académie de Paris

James Walters
Professeur
Académie de Besançon

Anne Menenteau
Professeur, formatrice
Académie de Créteil

Frédéric Davignon
Professeur, formateur
Académie de Montpellier

Cadrage pédagogique
Mélanie Herment

Précis grammatical
Sandrine Oriez
Maître de conférences
en linguistique anglaise
Université Rennes 2

didier

Remerciements

Les auteurs et l'éditeur remercient très chaleureusement Mathieu Chadefaux et Réjane Lorre, relecteurs critiques, pour leurs précieux conseils.
Ils remercient également tous les collègues formateurs et les enseignants rencontrés pour la richesse de leur réflexion sur l'enseignement des langues vivantes, ainsi que les collègues qui ont accepté de tester avec leurs élèves les chapitres de ce manuel.
Enfin, ils remercient chaleureusement les élèves britanniques de la Highgate School à Londres qui ont contribué, par leurs témoignages, à donner au projet son identité culturelle.

Edition : Rebecca Govin
Responsable éditoriale : Catherine Laurent
Conception de la couverture : Nicolas Piroux
Conception maquette intérieure : Primo&Primo
Mise en page et adaptation : Isabelle Aubourg, Danielle Mourain
Iconographie : Jade Vincent, Maria Mora
Cartes, schémas et illustrations : Stephen Collins, Johanna Crainmark, Antoine Levesque, Ulla Puggard, Mandy Norman, Jackie Parsons, Simon Spilsbury, Ahoy There, Patswerk
Photogravure : RVB photogravure

PAPIER À BASE DE FIBRES CERTIFIÉES

éditions didier s'engagent pour l'environnement en réduisant l'empreinte carbone de leurs livre Celle de cet exemplaire est de :
1,2 kg éq. CO_2
Rendez-vous sur www.editionsdidier-durable.fr

Achevé d'imprimer en avril 2019 en Italie par L.E.G.O. S.p.a. (Lavis)

Bienvenue en 1re

Et bienvenue dans *In Full Swing*!

14 chapitres pour…

Le monde bouge et se réinvente. Participez aux débats, exprimez-vous, créez… en anglais !

Découvrir et s'interroger

Les pays anglophones nous étonnent par leurs spécificités : où se situe la frontière entre vie publique et vie privée aux États-Unis ? Pourquoi les classes sociales occupent-elles une place si importante au Royaume-Uni ? Ces pays sont souvent à la pointe des débats sur la société de demain : intelligence artificielle, activisme sur les réseaux sociaux, *fake news*…
Slogans percutants, humour, poésie… la langue anglaise donne à toutes ces questions une saveur particulière !

S'impliquer dans des projets

Collaborer à un blog de critiques de films, imaginer un dialogue avec une intelligence artificielle, défendre une cause sur les réseaux sociaux… autant d'occasions de prendre la parole et d'agir !

Progresser en anglais

Chacun à votre rythme ! Les nombreux outils de la collection sont là pour vous aider : fiches *Work your way* du site compagnon, ressources en langue du manuel, exercices interactifs sur la plateforme…

Préparer le bac

De la méthodologie et des entraînements pour être prêt et confiant le jour des épreuves.

Nous vous souhaitons une très bonne année de 1re… *in full swing* !

Les auteurs

SOMMAIRE

14 chapitres pour explorer la thématique...

GESTES FONDATEURS ET MONDES EN MOUVEMENT

Audios et vidéos	Langue & méthode	Tâches
Audios • Michael O'Neil (English language specialist) on "the magical powers of English" • *These Boots are made for walkin'* (song) • *How to create amazing slogans* • *Verb Your Enthusiasm*, Brian Bilston (poem) **Vidéos** • History of the English language, Video Rouse	**Grammaire** • Les déterminants • Le lien entre deux verbes **Lexique** • Les mots et leurs qualités • La publicité, la poésie et la musique • Les formes contractées dans la langue orale **How to** boost your listening skills	**Training tasks** Play with words (tweets, verbing, portmanteau words) Present a song with great rhythm Create a slogan Take part in the "World Cup for languaging weirdly" **Final task** English Language Day! Create the class's glossary Act out a scene Create a slogan for a wristband Write and perform a poem **ÉVALUATIONS**
Audios • Annie talks about euphemisms • 6-word sentences **Vidéo** • Extract from a speech given by Donald Trump	**Grammaire** • La dérivation • Les *phrasal verbs* **Lexique** • Le discours politique et ses effets	**Training tasks** Analyse Newspeak words and create new ones 6-word challenge! Create euphemisms to talk about situations at school **Final task** Watch an extract from a speech and write about it Create a piece of artwork to illustrate "the power of words" **ÉVALUATIONS**
Audios • *Censorship on social media*, NPR **Vidéos** • *Unpresidented*, The Washington Post • *The news story that panicked a city* • *Facebook's new fact-checking feature*, Facebook website • Media literacy classes in the USA	**Grammaire** • Exprimer une opinion • Les dénombrables et les indénombrables **Lexique** • Les acteurs de l'information et leur public • La désinformation et les moyens de la démasquer **Prononciation** • Les verbes de deux syllabes • *Should, would, ought to* **How to** take part in a debate	**Training tasks** Fact or fake? Check a story on a fact-checking website Debate: Should social media be regulated? Check your fake-news spotting skills **Final task** Create a hoax to raise awareness about a cause Debate about fake news **ÉVALUATIONS**

SOMMAIRE

Axe et thématique | Textes et images

How do TV series handle reality?

Fictions et réalités

This is Us, Downton Abbey, Black Mirror, The Crown... Que disent les séries TV de notre passé, de notre présent ou de notre avenir ? Ce qu'elles nous montrent correspond-il à la réalité ?

Ancrage culturel

Des séries culte britanniques et américaines et ce qu'elles disent de ces pays

Textes

- *Testimony of an Instagram star*, buzzfeed.com
- *Tripadvisor, why did you ruin my life?* tripadvisor-warning.com
- *Why we get emotionally attached to TV shows*, theodysseyonline.com
- Comments about *This is us*
- *Downton Abbey: The true story of servants*, The Daily Express

Images

- Stills from TV series
- Real life servants in the UK

CHAPITRE FLASH

How can young people use the Internet to make their voices heard?

Citoyenneté et mondes virtuels

La génération #never again s'est emparée des réseaux sociaux pour faire entendre sa voix et changer la société : récit d'un engagement et d'un combat par ceux qui l'ont mené.

Ancrage culturel

Le débat constitutionnel et citoyen autour des armes à feu aux États-Unis

Textes

- *"How it all began"*, Cameron Kasky (extract from *Glimmer of Hope: How Tragedy Sparked a Movement*, March for Our Lives)

Images

- Pictures from the #neveragain movement

To what extent are guns embedded in American culture?

Territoire et mémoire

Cinéma, musique, langage courant... Aux États-Unis, les armes font feu de tout bois. Une « love story » qui remonte à la conquête du territoire.

Ancrage culturel

- La place des armes dans la vie quotidienne
- Le second amendement
- La conquête du territoire américain
- La NRA et le rôle des lobbies

Textes

- *Gun Love*, Jennifer Clement
- The Second Amendment (law)
- Extract from Donald Trump's speech at the NRA convention, May 2018

Images

- Movie posters and video game covers
- Paintings about landmarks events in American history
- *The NRA doubles down* (infographic)

How much power should we give to AI?

Innovations scientifiques et responsabilité

Au pays des GAFA, questions et débats sur la place à donner à l'intelligence artificielle et les responsabilités de chacun.

Ancrage culturel

- Les GAFA
- Le rôle de la science-fiction anglophone pour questionner la société
- *AI, the new frontier?*

Textes

- *Demon Seed*, Dean R. Koontz
- *Ex Machina*, Alex Garland (script)
- *Amazon's Alexa recorded private conversation*, The Guardian
- *Alexa, what is there to know about love?*, Brian Bilston (poem)

Images

- Pictures of next generation robots
- *What a virtual assistant can do*
- Stills from the films *Her* and *Ex Machina*

Audios et vidéos	Langue & méthode	Tâches
Audios • Annie & Mark talk about TV series • An interview with Charlie Brooker, author of *Black Mirror* **Vidéos** • The Coffee Shop scene, extract from the series *Black Mirror* (*Nosedive* episode) • Extracts from the series *This is us* • Trailer of the series *The Crown*	**Grammaire** • Le discours indirect • Les pronoms relatifs **Lexique** • La fiction et l'audiovisuel • Les genres • Les téléspectateurs **Prononciation** • Les diphtongues • Les mots en *-ic* • Accentuation et intonation pour exprimer son opinion	**Training tasks** Write a dialogue and act it out Give your opinion about a TV series Write a diary entry **Final tasks** Pitch a TV series about teenagers The producers of *Black Mirror* are looking for new ideas! Record your worst 'digital nightmare'! ÉVALUATIONS
Vidéos • Alex Wind's speech, Washington D.C., March 24th, 2018	**Grammaire** • Le récit au passé • *Be going* + *to* + BV **Lexique** • L'activisme sur les réseaux sociaux : participants, actions et médias	**Final tasks** Join the movement! Write a review of Kasky's *"How it all began"* narrative Share your favourite passage Send a message to the *March for our Lives* students Present your favourite quotes Act out an interview with Cameron Kasky ÉVALUATIONS
Audios • Mark talks about gun culture in the USA • The history of guns in the USA (audioguide) **Vidéos** • Promotional film for the NRA	**Grammaire** • L'expression du but • L'expression du contraste **Lexique** • Les armes à feux et leurs propriétaires • La culture des armes et les lobbys **Prononciation** • Les sons /ʊ/ et /uː/ • L'accent de mot **How to** get better at speaking	**Training tasks** Post a review for a movie or a video game Design and present a book cover Make up the caption of a picture for an exhibition **Final tasks** Record a story for an art project Write a new passage for *Gun Love* ÉVALUATIONS
Audios • Mark's commentary • AI weapons **Vidéos** • *Next Generation Robots* • Deep sea exploration • *Emma: a Customer Assistant* • Driverless Cars • Trailer of the film *Her* • *Amazon's Alexa*, cnet news • Trailer of the film *Ex Machina* • *Sophia* on Tonight Showbotics	**Grammaire** • Envisager l'avenir • Les énoncés interrogatifs **Lexique** • L'intelligence artificielle : les perspectives et les menaces • Opinions et sentiments **Prononciation** • Suffixe et accentuation • L'intonation dans les questions **How to** write a dialogue	**Training tasks** Share an anecdote about AI Chat with a virtual assistant Record a questionnaire Call customer service Write a script **Final tasks** A scene involving a human & an AI Debate: "Should AI robots be granted rights?" ÉVALUATIONS

SOMMAIRE

Audios et vidéos	Langue & méthode	Tâches
Audios • Understanding the British class system • Chav stereotypes: funny or offensive? • Supermarkets and the class system • Grime: working-class music, middle-class fans? **Vidéos** • *The Class Sketch*, The Monty Python • *#shoppingproblems*, BBC Comedy • *Posh Mum* (TV shows) • *"Accentism"*, RT London • J. McAvoy about "The Class Ceiling"	**Grammaire** • Le comparatif • Le superlatif **Lexique** • Les marqueurs sociaux • La mobilité sociale • Sentiments et opinions **Prononciation** • Sons voyelles • Le lien entre deux sons consonnes • Le comparatif	**Training tasks** Write a #middleclassproblem tweet *Posh Mum:* write or tell a story! Give your opinion on a radio show Present a collage about social markers Bring a scene to life **Final tasks** Create a parody news report Write a short anecdote about social classes ÉVALUATIONS
Vidéos • *I, Daniel Blake* (trailer and extracts) • Ken Loach's speech at the BAFTA ceremony, 2017 • Jeremy Corbyn during Prime Minister's Questions	**Grammaire** • La structure causative • La proposition infinitive • Exprimer la quantité **Lexique** • La justice et l'injustice sociale • La politique et le pouvoir • L'emploi et le chômage	**Training tasks** Has Ken Loach reached his goal? Discuss. Write a memo about Ken Loach's speech React to a post **Final tasks** Should *I, Daniel Blake* be selected for an award? Discuss with the jury Promote the film for a festival ÉVALUATIONS
Audios • Mark talks about immigration issues in the USA • Mark's comment on the Ancestry map • An interview with María Rocha, NPR **Vidéos** • *Illegal* (short film) • Trailer of the film *Documented* • Barack Obama's speech, 2013 • *What is DACA?*, CNN	**Grammaire** • La voix passive • L'hypothèse **Lexique** • La situation des migrants aux États-Unis • Les motivations et les sentiments • La mobilisation **Prononciation** • Les sons /ɑː/ et /eɪ/ • Les chiffres **How to** listen and take notes	**Training tasks** Be a reporter American icons: guessing game Comment on a picture **Final tasks** Create and present a magazine cover Write a speech ÉVALUATIONS
Audios • *Dirty Laundry*, Don Henley (song) **Vidéos** • Trailer of the film *The Scarlet Letter* • Apple and the right to privacy	**Grammaire** • Possibilité, permission, obligation • Les adverbes **Lexique** • La vie privée : aspects, attitudes et sentiments • Les atteintes à la vie privée **Prononciation** • Les noms, les adjectifs et les verbes de deux syllabes • Les adverbes **How to** read a literary text	**Training tasks** Write and act out a dialogue Create a newspaper front page Post a comment on Apple's website Write a tip about privacy **Final tasks** A survival guide for international students Defend your right to privacy! ÉVALUATIONS

SOMMAIRE

Audios et vidéos	Langue & méthode	Tâches
Vidéos • *Have you ever dreamed of flying in your car?* BBC • *Star Trek gadgets that now exist,* BuzzFeed • *Barack Obama on the true meaning of Star Trek*, Wired	**Grammaire** • Le superlatif • La possibilité • L'évocation de l'avenir **Lexique** • Le progrès scientifique et les inventions • La fiction et les super-pouvoirs **Prononciation** • Les formes faibles • Les noms composés **How to** write an essay	**Training tasks** Write an email to Michio Kaku Shoot a video clip about a gadget from *Star Trek* Write a new scene for *The Invisible Man* Create and present a piece of art in the manner of Liu Bolin **Final tasks** Contribute to *Physics of the Impossible*: write a text about a scientific "impossibility" Tell the world about a new technology! ÉVALUATIONS
Vidéos • *Discover a Detroit's landmark* • *The Golden Era* • Motown • *The 1967 riots* • *The Detroit Mower Gang* • *Letter to Detroit, Eminem*	**Grammaire** • Prétérit vs *Present Perfect* • *For, since, ago* **Lexique** • Le paysage urbain • L'ambiance de la ville et ses habitants • Le déclin et la renaissance **Prononciation** • Le déplacement d'accent • *Slam poetry*	**Training tasks** Create a Detroit Motown playlist Create a timeline Record the voice over for a video **Final tasks** Prepare a presentation to attract new businesses to Detroit Write a letter to a city ÉVALUATIONS
		Final tasks Fool your friends! Write a story and share it with your classmates. Have them guess if it's true or false!

1

THE MAGIC OF ENGLISH

REACT

1. **Look at the picture.**
   a. Can you link the words produced by the wand with the title "the Magic of English"?
   b. Is there anything you particularly like about the English language?
2. **Listen to Michael O'Neil.** IFS1002
   Had you ever thought about the "power" he mentions? What do you think about it?

Micheal O'Neil, English language specialist, will be your guide and take you, step by step, through the different "magical powers" of English!

AUDIO
The great attraction of the English language

Power 1
Simplicity

DEBRIEF

What could explain the success of the English language throughout the world?

1 The powers of English

Power 2 Brevity

1 a. Look at documents A and B.
Message A consists of 5 words. Translate it into French. How many words are needed? Do the same with message B. What do you conclude? → **YP 21**

b. Listen to Micheal O'Neil and check.
What other examples of "brevity" does he give? Can you think of others? IFS1003

A

⇅ Trisha Tarr retweeted

patricia smart • 13h

First time voting. Feeling proud.

B

New York Times 1h

Hugo Boss is reissuing the white suit that it created for Micheal Jackson's 1982 blockbuster album "Thriller"

Micheal Jackson's 'Thriller' Suit is Back

AUDIO Michael O'Neil 1

YOUR TURN

Write a tweet IN PAIRS

- Think of an event.
  sports | politics | entertainment
- Talk about it to a friend who will write a tweet about it. Then swap roles.

Power 3 Creativity

Verbing

1 Read the cartoon. ▲

a. How many examples of verbing can you find?

b. Use "access" in two sentences: first as a noun, then as a verb.

c. Can we do the same in French?
What does it show about the English language?

YOUR TURN

Verb a famous person!

SHE SPENT THE NIGHT LADY GAGAING.

- Choose a celebrity and "verb" their name.
  Use the verb you have created in a sentence.
- Have the class guess what you mean.

Portmanteau words

2 Look at the picture. ▶
It contains an example of a "portmanteau word".
a. What do you think it means?
b. Try to explain what a portmanteau word is.

3 Listen to Michael O'Neil. IFS1004
a. Check your definition.
b. Pick out two examples and write them down:
- in their portmanteau form
- as two separate words

AUDIO Michael O'Neil 2

YOUR TURN

Fantabulous!
- Invent two portmanteau words.
- Have the class guess their meanings.

Power 4 Diversity

> *"Personally, I would be highly suspicious of anybody who could converse with snakes, as serpents are often used in the worst kinds of Dark Magic, and are historically associated with evil-doers."*
>
> J.K. Rowling, *Harry Potter*

1 Read the quote.
What words helped you understand it? What is their origin? Any idea why they are so frequent in English?

2 Watch the video and check. IFS1005

VIDEO The history of the English language

Power 5 Musicality

The **O**rigin of this **WORD** is **INT**eresting
■ ■ ■
L'origine de ce mot est intéressante.

AUDIO Michael O'Neil 3

1 Listen to these sentences. ▲ IFS1006
Pay attention to:
- the word stress
- the rhythm

What do you notice?

2 Listen to Michael O'Neil to find an explanation.
IFS1007

DEBRIEF For you, which power contributes most to the "magic of English"?

And now discover artistic ways of using these powers!

2 It's got rhythm...

AUDIO
Listen to the song!

These boots are made for walkin'

You keep sayin' you've got somethin' for me
Somethin' you call love, but confess
You've been a-messin' where you shouldn'ta been a-messin'
And now someone else is gettin' all your best

CHORUS
These boots are made for walkin'
And that's just what they'll do
One of these days these boots are gonna
Walk all over you. Yeah.

You keep lyin' when you oughta be truthin'
And you keep losin' when you oughta not bet
You keep samin' when you oughta be a-changin'
Now what's right is right, but you ain't been right yet.

CHORUS
You keep playin' where you shouldn't be playin'
And you keep thinkin' that you'll never get burnt, ha!
I've just found me a brand new box of matches, yeah
And what he knows, you ain't had time to learn

CHORUS
Are you ready boots? Start walkin'!

Written by
Lee Hazlewood
and recorded by
Nancy Sinatra (1966)

1 Listen to the song, concentrating on the rhythm. e IFS1008

a. Tap your desk regularly each time you hear a stressed syllable. What do you notice about words such as "boots" and "walk"?
→ YP 2a

b. Focus on verse 1. How many "beats" are there in each line? What about the chorus?

c. Which words carry the "beats" in the other verses? What can you say about these words?

2 Now focus on the typically English transformations highlighted in pink and green.

a. Explain how they are constructed.

b. What is the effect produced? → YP 28

c. Discover the section below to learn more.

3 Listen to the song again, focusing on the lyrics.

a. Explain:

- the romantic situation of the singer
- the role played by the boots

b. Would you say the rhythm reflects the meaning of the song? How?

Changing the language to keep the rhythm

- Listen to the recording. e IFS1009
- Use it to comment on the following examples:

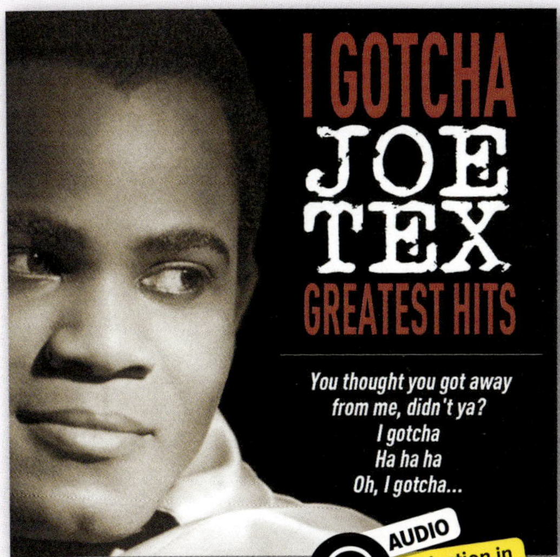

AUDIO Reduction in oral English

DO YOU WANNA COME?

NO THANKS. I'VE GOTTA GO.

YOUR TURN

Beat it!

- Find a song in English which you think has great rhythm.
- Present it in class explaining how the rhythm serves the meaning.

HAVE YOUR CLASSMATES DRUM THE BEAT!

3 It sells

1 **Read the slogans.**
Which ones do you know?
Say what brand or product they advertise.

2 **Choose your two favourite slogans.**

a. Analyze them. Do you understand the reasons for their success?

b. Share with the class. → **YP 21, 25**

3 **Recap.** All together list your "golden rules" for a good slogan.

4 ***IN GROUPS*** **a.** Discover more about what makes a great slogan.

b. Compare your findings with the other groups'.

GROUP 1

AUDIO How to create amazing slogans

- **Listen to the recording.** IFS1010

  a. Do the slogans above respect the advice given?

  b. Complete your own "golden rules" if necessary.

‘The Real Thing’?
The language of advertising slogans

Love them or hate them, stand aloof from them or engage with them, claim immunity from their persuasions or celebrate their memorability, there is no denying that the language of advertising slogans is pervasive[1], influential and ubiquitous[2]. It is estimated that the average western consumer is subject to 5,000 daily advertising messages across all forms of media. This makes it the most universal of creative literary forms.

What is the purpose of the advertising slogan? A clue lies in the etymology of the word advertise itself – which has its root in the Latin verb ‘advertere’ – to turn towards. Slogans are a way of capturing the attention and taking the attention onwards to a predetermined destination.

It was not always so. Advertising’s early words and images were simply to convey information: to describe products, how they worked, what they did, and their availability. Its modern role as an instrument of persuasion, as a literary form to convey meaning and significance, came later in the 20th century.

To keep the consumer ‘turning towards’ the desired destination, the advertising slogan has to first of all grab attention. Then it must embed[3] itself in the memory.

To state the obvious, advertising words must be memorable. To be memorable, the words, phrases, and slogans must be repeated. (Even the word used for the basic text of an advertising message – copy – connotes replication and reproduction). To be recalled and repeated, to be passed along to others, to be used and reused, is the ultimate destination – the golden journey of an advertising slogan passing from the advertisers’ creative notebook to the nirvana of becoming a popular expression. Take ‘the customer is always right’ for a neat example of something that began life as an advertising slogan for Selfridges Store in 1910 and now is ingrained in the shopper’s lexicon.

It is essential in a noisy and crowded world that a slogan stands out. Take the Apple slogan of the 1990s ‘Think Different’ – which used the adjective “different” rather than the expected (and more grammatically correct) adverb “differently”. To be memorable the phrase and the image that goes with it must be differentiated.

The word form of the slogan enables memorability.

Charles Doyle, *Oxford Dictionaries – Language Matters* (20th October, 2011)

1. impossible to avoid **2.** omnipresent **3.** fix

GROUP 2

- **Focus on the text above.**
  Read only the first sentence of each paragraph. Do you understand what this text is about?
- **Read the whole text.**
  a. Can you find points in common with your list of “golden rules”?
  b. What new information does the text contain?
- **Focus on the Selfridges’ slogan (l. 24-25)**
  a. Explain why it is quoted here.
  b. Can you think of similar examples?

DEBRIEF

Is the English language particularly suited to writing advertising slogans? Explain, giving concrete examples.

YOUR TURN

Advertise it!

Create a slogan for:

a place | a thing | a celebrity | ...

4 It "funs"! ☺

Verb Your Enthusiasm

I remember when it first circumstanced,
this problem that routines with my words:
I was in the kitchen, plating my food,
when my nouns conversioned to verbs.

I friended others with similar troubles
and we workshopped together for days.
Dialoguing in search of solutions,
as the long hours flipcharted aways.

I now diarise each time they event.
Are they nerbs or vouns? I'm not sure.
The doctors cannot medication me.
Even to poem provisions no cure.

At a World Cup for languaging weirdly
or a verbing-renowned Olympics,
I'd have podiumed – I'm in no doubt –
if it weren't for those medalling kids.

Brian Bilston, 2016

AUDIO A reading of the poem

1 Read the poem.

a. What powers of English have been used?

b. What do you think of the result?

2 Pick out an expression you like. What makes it attractive?

3 Choose a verse.

a. Practise saying it aloud, trying to convey its meaning.

b. Now listen to the recording of the poem and compare with your own interpretation.

e IFS1011

YOUR TURN

Take part in the "World Cup for languaging weirdly"

- Are you one of "those medalling kids"? You can verb your:

mood | tastes | hobbies | dreams | favourite movie | best holidays | ...

- You can also create portmanteau words. ☺

FINAL TASK

Celebrate English Language Day!

WHAT A WONDERFUL WORD!

- What is your favourite English word? Explain why you like it. Is it because of its sound / meaning / both ?
- Put your favourite words together to create the class's glossary.

BEWILDERED

I like 'bewildered' because it sounds exactly like what it means - confused and distracted.

ON STAGE! IN GROUPS

- Choose a scene from a film, series or musical that you particularly like.
- Pay attention to the way the actors say their lines and try to imitate them as best as you can!
- Why not add... an extra line / a new character / ...

Act it out in front of the class!

A WRISTBAND TO CELEBRATE

- Imagine a slogan to celebrate: your sports team / your school / your class / ...
- Follow the instructions about how to make a wristband. e IFS1012
- Write your slogan on it.

A POEM FOR THE DAY

- Think of an idea or a feeling you would like to express.
- Choose the "magical powers" of English you wish to use:

RHYMES PORTMANTEAU WORDS VERBING reductions

- Write your poem then read it to the class!

GRAMMAR

Pour mieux jouer avec la langue anglaise,
il faut en connaître les règles !
Commençons par les déterminants et
la façon de relier deux verbes.

1 Les déterminants : Ø ou *the* ?

❶ Something you call Ø **love** [...]

❷ "Maybe we can eventually make Ø **language** a complete impediment to understanding."

❸ **The language of advertising slogans** is influential.

❹ Ø **Slogans** are a way of capturing the attention.

❺ Take **the Apple slogan of the 1990s** 'Think Different'.

❻ Ø **Adversing's early words and images** were simply to convey information.

- On choisit l'article zéro Ø lorsqu'on veut renvoyer à un ou plusieurs éléments en général. On utilise l'article ***the*** pour renvoyer à un ou plusieurs éléments précis.
- Ainsi dans l'énoncé ❷ il s'agit du langage en général, et dans l'énoncé ❸ du langage de la publicité. De même en ❹ on évoque les slogans en général, et en ❺ un slogan particulier.
- Attention à l'énoncé ❻ : alors qu'en français on dirait « Les mots et les images des premières publicités », en anglais *Advertising's* suffit à déterminer *early words and images* : on n'a donc pas besoin du déterminant *the*.

→ Précis 2, 3, 4 p. 232-233

2 Le lien entre deux verbes

❶ Great slogans **make** the customer Ø **feel** smart, or unique, or happy.

❷ You **keep saying** you've got something for me. You **keep lying** [...].

❸ I **like to verb** words.

- Lorsque deux verbes se suivent, trois constructions sont possibles :

V1 Ø V2	C'est le cas de ***make*** ❶ et de ***let*** *("Let it be")*.
V1 V2-*ing*	C'est le cas de nombreux verbes : ***keep*** ❷, ***imagine*** *("Imagine saying something like this!")*, ***mind*** *("Would you mind closing the door?")*, etc.
V1 *to* V2	C'est aussi le cas de nombreux verbes : ***like*** ❸, ***want*** *("I want to go there.")*, ***remember*** *("Remember to call her!")*, etc.

Comment choisir ?

Certains verbes admettent deux constructions. C'est par exemple le cas de *remember* :

- ***Remember to call** her!*

On choisit V1 *to* V2 lorsque V2 apporte une information nouvelle : la personne à qui on parle ne sait pas ce qui va suivre V1.

- *What a great song! I **remember listening** to it when we were in England.*

On choisit V1 V2-*ing* lorsque V2 est déjà sous-entendu par le contexte, ou antérieur à V1.

PRACTISE ONLINE

WORDS

Special effects

- be **mem**orable
  eye-catching / catchy
  ef**fec**tive
  popular / at**trac**tive
- rhyme
- have **rhy**thm / musi**ca**lity
  /ˈrɪðəm/
- con**vey mea**ning
- catch / grab / **cap**ture at**ten**tion
  /ˈkæptʃər/

IFS1013

Often heard in spoken English...

- **got**ta /ˈɡɒtə/ — *got to*
- **gon**na /ˈɡənə/ — *going to*
- **wan**na /ˈwɒnə/ — *want to*
- **got**cha /ˈɡɒtʃə/ — *I have got you*
- **could**a — *could have*
- dun**no** /dəˈnəʊ/ — *I don't know*
- **gim**me /ɪ/ — *give me*
- **lem**me — *let me*
- ain't /eɪnt/ — *isn't / aren't*
- ya — *you*
- er — *her*
- im — *him*
- em — *them*
- 'n' — *and*

IFS1014

Imagination & Inspiration

Advertising

- an **ad**vert, an ad
  /ˈædvɜːt/
- a **slo**gan
- TV com**mer**cial
- con**su**mer / **cus**tomer
  /juː/ /ʌs/
- a **bill**board
  /ɔː/

Poetry

/ˈpəʊɪtri/

- a **po**em
- a verse
- a line
  /aɪ/
- the **po**et

Music

- a song
- the **ly**rics
- the **cho**rus
- the **sin**ger
  /ˈsɪŋər/
- the interpre**ta**tion
  /ɪntɜːprəˈteɪʃən/

IFS1015

TEST YOUR SKILLS

OBJECTIF BAC

Listening & Writing

» **Listen** to the document three times and report what you have understood. IFS1016

» **Write** about the same topic, following your teacher's instructions.

Durée 1'30

AUDIO Words on the move

"The English language is a work in progress. Have fun with it!"
Jonathan Culver

Speaking

» **React to a document.**

- Your teacher will give you a set of two documents.
- In your opinion, which one best illustrates the notion of ART AND POWER?
- Explain why.

"I FIND THE EASIEST WAY TO EXPAND MY VOCABULARY IS TO MAKE UP WORDS."

HOW TO... boost your listening skills

Understanding a spoken message is a skill that can be improved, like writing and speaking. You need strategies... and practice!

Trust yourself

Strategies

Practise with this document IFS1010

Anticipate what you may hear

- To do this, **you can use**: *the title • the picture • the first few seconds of the document*
- **Accept the unexpected!** You may well end up hearing something that you had not anticipated. So remain open-minded ☺

What do you expect to hear? Advice? A list of instructions? A tutorial?

IFS1011

Remember: English's got rhythm!

- **The words which carry the meaning are stressed** (nouns, verbs, adjectives, adverbs...)
- **"Grammatical" words** are generally **unstressed**, except when the speaker wants to insist on them.

Make sense of the intonation!

- **Rising intonation** ↗ is generally used when asking for information (doubt) and **falling intonation** ↘ when giving information (certainty).

"So **what**? I'll **make** my **slogan shorter**? Will that **really make** the **difference** in them **remembering** it?"

"If you **really** want an **amazing slogan**, you **need** to **maximize** it in **every** way."

"Did you just sing a little tune in your head?"

Listen to English regularly

- Listen or watch, with or without subtitles, it doesn't matter, as long as you **get to hear English**.

→ *You can even set up your devices or social media in English* ☺

GOLDEN RULES

- **Trust** yourself: you *will* understand.
- **Accept** that you will not understand everything.
- **Listen** to English as often as possible.

THE POWER OF WORDS

VIDEO Commentary

REACT

1. **Look at the illustration.** Explain the situation:

   the place | the people

   What makes you think this?

2. **a.** Judging from the audience's reactions, what do you think the speaker's message is? Finish his sentence!

   b. Check with the original. e IFS1053

DEBRIEF

- Why do you think politicians are sometimes tempted to not tell the truth?
- Listen to the recording. Compare with your own answers. e IFS1054

1 Newspeak

"A machine-gun spraying forth bullets..."

In the totalitarian state of Oceania, governed by Big Brother, a language called Newspeak has been created as a way of spreading the regime's political propaganda.

In Newspeak [...] what was required, above all for political purposes, was short clipped words of unmistakable meaning which could be uttered rapidly and which roused the minimum of echoes in the speaker's mind. The words of the B vocabulary even gained in force from the fact that nearly all of them were very much alike. Almost invariably these words – *goodthink, Minipax, prolefeed, sexcrime, joycamp, Ingsoc*[1], *bellyfeel, thinkpol*, and countless others – were words of two or three syllables, with the stress distributed equally between the first syllable and the last.

The use of them encouraged a gabbling[2] style of speech, at once staccato and monotonous. And this was exactly what was aimed at. The intention was to make speech, and especially speech on any subject not ideologically neutral, as nearly as possible independent of consciousness.

For the purposes of everyday life it was no doubt necessary, or sometimes necessary, to reflect before speaking, but a Party member called upon to make a political or ethical judgement should be able to spray forth the correct opinions as automatically as a machine-gun spraying forth bullets. His training fitted him to do this, the language gave him an almost foolproof[3] instrument, and the texture of the words, with their harsh sound and a certain wilful ugliness which was in accord with the spirit of Ingsoc, assisted the process still further.

So did the fact of having very few words to choose from. Relative to our own, the Newspeak vocabulary was tiny, and new ways of reducing it were constantly being devised. Newspeak, indeed, differed from most all other languages in that its vocabulary grew smaller instead of larger every year. Each reduction was a gain, since the smaller the area of choice, the smaller the temptation to take thought. Ultimately it was hoped to make articulate[4] speech issue from the larynx without involving the higher brain centres at all.

George Orwell, *Nineteen Eighty-Four* (1949)

1. English Socialism
2. gabble: talk rapidly and unintelligibly
3. infallible
4. clearly expressed and easily understood

1 **a. Comment on the poster.** What type of fiction do you associate with it?

b. Read the title and the introduction. What can you imagine about Newspeak?

2 **a. Read the text.** Pick out references to the characteristics of Newspeak:

sound | vocabulary

b. How does it serve the regime's purpose?

WORK your WAY — Read the text above or use a guided version. IFS1055

YOUR TURN

Do you speak Newspeak?

- Try to understand how the examples of Newspeak from the text were created and what they could mean in this context.
- Why not invent your own Newspeak words?

Standard English	Newspeak
English + Socialism	Ingsoc
...	...

2 Trump's "77-word" vocabulary

www.inverse.com

Spitting out words

By Sarah Sloat, February 7, 2017

There's not much variety to the words President Donald Trump spits out, but we know which ones are his: To Americans, words like "loser", "sad", "horrible", "weak" and "stupid" have become ubiquitous with Trump in 2017. This is likely what led the writer Phillip Roth to angrily call out Trump's "77-word" vocabulary in the most recent issue of *The New Yorker*. Roth's assessment of Trump's small vocabulary size may be correct, but we should be careful not to assume it means that the President is dumb. [...]

It's become increasingly apparent to researchers that a non-expansive vocabulary isn't necessarily the sign of a failing mind; rather, it might be the hallmark of a person sly enough to hook his listeners and persuade them using only a few words. [...]

Geoffrey Nunberg, a professor at the University of California-Berkeley, wrote in *The Los Angeles Times* that Trump's repetitions and digressions come off as "spontaneous and genuine" to people listening at a rally." Like most people who attend political rallies, Trump's audience came there to connect — "they were already convinced," Nunberg said.

Repetition is considered a rhetorical strategy proven to produce emphasis, clarity, amplification, and emotional effect. Audiences judge spoken content differently than words they read on a page. By repeating phrases, which may look less intelligent later transcribed on paper, the speaker guarantees that their audience walks away with their most important points in mind. When Trump said in the final presidential debate that "Iran should write us a letter of thank you, just like the really stupid — the stupidest deal of all time, a deal that's going to give Iran, absolutely, nuclear weapons," he made sure that listeners linked "stupid" and "Iran" together. His statements provide no context for what he's saying, but by mashing words together he creates an emotional platform to use against his opponent. [...]

And that level of manipulation is anything but dumb.

Inverse.com

1 Focus on the titles and illustration. What do they imply about Donald Trump?

2 Read the article.

WORK your WAY — Read the article above or a guided version. IFS1056

a. Pick out references to Trump's language:

characteristics

effect produced on his audience

b. Pick out two different ways of analyzing Trump's use of language.

3 React. What is your own analysis?

DEBRIEF

How can words be used to manipulate? Draw examples from both texts.

YOUR TURN

The 6-word challenge

Use a maximum of six content words to convince your classmates to try something new:

food | sports | music | ...

TIP

- You can say a lot with only a few words! It's all about the choices you make:

repetitions | comparatives and superlatives | word stress | sentence structure | ...

- Listen to a few examples. IFS1057

3 Doublespeak

The defence of the indefensible…

In our time, political speech and writing are largely the defence of the indefensible. Things like the continuance of British rule in India, the Russian purges and deportations, the dropping of the atom bombs on Japan, can indeed be defended, but only by arguments which are too brutal for most people to face, and which do not square with[1] the professed aims of the political parties. Thus political language has to consist largely of euphemism, question-begging and sheer cloudy vagueness.

Defenceless villages are bombarded from the air, the inhabitants driven out into the countryside, the cattle[2] machine-gunned, the huts set on fire with incendiary bullets: this is called *pacification*. Millions of peasants are robbed of their farms and sent trudging along the roads with no more than they can carry: this is called *transfer of population* or *rectification of frontiers*. People are imprisoned for years without trial, or shot in the back of the neck or sent to die of scurvy[3] in Arctic lumber camps: this is called *elimination of unreliable elements*. Such phraseology is needed if one wants to name things without calling up mental pictures of them.

The great enemy of clear language is insincerity. When there is a gap between one's real and one's declared aims, one turns as it were instinctively to long words and exhausted idioms, like a cuttlefish[4] spurting out ink. In our age there is no such thing as "keeping out of politics." All issues are political issues, and politics itself is a mass of lies, evasions, folly, hatred, and schizophrenia. When the general atmosphere is bad, language must suffer.

George Orwell, *Politics and the English Language* (1946)

1. correspond to
2. *bétail*
3. *scorbut*
4. *seiche*

TIP

George Orwell wrote, "Good prose should be transparent, like a window pane".

- Note how Orwell often uses an opening statement, followed by several examples to clarify and back up his argument (e.g. paragraphs 1 & 3).

1 Look at the title and imagine all you can about the article.

How? By whom?

The defence of the indefensible…

What? When? Where?

2 Read the text. Check your ideas and complete your notes.

WORK your WAY — Use the text above or a guided version.

DEBRIEF

"When the general atmosphere is bad, language must suffer." Do you agree? Can you think of any great political speeches that were made during "bad times"?

YOUR TURN

The art of euphemism

Create euphemisms to talk about situations at school.

e.g. *"I'm giving you both detention."* → *"You are invited to spend quality time on the premises."*

FINAL TASK

Language analysis

Analyse a political speech.

1 Get ready

- Watch an extract from a speech delivered by Donald Trump about Kim Jong Un in August 2017. e IFS1058
- Analyse it using what you have learned in the chapter.

2 Action!

- Write a short analysis of it.

TIP
- Read Sarah Sloat's article again (p. 27).
- Pick out expressions that you can use to quote or analyse Donald Trump's speech: "Trump's repetitions come off as..." "Repetition produces emphasis, clarity..."

VIDEO Donald Trump's speech (2017)

or

Art as Activism

Create a piece of artwork to illustrate "the power of words".

1 Get ready

- Decide if you want to represent the power of words in a positive or a negative way.
- Choose an art form:

cartoon (p. 25) poster (p. 26) illustration (p. 27-28)

2 Action!

- Create your poster.
- Present it to the class.

GRAMMAR

Dans ce chapitre, on explore la manière dont les mots sont utilisés et les phrases construites pour convaincre ou manipuler. Pour cela, on a besoin de la **dérivation** et des ***phrasal verbs***.

1 La dérivation

- La dérivation consiste **à former un nouveau mot** en lui ajoutant un **préfixe** (en début de mot) ou un **suffixe** (en fin de mot) à partir d'un mot-racine.
- Les **suffixes** peuvent **changer la nature** du mot-racine :

verbe → nom	*eliminate → elimin**ation***	*manipulate → manipul**ation***
verbe → adjectif	*rely → reli**able***	*depend → depend**ent***
adjectif → adverbe	*automatic → automatic**ally***	*angry → angr**ily***
adjectif → nom	*ugly → ugli**ness***	*free → free**dom***

- Les **préfixes** ne changent pas la nature du mot mais ils en **modifient le sens**. Parmi les préfixes les plus courants figurent les préfixes négatifs : ***in**sincerity, **un**pleasant, **dis**appear, **a**moral...*

2 Les *phrasal verbs*

1. "A machine **spraying forth** bullets..."
2. There's not much variety to the words President Donald Trump **spits out**.
3. By repeating phrases, the speaker guarantees that their audience **walks away with** their most important points in mind.
4. Trump's repetitions and digressions **come off** as "spontaneous and genuine".
5. Defenceless villages are bombarded from the air, the inhabitants **driven out into** the countryside.

- Dans tous les énoncés ci-dessus, on trouve un **verbe** suivi d'un petit mot (une **particule**) qui **modifie le sens de ce verbe**.
- Ainsi le verbe *come* peut avoir, selon la particule qui le suit, des sens bien différents :
  come in (entrer),
  come back (retourner),
  come through (réussir, parvenir),
  come up (with) : imaginer, inventer
  come off 4 : ici « être perçu comme »,
  ... etc.
- Ces verbes, que l'on appelle des *phrasal verbs* ou verbes à particule, sont très fréquents en anglais. Les particules les plus courantes sont : *out* 2 5, *away* 3, *off* 4, *on, in, up, back, down, over, about, through, around, along.*
- La particule peut être suivie d'une **préposition** 3 5.

Place de la particule
- Si le complément est un **nom**, la particule peut se placer avant 1 ou après 2 ce nom.
- Si le complément est un **pronom**, la particule se place obligatoirement **avant ce pronom** :
  *Can you **switch off** the light, please?*
  *Can you **switch** it **off**?*

→ Précis 35 p. 249

PRACTISE ONLINE

WORDS

Political Speech

- use **eu**phemisms /ˈjuːfəmɪzm/
  - repe**ti**tions
  - di**gres**sions /daɪˈɡreʃn/
  - a **li**mited vo**ca**bulary
  - **sim**ple words
  - ≠ long, **com**plicated words
- re**peat phra**ses
- make a **state**ment /ˈsteɪtmənt/
- tell the truth ≠ tell lies / lie
- a po**li**tical **ral**ly
- the **spea**ker
- an **o**rator /ˈɒrətə/
- the **au**dience

IFS1057

Effects

- ma**ni**pulate
- per**suade**, con**vince** /pəˈsweɪd/
- hook your **lis**teners
- pro**duce** an e**mo**tion
- cre**ate** an ef**fect**

IFS1058

Attention aux faux-amis

- **is**sue:
  1. *numéro d'un journal,*
  2. *problème*
- at**tend**
  = be present
- a**chieve**
- de**ceive**
- **sen**sible
- **ac**tually
- e**ven**tually

IFS1059

TEST YOUR SKILLS

OBJECTIF BAC

Listening & Writing

- **Listen** to the document three times and report what you have understood. IFS1060
- **Write** about the same topic, following your teacher's instructions.

Durée 1'30

AUDIO The Language of Politics

▶ British actor, writer, presenter and comedian Stephen Fry

Speaking

- **React to a document.**
  - Your teacher will give you a set of two documents.
  - In your opinion, which one best illustrates the notion of **ART AND POWER**?
  - Explain why.

3

EXTRA! EXTRA!! EXTRA!!

REACT

1. **Look at the front page of the newspaper and read the caption underneath.**
   a. What do you think of it?
   → YP 2
   b. Imagine all you can about this front page:
   who created it | why | the impact
2. **Watch the video.** IFS1104
   Check your answers to question **1b**.

VIDEO
Unpresidented

▲ Washington D. C., Jan 2016

DEBRIEF Do you agree with what The Washington Post reporter has to say about the credibility of news sources?

1 The Central Park Zoo Escape

1 Look at the documents below.

a. Find everything you can about the

AWFUL CALAMITY.

b. Imagine people's reactions when reading the news in 1874.

2 Class survey. Do you think the event really happened? → **YP 2a, 21**

3 Watch the video (2'26"→ 4'30"). e IFS1105

a. Pick out information to complete your understanding of the situation:

reasons for publishing the story	reasons for the impact it had

4 React. Do you think this would work today? → **YP 37**

A

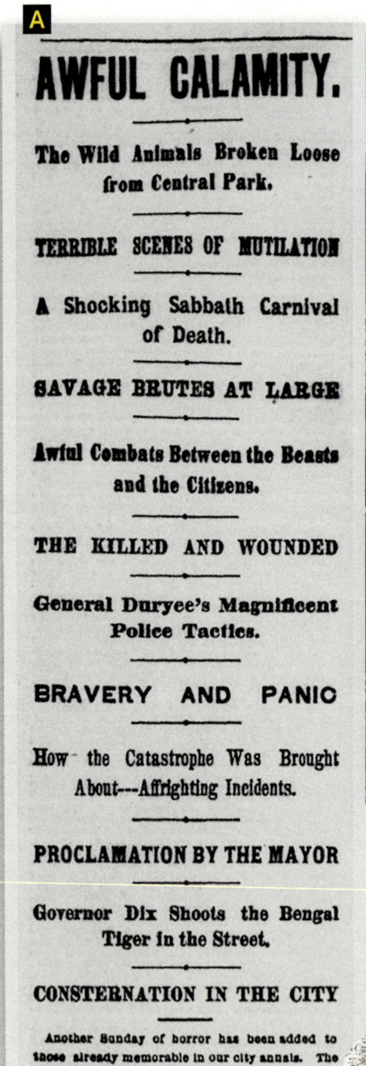

AWFUL CALAMITY.

The Wild Animals Broken Loose from Central Park.

TERRIBLE SCENES OF MUTILATION

A Shocking Sabbath Carnival of Death.

SAVAGE BRUTES AT LARGE

Awful Combats Between the Beasts and the Citizens.

THE KILLED AND WOUNDED

General Duryee's Magnificent Police Tactics.

BRAVERY AND PANIC

How the Catastrophe Was Brought About---Affrighting Incidents.

PROCLAMATION BY THE MAYOR

Governor Dix Shoots the Bengal Tiger in the Street.

CONSTERNATION IN THE CITY

Another Sunday of horror has been added to those already memorable in our city annals. The

▲ New York Herald, 1874

VIDEO The news story that panicked a city

B

EXTRA! EXTRA!! EXTRA!!

ILLUSTRATING THE AWFUL CALAMITY

DESCRIBED IN THE

NEW YORK HERALD.

THE WILD ANIMALS BROKEN LOOSE FROM CENTRAL PARK!!

Terrible Scenes of Mutilation!!

SAVAGE BRUTES AT LARGE!!!

▲ Harper's Weekly, 1893: 20th anniversary of the news story

2 Crisis actors?

Paul James
6 hrs

So Called “Student”. But actually a CRISIS ACTOR, David Hogg, was on camera months ago, pretending to be a high school student in California. Now, suddenly, he is a high school student in Florida???

Like   Share   < / > Embed

Question ③ (comment) — Question ② (both pictures) — Question ① (bottom picture)

◂ **David Hogg** is one of the founding members of the #Never Again movement, which promotes greater gun control in the US.

1 Focus on the bottom picture. ▴
Pick out elements to explain the context:
people | place | event

2 Compare the two pictures:
place | time | caption → YP **12a, 15**

3 Focus on the comment.

a. Make links between the comment and the images.

b. Analyze the message closely to identify Paul James's opinion. Share with your friends: do you all agree?

4 GROUP TALK

Discuss the definition of “crisis actor”.

In your opinion, why did Paul James publish this post?

YOUR TURN

Fact or fake? IN GROUPS

Is Paul James' claim above fake news?
Check the story on the following websites:

www.factcheck.org | www.snopes.com | www.politifact.com.

WORK your WAY You can browse the websites **or** read the extracts provided. IFS1106

Fact-checking websites
Snopes (launched in 1994), PolitiFact (2007) and FactCheck (2003) are among the most reliable fact-checking websites.
These websites provide fact-checking services about both political and non-political subjects.

DEBRIEF What can the reasons be for spreading fake news? Do you think it can sometimes be acceptable?

3 Should social media be regulated?

IN GROUPS

1. Do you think social media should be regulated? Why? → YP 37, 38

Conduct a survey in class and write the results on the board.

2. **IN GROUPS** You're going to discover the views of some American people on the subject.

a. Read or listen to your document then discuss with your group: do you agree with the views expressed?

b. Get ready to share what you have learned with the class: take notes about the document (facts, quotes).

TIP
Look at the *Background* section to have a better understanding of the different points of view.

DEBRIEF

What seems to be of prime concern for the American people?

Do you share this concern?

Conduct a second survey in class: has anyone changed their minds?

GROUP 1

THINK THE VOTE

Is regulating social media the most effective way to prevent fake news?

YES

Anna from **Kentucky**
Yes, regulating social media is clearly the most effective way to prevent fake news. Since social media is the main source for all news, putting restrictions on certain posts would be the most effective way. Our right to free speech would not exactly be violated considering what's being posted are false stories.
REPLY

Haley from **Texas**
People from ages three to one hundred and three use the Internet. Fake news is a widespread issue, especially for children.
Children do not have the ability to pull the truth out of a lie, they simply take everything they read to heart. This creates an entire generation of people who are commonly misinformed, usually finding out the truth years later, if they ever get the truth. This is leading our country to a generation of half extremely gullible, half extremely distrusting adults. That is no way for a free country to be, so news online should be regulated–websites such as Wikipedia, Buzzfeed, and any other site that pumps out a continuous stream of "news".
REPLY

NO

thinkthevote.com

GROUP 2

AUDIO
Censorship on social media (NPR, 2018)
IFS1107

Facebook, Spotify and YouTube closed the account of the conspiracy theorist Alex Jones.
This NPR programme discusses Twitter's decision and the regulation of social media.

Background

What the law says

The First Amendment
"Congress shall make no law respecting an establishment of religion, or prohibiting the free exercise thereof; or abridging the freedom of speech, or of the press, or of the right of the people peaceably to assemble, and to petition the Government for a redress of grievances."

The American Constitution
It was composed by the original 13 states and ratified in 1789. In 1791, 10 articles were added, listing basic rights many people had wanted to include in the original Constitution. These first 10 amendments are known as the Bill of Rights.

▲ **George Whashington** (1732-99)
He was an American political leader, military general, statesman and Founding Father. He was the first President of the US.

GROUP 3

% of U.S. adults who say ...

U.S. govt. should take steps to restrict false info online, even if it limits freedom of info	**Freedom of info should be protected,** even if it means false info can be published
39%	58%

% of U.S. adults who say ...

Tech companies should take steps to restrict false info online, even if it limits freedom of info	**Freedom of info should be protected,** even if it means false info can be published
56%	42%

Note: Respondents who did not give an answer are not shown.
Source: Survey conducted Feb. 26-March 11, 2018.
"Americans Favor Protecting Information Freedoms Over Government Steps to Restrict False News Online"
PEW RESEARCH CENTER

YOUR TURN

Battle time!

Join the discussion about the regulation of social media.

- **Team A** is in favour of regulating social media.
- **Team B** is against.

TIP See *How to* p. 46.

FOR & AGAINST

- Stand up.
- **Team A** gives an argument and **Team B** answers it.
- Once a student has spoken, he or she sits down and cannot speak again.
- A jury will decide which team has been the most convincing.

4 Facebook *vs.* fake news

VIDEO
Facebook's new fact-checking feature

1. **Before watching.** What do you know about the role Facebook plays regarding fake news?
2. **Look at the title of the video.** Imagine all you can about this feature.
3. **Watch the video.** e IFS1108 Explain what you have understood about this feature. ▸ *i*
4. **IN PAIRS** Has the feature evolved since it was launched? Check it, test it, rate it!

5 How to spot fake news?

1. **Look at the cartoon.**
   a. Imagine the answer the man could give.
   b. Check the original cartoon. e IFS1109
2. **Read the infographic (p. 39).**
   a. Does it contain any of the answers you came up with?
   b. Do you ever apply any of these techniques?

6 Fake news classes

1 Before watching. How would you answer the question above? What is the most frequent answer in the class?

2 Watch part 1. IFS1110

a. Explain what is going on:

where? who? what?

b. Would you like to have this type of class?

3 a. How would you answer the following questions?

How do you avoid fake news?

What are some reliable sources?

b. Watch part 2. IFS1111 Pick out the boys' answers to these questions. Compare with your own answers.

4 Look at the infographic. ▶

a. Tick the items that are mentioned in the video. IFS1123

b. Add a new technique in the infographic and illustrate it!

YOUR TURN

Check your fake-news spotting skills

- Read three articles and determine what type of information they are. IFS1112
- For each text, explain what techniques you have applied to check the piece of news.

DEBRIEF

Are media literacy classes a good way to fight fake news? Are they enough?

7 Alternative facts

From the encyclopedia of alternative facts

Frankenstein was the monster's name.
There's no such thing as climate change.
A solero is a type of hat.
The planet is not round but flat.

Six is the legal drinking age.
Women are paid an equal wage.
Elvis was influenced by Take That.
The planet is not round but flat.

Achilles had a dodgy knee.
Terror comes from refugees.
Insomnia affects most cats.
The planet is not round but flat.

There are no fascists on the rise.
A politician never lies.
It's impossible to change a fact.
The planet is not round but flat.

Brian Bilston, 2017

AUDIO
A reading of the poem
IFS1113

1. **Read the poem.**
   What do you think of it? Do you like it?
2. **a.** How would you define an "alternative fact"?
   b. What do you think of those listed in the poem?
3. **IN PAIRS** Choose one or two of the following activities to do:

LITERARY ANALYSIS
- Pay attention to the structure of the poem:
  last lines of each stanza
  last stanza
- What effect is created?

DISCUSSION
Discuss some of the facts mentioned in the poem.

ENCYCLOPEDIA
Think of other alternative facts and add your own stanza to the poem.

Where does the term "alternative facts" come from?
Kellyanne Conway, an advisor to President Donald Truump, used the euphemism *alternative facts* when she was a guest on NBC's Meet the Press on January 22, 2017. She used this term to describe false statements made by the press secretary Sean Spicer on January 21, 2017, the day after Donald Trump took office. The NBC host reacted immediately, saying "*Alternative facts* are not facts. They're falsehoods."

FINAL TASK

Create a hoax

An NGO* is looking for brilliant ideas to raise awareness about their cause. Create a hoax to catch people's attention! IN PAIRS

* non-governmental organisation

1 Get ready

- Think about the cause you want to defend.
  climate change | endangered species | the living conditions of animals in zoos | ...

2 Action!

- Create a fake newspaper front page.
- Write a note to present it to the members of the organization explaining why your idea will have a great impact on people.

TIP Look at the front pages again (on p. 33 and 34).

or

Take part in a debate

You are studying in an American high school, and have been invited to take part in a debate.

1 Get ready

- You are going to be given one of these motions: ▸
- Team up with your partners and get ready to debate:
- Prepare useful notes: facts | statistics | experts' opinions and quotes | ...
- Think about your opinion and arguments.
- Practise expressing your opinion:
  – review useful vocabulary
  – practice using a convincing intonation,
  – practice nuancing your opinion,
  – anticipate what the other team might say.

TIP Use *How to take part in a debate* p. 46.

Fake news cannot be censored because judging what is "fake" and what is not is too difficult.

Publishing fake news should be regarded as a crime, as much as hate speech.

Fake news have to be fought, even if it means restricting people's freedom of speech.

2 On stage!

→ You have 5 minutes to consult with your team, then you can start debating.

→ Two moderators will make sure that the debate runs smoothly and that each side has equal speaking time.

WORDS

PRACTISE ONLINE

Misinformation

- false **sto**ry, /fɒls/ false infor**ma**tion, false news, fake news ≠ **cre**dible infor**ma**tion
- a prank, a hoax /əʊ/
- a **ru**mor /ˈru·mər/
- a cons**pi**racy **the**ory /θ/
- unre**li**able /aɪ/ ≠ re**li**able, trust**wor**thy /ð/
- go **vi**ral /aɪ/, spread (online)
- spread fake news

IFS1114

Readers

- be **gul**lible, na**ive**, **ea**sily fooled, easily **chea**ted /tʃiːtid/ ≠ be well-in**for**med, dis**cer**ning
- take **so**mething at face **va**lue = regard sth as true without questioning it ≠ question what you read
- have **bi**ases /ˈbaɪəsiz/ / be **bi**ased /ˈbaɪəst/ = have **pre**judices / be **pre**judiced
- be dis**trus**ting = be sus**pi**cious

IFS1115

FAKE NEWS

Fighting misinformation

- in**ves**tigate
- check your facts, check the source /sɔːs/ / the **au**thor / the date
- check the **a**ccuracy of the infor**ma**tion pro**vi**ded
- check the credi**bi**lity of a source
- de**ci**pher /aɪ/ between real and fake news
- use a **fact**-checking site
- de**bunk** /diːˈbʌŋk/ / ex**pose** misinfor**ma**tion = show that sth is not true, prove sth false
- pre**vent** / re**strict** false news **on**line
- **cen**sor /ə/ (s.o., a piece of information...)
- **re**gulate **so**cial **me**dia **plat**forms
- teach **me**dia **li**teracy /ˈlɪtərəsi/, intro**duce** **me**dia **li**teracy **cour**ses /kɔːsiz/

IFS1116

Actors

- tech **gi**ants /ˈdʒaɪnts/ / **so**cial **me**dia /ˈmiːdiə/
- **main**stream **me**dia ≠ in**de**pendent **me**dia
- **pu**blic o**pi**nion
- **fact**-checkers
- a **news** outlet / a **me**dia outlet

IFS1117

EXERCISES

1 Odd one out

Which word doesn't fit?

1. unreliable, trustworthy, fake, false
2. gullible, discerning, naive, easily fooled
3. biased, prejudiced, objective, partial

2 Campaign

a. Complete this "message to our customers".

First try to do it from memory, then check with the mindmap.

b. Create a similar poster for another social media!

3 Promote media literacy in your school!

You think media literacy should be taught in your school. Prepare your arguments before meeting the Principal.

4 News consumers also bear responsibilities!

Complete the document below with the following words. Don't forget to use the right verb forms!

credibility – accuracy – spread false – information – investigate – outlets – misinformation – false information

RESPONSIBILITIES

News consumers also bear responsibilities.

News consumers should avoid ______, including reposting or sharing information without first reading it through, and by ______ the ______, provenance, and ______ of the information.

News consumers should report instances of ______ to platforms and ______ that publish them to facilitate more effective efforts to avoid the promulgation of ______.

Pen America - News Consumers' Bill of Rights and Responsibilities

5 Front page

Use words from the mindmap on p. 42 to write a short paragraph about this front page. Think about:

- the type of information
- the readers
- what you think the readers' reaction should or shouldn't be

6 Opposite meaning

En anglais on peut transformer un nom en son contraire en lui ajoutant un préfixe négatif.
Voici les plus courants :

dis – il – im – in – mis – un – ir

e.g. *happy → unhappy* *relevant → irrelevant*

Using negative prefixes, change the following words:

information – reliable – true – accurate – trusting

Pronunciation

PRACTISE ONLINE

7 Two-syllable verbs

IFS1118

- Les verbes de deux syllabes sont souvent accentués sur la 2e syllabe :
  e.g. *decide* (•●) *compare* (•●)
- Il y a cependant de nombreuses exceptions :
  e.g. *answer* (●•) *listen* (●•)

a. How would you pronounce the following verbs?

prevent – restrict – question – distrust – allow censor

•●	●•

b. Listen and check.

GRAMMAR

Faut-il réguler l'information ou protéger avant tout la liberté d'expression ? Pour en parler, on est amené à **exprimer son opinion**. Et pour parler d'information, de preuves et de nouvelles, mieux vaut connaître les noms **indénombrables** en anglais !

1 Exprimer une opinion

1. Putting restrictions on certain posts **would be** the most effective approach.
2. Our right to free speech **would** not exactly **be** violated.
3. The US government **should take** steps to restrict false information online.
4. Freedom of information **should be** protected.
5. Professional journalists **ought to be trained** to observe events with objectivity and detachment.

Prononciation
- *would* et *should* se prononcent avec le son voyelle de *book*.
- On ne prononce pas la lettre « l » : /wʊd/ /ʃʊd/

- *Would*, *should* et *ought + to* sont des **auxiliaires de modalité**. Comme tous les modaux, ils permettent à l'énonciateur de donner son point de vue sur un événement et sont obligatoirement suivis d'une **base verbale**.
- Ils sont au **Prétérit**, ce qui signale ici un décalage par rapport à la réalité des faits : il est question d'irréel, de ce qui n'est pas encore arrivé.
- *Would* 1 2 est le Prétérit de *will* : il combine donc l'idée de forte probabilité avec la valeur d'irréel du Prétérit (= « ... serait sans doute la solution la plus efficace »).
- *Should* 3 4 permet à l'énonciateur de formuler un conseil ou d'exprimer une opinion personnelle.
- *Ought + to* 5 est comparable à *should*, mais le jugement se veut plus objectif, comme émanant de la morale ou de la société en général (→ *« En principe, les journalistes... »*).

→ Précis 28, 29 p. 244-245

2 Dénombrables et indénombrables

1. Fake **news** **is** a widespread issue, especially for **children**.
2. The good **news** **is** that tech companies are now developing fact-checking tools.
3. The US government should restrict false **information** online.
4. **Is** there enough **evidence** that something definitely happened?

- En anglais comme en français, certains noms sont **dénombrables** (on peut les compter et les mettre au pluriel. Ex : *one child → three children*) et d'autres **indénombrables** (ex : *anger, water, knowledge...* : on ne peut pas les dénombrer, ils forment un tout).
- Attention cependant : quelques noms dénombrables en français sont indénombrables en anglais. C'est le cas de *news* 1 2, *information* 3, *evidence* 4.

→ Précis 1 p. 232

Indénombrables : à retenir !
- On ne peut pas les mettre au pluriel. Ils sont donc toujours suivis d'un verbe conjugué au singulier : *Is there enough evidence ?* 4 → *« Les preuves sont-elles suffisantes ? »*
- Ils ne s'emploient pas avec l'article *a* ni avec un chiffre *(one, two...)*.
- Si on veut parler d'un élément précis, on fait appel à la tournure *a piece of* : *This piece of news is quite interesting.* Cette information est très intéressante.

EXERCISES

Exprimer une opinion

❶ You are the Facebook administrator!

Give at least three rules of good practice users should respect in order to prevent the spread of fake news on the platform.

❷ *Should or ought to?*

a. For each of the following sentences, justify in French the choice that was made.

e.g.: Journalists *should not* be allowed to put words into your mouth.
→ *La personne qui parle donne son point de vue : selon elle, les journalistes ne devraient pas avoir le droit de nous faire dire ce qu'on n'a pas dit.*

1. Reporters ought to keep a professional distance from their sources.
2. Media platforms should regulate this kind of speech.
3. We ought to encourage media literacy.
4. We shouldn't trust everything we read.
5. You really shouldn't try this fact-checking website.
6. The preservation of the First Amendment ought to be of the utmost importance to any advocate of free speech.

Les noms indénombrables

❸ A free bit of advice!

Ø | a/one piece of | ?

Choose how to complete the following sentences:

1. ... advice: read the whole text before starting to fill in the answers.
2. I always follow my doctor's ... advice.
3. It is preferable to delay broadcasting ... news briefly to be able to place it in its context and help the listener to be better informed.
4. To anyone encountering Mrs Merkel for the first time, I have ... advice: don't underestimate her perseverance and the strength of her convictions.
5. In this troubled context, I shall single out ... very good ... news.

❹ No news is good news

Complete each sentence with the appropriate form.

1. ... bad news, because I was so happy and now the score is one all. *This is / These are*
2. And ... the good news – you don't have to pay extra money for this. *here is / here are*
3. A teacher once told me to trust my skills. ... such good. *This was / These were*
4. All of the advice given in this book ... interesting. *is / are*

❺ French speakers beware!

How would you say the following in English?

1. *Les conseils* donnés dans cette vidéo sont utiles.
2. Avez-vous suivi *l'actualité* cette semaine?
3. A-t-on *des preuves* que ceci s'est réellement passé ?
4. Rien ne prouve que *cette nouvelle* est vraie.

Pronunciation

Practise Online

❻ Should, would, ought to IFS1119

a. Listen and practise repeating these modal verbs.

should	would	ought to
/ʃʊd/	/wʊd/	/ɔːt tuː/

b. Now practise pronouncing these sentences :

1. You should try this fact-checking website.
2. Putting restrictions on certain posts would be the most effective way.
3. Wouldn't it be great if the news we read was more reliable?
4. Schools ought to encourage media literacy.

Rhythm & Sounds

Listen then say these sentences out loud, imitating the rhythm of the native speaker. IFS1120

- Facebook, Spotify and Youtube among others removed Jones's account from their platforms.
- The handling of Alex Jones and his infowars poses a big question: what is the responsibility of social media platforms to moderate misinformation or incendiary viewpoints?

HOW TO... take part in a debate

We don't always agree on everything... thankfully! So being able to express an opinion and react to others is essential.

Don't panic if you can't find the word you're looking for. You can reformulate!

Strategies

Make sure you understand the topic

- Check you understand all the words in the debate topic. Think about what you know about the **subject** so far.
- Here, the topic of the debate is a **question**, and you are encouraged to **give your opinion**.
- Think about the questions that the subject will raise.

Do you think that social media should be regulated?

Why "should"? What would be the advantages? The drawbacks?

Who would regulate them?

Express clear, nuanced opinions

- Listen to Year 12 students taking part in a conversation about social media and fake news. IFS1121
  → How does the first girl, Keana, express her opinion? Do you think it is effective? Why?

Golden rules!
- Nuance your opinion
- Acknowledge other people's opinions even if you disagree with them
- Provide at least ONE example for each argument

AUDIO Should social media be regulated?

Anticipate your opponents' answers

- You can prepare your ideas beforehand and use your notes during the debate. Most debaters do.

1. My opinion	2. My arguments	3. My opponents' arguments	4. My counter-arguments
	1.		
	2.		
	3.		

Each speaker has a role!

FOR THE DEBATERS

- Listen to the rest of the discussion. What happens?

Listen to how each debater:
- expresses their **opinion**,
- introduces their **arguments / examples**,
- **reacts** to what the others have said.

FOR THE MODERATOR

Your job is to:
- introduce the topic and the debaters
- make sure the debaters stay on topic,
- make sure that each team gets to speak roughly the same amount of time,
- remind the speakers to remain polite and respectful.

YOUR TURN!

Now join the discussion: react to what the British students said, and express your thoughts on the topic.

OBJECTIF BAC TEST YOUR SKILLS

Listening & Writing

Listen to the document three times and report what you have understood. e IFS1122

Write about the same topic, following your teacher's instructions.

AUDIO Fact checkers

Durée 1'30

Reading & Writing

Your teacher will give you several documents.

- Read them carefully and follow the instructions.

Speaking

React to a document.

- Your teacher will give you a set of two documents.
- In your opinion, which one best illustrates the notion of **CITIZENSHIP AND THE DIGITAL WORLD**?
- Explain why.

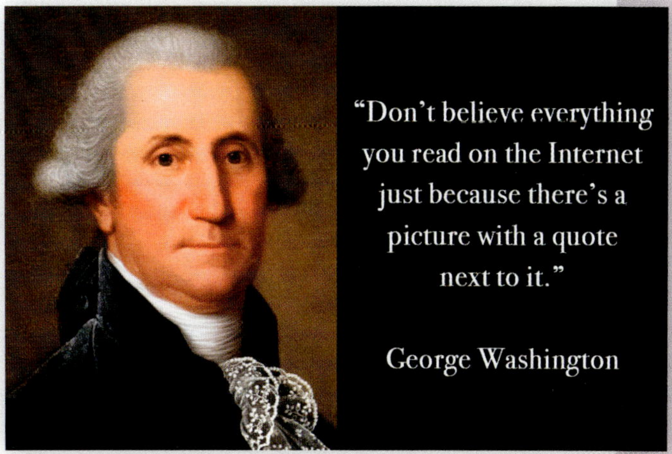

4

THIS IS US

REACT

1. Look at the photo. What do you think about it? → **YP 4, 6a, 29**
2. Can you see any possible link between the photo and the title? Explain your answer.

AUDIO Commentary

DEBRIEF

Listen to the commentary. What new information did you learn? Sum up the speaker's reaction to the photo and compare it with your own. ISF1155

1 Rate a friend

VIDEO
A scene from the series *Black Mirror*

▲ The Coffee Shop scene (extract from the *Nosedive* episode)

1 Have a close look at the two stills above.
Say all you can imagine about:
the people | the world they live in | the story | ... → YP 20

2 Watch the video and check your ideas. (1'56→3'03) e ISF1176

a. What can you say about the relationships between people in this world?

3 React. Do you find this world rather:
pleasant | disturbing | ... ? Why? → YP 18

4 The two pictures below appear later in the episode. Imagine what happened to Lacie.

An interview with Charlie Brooker

VIDEO
An interview with the author of *Black Mirror*

5 Watch the video. e ISF1156

a. Pick out what Charlie Brooker says about the series:
purpose | when it is set | title | ...

b. Do you think it was a good idea to create this series?

6 React to Charlie Brooker's statement:

“My stories feature the way we might be living in 10 minutes time if we're clumsy.”

YOUR TURN

On stage! IN GROUPS

Lacie's rating is now 1.3. She's desperate to get some 'up' votes!

- Imagine what she will do:
  be particularly nice to someone | be helpful | ...
- Write the dialogue, then act it out!

WORK your WAY Use only your imagination or use the help provided. e ISF1157

2 Digital nightmares?

Text 1

An 18-year-old Instagram star says her "Perfect Life" was actually making her miserable

This is Essena O'Neill, an 18-year-old from the Sunshine Coast of Australia. Over the past several years, O'Neill has built a social media empire. She explained that when she was in high school, she started posting on a blog, YouTube and social media and was rapidly consumed by it.

She soon became an online sensation. She said she at one point had more than half a million followers on Instagram and more than 250,000 YouTube subscribers alone. To her thousands of fans it seemed like she had it all. But, O'Neill wrote, she was totally unhappy.

▲ Essena O'Neill in 2015

Recently, O'Neill decided she had had enough. She said she realized she wasn't living an authentic life. "I was addicted to what others thought of me," she wrote. "I was severely addicted. I believed how many likes and followers I had correlated to how many people liked me. I didn't even see it happening, but social media had become my sole identity. I didn't even know what I was without it."

So she has decided to make a change. O'Neill announced to her followers last week that she is quitting social media and edited the captions on her "perfect photos" to tell the truth behind the pictures. O'Neill wrote that she would spend hours trying to get the "perfect" selfie, and then would edit it using several different apps. Now, O'Neill is asking others to challenge themselves by quitting social media for a week. She has created a website, LetsBeGameChangers.com, to tell her story and encourage others to be present and live authentically.

buzzfeed.com November 2, 2015

Text 2

tripadvisor WHY did you ruin my life?

When her children left home, Mary turned her house into a Bed and Breakfast. Things went well for a few years but one day her world came crashing down.

Another B&B opened just 2 miles from Mary; it was no big deal thought Mary, she even recommended it to people that came to her, when she was full. One day a returning guest told her that she had 2 very bad reviews on TripAdvisor. Mary had never heard of TripAdvisor. The returning guest showed Mary the 2 bad reviews (there were only 2 reviews about Mary's B&B and both were bad) – they were both posted by an anonymous person. Coincidence or not, within 8 months of opening the doors of the new B&B, they had already managed to get 8 fantastic reviews. Mary no longer manages to fill 3 rooms during the weekend, she is actually lucky to get one room occupied. All the love and hard work Mary put into her B&B was destroyed by LIES posted by someone that had obviously NEVER stayed at her B&B. The site TripAdvisor allows these lies and libel reviews to be posted without any form of validation.

Adapted from tripadvisor-warning.com March 6, 2011

1 **Read the titles of the two documents above.** What common point you can see?

2 IN GROUPS **Choose one of the texts.**

WORK your WAY — Work on the text above or use a guided version. ISF1158

a. Pick out what is said about:

- the main character
- her experience
- the consequences on her life

→ YP 17, 18

b. Share your findings with the class.

DEBRIEF

Can you see a link between the two texts and the *Nosedive* episode? Explain.

3 Is this us?

VIDEO Extracts from the TV series *This is us*

▲ *This Is Us* is an American television series that premiered on NBC in September 2016.

1 a. Look at the picture above. Imagine:

- who these people are
- how they are related
- what this series is about

→ YP 21

b. Watch the extracts and check your guesses. What else did you learn about the series?

2 *"This is US"* → Can you imagine why this title was chosen for the series?

3 Now listen to viewers' reactions. ISF1159

a. What do they have in common?

b. How did these viewers relate to the characters?

4 Look at the title of this article. ▶ Give your point of view. Discuss with your classmates.

5 Read the article and compare with your opinion. How do you relate with the heroes of *your* favourite TV show?

YOUR TURN

Interview *IN PAIRS*

- You are being interviewed about your favourite TV series. Get ready to talk about it, your neighbour will record you!
- Then change roles.

Why we get emotionally attached to TV shows

It's all because we are emotionally involved in the show. But why do we get so attached? The easy answer would be because we connect to the characters, but I don't think a lot of people identify with a demon-killing ghost hunter. But, hey that's just me. I don't know your life. We connect with a show because the writers have a way of making the people in the shows seem real. I mean, as real as they can be. TV shows are an escape from our everyday lives. For 30 minutes to an hour, we can sit down and watch our fantasy lives unfold. We get so attached to these characters' lives because we want to be able to live their lives.

Elizabeth Rodriguez,
theodysseyonline.com,
July 27, 2015

4 This is NOT us!

Previously TV — **THIS IS US** — SHOWS | FORUMS | PODCASTS

Mary1233
I like this show, but I don't LOVE it. I haven't cried once. I think it's cheez whiz. Nicely done cheez whiz, but still. I never meant to watch it, it was the twist all the critics were raving about that got me here. I do feel compelled to stay, though, even if it's unlikely to ever be my fave show.

Chris1192
I too think it's overly cheesy… Don't like that every scene is some drama and it gets resolved in that scene. But I will watch, because Justin! And some stuff is good. But I agree, not my fave show.

MelDib
I'm an awful person. I don't like Kate. She is just too big. She is sooo overweight. It would be great if her weight problem was a bit more realistic. A large portion of Americans are overweight, myself included, I wish that character were more relatable.

RebDouble
I do not care about William's cat. There. I said it.

AlexOne
I don't understand people's endless tears over characters they've known for half a dozen episodes. Or rather: I think people ENJOY watching manipulative cheese and talking about how it made them cry and cry. Some of the speeches on this show are painfully artificial and deliberately tearjerky!

forums.previously.TV, 2016

1 Read the first sentence of each comment.
What do you notice?

2 a. Choose two comments.
For each one, find out:

what the viewer thinks | the reason they give

b. Share with the class.

TIP

- When you take part in a forum, you **give your opinion**. Look at the text and pick out the expressions which allow you to do so:
  – verbs (love, like…),
  – adjectives (*good, fave, cheezy…* → are they positive/negative?)
- **Infer the meaning** of unfamiliar words by analysing:
  – their construction *(over/weight, tear/jerky…)*
  – the context *("people's endless tears […] tearjerky"…)*
- **Check the meanings** of the words you don't know on an online dictionary.

3 React. Based on the "best of" you've seen for this series, do you agree with these comments? Would you like to watch this series?

DEBRIEF

According to Chrissy Metz, an actress in the series *This is us*: "This is happening in the real world. We want to see ourselves on TV, we want to relate to those stories."

Do you agree?

YOUR TURN

Forum *IN GROUPS*

- Choose a TV series you all know.
- Give your opinion (positive or negative) about it on a forum-like page.
- Then pass it on to your group-mates. They will add their own opinions and react to yours.

5 Downton Abbey

Downton Abbey
A British historical TV series which depicts the lives of an aristocratic family and their domestic servants. It is set in the fictional Yorkshire country estate of Downton Abbey, between 1912 and 1926.

▲ Actress Maggie Smith in *Downton Abbey*

1 Look at this picture and the information above. Say all you understand about:

- the time when the woman lived
- her social background
- her personality
- the relationships between masters and servants at the time

2 a. Look at the pictures on p. 55. Which characters belong to: fiction / reality ?

b. Focus on the title of the article and the caption beneath the picture *("Forget the polished image...")*. What can you infer from this? → YP **20**

3 a. Read the article and check your ideas.

WORK your WAY Work on the text p. 55 **or** use a guided version. ISF1160

b. Pick out the following information:

Servants → *Social rights*, *Salary and free time*, *Work*, *Living conditions*, *Clothes*, *Status and relationship with employers*

c. Conclude about the "true story of servants". → YP **34**

DEBRIEF
How can historical TV series influence our vision of the past?

YOUR TURN

A diary

- You are Margaret Powell (text p. 55, l. 50-58).
- Write an entry in your diary. Describe your working day, using information from the text.

WORK your WAY Use only your imagination **or** use the help provided. ISF1161

The real life Downton Abbey: The true story of servants

At the turn of the 20th century when the population of Britain was only 36 million there were 1.5 million servants. That is more than worked on the land or in factories. Our image of this under-class is based on television programmes such as *Downton Abbey* and *Upstairs Downstairs*. Servants are portrayed as a loyal and largely contented breed[1]. These rose-tinted depictions would also have us believe that mutual respect existed across social boundaries.

▲ Forget the polished image of *Downton Abbey*, life below stairs was sadistic and miserable.

In fact, as a new BBC series reveals, their lot could be miserable, degrading and exhausting. Servants were badly paid and often lived in squalor[2]. In the worst homes life was little better than a form of silver-service slavery.

In the big country houses or the great London mansions servants were crammed[3] into shared bedrooms and beds with no bathroom or lavatory facilities. They wore white gloves to serve at table to conceal their grubby[4] hands. [...] Servants worked 17-hour days with time off limited to church on Sunday morning and one afternoon a week. Social historian Dr Pamela Cox, who presents *Servants – The True Story Of Life Below Stairs*, says: "Country houses wouldn't have been able to function without a vast hidden army of servants. However the contrast between the sumptuous family areas and the dull, often squalid servants' quarters was stark. This was a deliberate ploy to demonstrate that they were a class apart."

Dr Cox, whose aim was to strip away some of the nostalgia surrounding this British class, adds: "The work was boring, repetitive and could also be very lonely. Servants were often left utterly exhausted but they had no unions or employment rights."

Invisibility and segregation were part of their job. In some stately homes, hidden passages kept servants separate from family members to spare them the embarrassment of encountering this under-class. Servants were expected to "know their place". Margaret Powell, a former servant who died in 1984, recalled in her memoirs: "I was confined to the basement, the backstairs and the miserable attic room that I shared with another maid and which was so cold in winter that the ice froze in the jugs of water we used for washing. I got up at 5.30 am to clean the fireplaces and front steps, polish the shoes and boots of everyone in the household."

In addition to wearing uniforms servants were expected to have matching hairstyles. Bizarrely in another stripping away of identity they were sometimes given generic names. Historical archives reveal that countless footmen were called William, Henry or James, which were considered "acceptable" names. A favourite maid's name was Sarah.

Adrian Lee, *The Daily Express*, Tuesday 25 Sept. 2012

1. a type of people **2.** extreme dirtiness **3.** *entassés* **4.** dirty

Upstairs, Downstairs

A British television programme about a rich family and their servants who live in London in the early 1900s. It shows the two different worlds of the upper-class people, who live 'upstairs' in the main part of the house, and of their servants who live and work in the lower part of the house (i.e. 'downstairs').

6 The Crown

VIDEO An extract from the official trailer of *The Crown*

▲ Queen Elizabeth II and her TV doppelganger Claire Foy in the British TV series *The Crown*

1 Focus on the two pictures above.
Who are the two women? Compare the pictures. → **YP 12, 15**

2 Now, watch the trailer. IFS1162

a. What can you say about:

the time period | the main characters | their feelings → **YP 2b, 23**

b. How is the Queen portrayed?

3 Read these comments. ▶
What do they reveal about the series?

DEBRIEF

Do you think it is possible for a TV series like *The Crown* to be faithful to reality?

***The Crown* on Netflix is riveting. And not completely true.**

Patricia Treble, Macleans.ca

It humanizes the Royal Family in a way that has never been seen before.

Gabriel Tate, *The Telegraph*

The Queen really liked it, although obviously there were some depictions of events that she found too heavily dramatized.

Royal source

***The Crown* displays Elizabeth as little more than a puppet, a polished dolly.**

Clarisse Loughley | *The Independent* | 7 Novembre 2016

FINAL TASK

Pitch a TV series about teens

HBO is looking for a brand new PG13 series about French teenagers called "This is Us". You and your team are invited to pitch an idea. *IN GROUPS*

1 Get ready

- Think about:

the characters / the actors | the settings (place/time) | the plot | the genre (drama, comedy...)

- Decide how you want teenagers to be portrayed.

2 Action!

- Organize your notes.
- Pitch your ideas to HBO!

or

Your life on screen!

The producers of *Black Mirror* are looking for new ideas. They want to hear about your story!

1 Get ready

- Think about a teenager's worst digital nightmare: ▶
- Imagine: the chain of consequences | your reactions

Your parents tagging you in excruciatingly embarrassing childhood pictures on FB

Sending a message to the wrong person

No wifi for 2 weeks while on holiday in the middle of nowhere

2 Action!

Record your story and send it to the producers. Will it be the next *Black Mirror* episode?

TIP

You can use Essena's experience as a model (text 1 p. 51).
"I was addicted to what others thought of me. Social media had become my sole identity"

WORDS

PRACTISE ONLINE

The story

Nouns
- the **cha**racters
- the lo**ca**tion
- the plot = the **sto**ry
- the **se**tting *(le cadre)*
- the time **per**iod /ˈpɪərɪəd/

Verbs
- de**pict** real life / his**to**rical e**vents**
- be set in the **pre**sent / in the past
- make **peo**ple think / laugh / dream…
- pre**dict** / **fore**tell the **fu**ture
- re**shape** the past = re**write** history /riːˈʃeɪp/
- pro**voke** / **trig**ger e**mo**tions
- be ad**dic**tive

Adjectives
- enter**tai**ning
- **cap**tivating, **ri**veting, ab**sor**bing /əbˈzɔːbɪŋ/
- **ac**curate, **faith**ful to re**a**lity /ˈækjʊrət/
  ≠ in**ac**curate
- in**struc**tive /ɪnˈstrʌktɪv/
- rea**lis**tic ≠ unrea**lis**tic /ˈrɪəlɪstɪk/
- **fright**ening, **sca**ry /ˈfraɪtnɪŋ/
- **wo**rrying, dis**tur**bing, un**set**tling
- **mo**ving, sad
  → a sob **sto**ry, a **tear**jerker
- kitsch, **chee**sy /ˈtʃiːzi/
- **ro**sy = opti**mis**tic
- dark = pessi**mis**tic
- **fa**mily-**friend**ly
- re**la**table

ISF1163

Genres
- **ac**tion
- ad**ven**ture /ədˈventʃə/
- crime **fic**tion, **mys**tery **fic**tion, **thri**ller
- **dra**ma ≠ **co**medy
- dys**to**pia /dɪsˈtəʊpiə/
- **fan**tasy
- his**to**rical **fic**tion, **do**cudrama /hɪˈstɒrɪk(ə)l/
- **hor**ror
- **ro**mance, ro**man**tic **co**medy
- **sci**ence-**fic**tion

ISF1164

TV shows

Viewers

Nouns
- the **au**dience
- the **view**ers, the spec**ta**tors
- a fan, a **fol**lower

Verbs
- **fol**low a show
- have a **fa**vourite show
- be ad**dic**ted = be **hook**ed
- con**nect** with / i**den**tify with / re**late** to a **cha**racter
- be e**mo**tionally in**vol**ved in a show /ɪˈməʊʃnəlɪ/
- live a life by **pro**xy

ISF1165

Broadcasting

The show
- a TV **se**ries, a TV show /ˈsɪəriːz/
- an **e**pisode, the next **e**pisode
- a **sea**son /ˈsiːzən/
- the **sea**son fi**na**le /fɪˈnɑːli/
- a **re**run = a**no**ther **show**ing
- a **trai**ler
- a ‘**best** of’
- a **tea**ser
- a **pro**mo reel /riːl/
  = a pro**mo**tional **vi**deo

The people involved
- an **ac**tor / **ac**tress = the cast
- a role, a **lead** role
- a di**rec**tor
- a **script**writer, a **screen**writer /ˈskriːnraɪtə/
- a pro**du**cer

ISF1166

EXERCISES

❶ The odd one out

a. In each line, one word is not connected to the others. Which one?

1. dystopia – follower – crime fiction – fantasy
2. unsettling – worrying – captivating – disturbing
3. promo reel – trailer – finale – teaser
4. audience – viewers – characters – spectators

b. Make 4 sentences with the words you have found in order to explain their meanings.

❷ User reviews

Complete with words from the mind map.

THE CROWN

★ **10/10** – *The Crown* is really … . I've learned so many things about Elizabeth II!

★ **10/10** – What an extraordinary treat. It's like reading a book you can't put down. I'm totally … !

★ **8/10** – *The Crown* is certainly a beautiful drama, but often historically … . Several scenes give entirely the wrong impression of what truly happened. Why do scriptwriters always need to … the past?

BLACK MIRROR

★ **10/10** – Despite being fictional and mostly sci-fi, it's so … in the scariest way!

★ **9/10** – Of course, the series doesn't explore any positive trends (where would the fun be in that?) – but clearly adopts a … , cynical point of view.

★ **9/10** – Although it's a dark look at what our world could become, *Black Mirror* is NOT a … , it is an actual mirror of a utopian idea gone terribly wrong.

❸ The great noun factory

Si l'on ajoute à un verbe le suffixe *-er* ou *-or*, on obtient un nom désignant la personne qui accomplit l'action :
speak → ***speaker*** / *translate* → ***translator***

a. Find at least four examples in the mind map on p. 58.

b. Now choose four verbs and try to turn them into nouns. Check your answers with your teacher.

❹ Guess my show!

Choose a series you know, then describe it to your classmates, using words from the mind map:

genre | setting | time period | plot | qualities | characters & cast

The show I'm thinking about is **not** a romance…

They must guess what show you are talking about.
Don't make it too easy! Start with general information, then give more precise details. ☺

Pronunciation

PRACTISE ONLINE

❺ Les diphtongues ISF1167

Une diphtongue est une voyelle double composée de deux sons voyelles. En voici quatre parmi les plus courantes :
/aɪ/ comme dans *crime*, ***I***, *my*, *science*
/eɪ/ comme dans *location*, *trailer*, *day*
/ɔɪ/ comme dans ***boy***, *voice*, *noise*
/aʊ/ comme dans ***now*** /naʊ/ ; ***how*** /haʊ/ ; ***out*** /aʊt/

a. Listen and practice pronouncing the words above.

b. Now listen to the following words and classify them.

pilot – reshape – enjoy – trailer – captivating – writer – down – voice – location – disappoint – how

/aɪ/	/eɪ/	/ɔɪ/	/aʊ/

Practise saying them in a loud voice.

❻ Words ending in *-ic* ISF1168

a. Listen to the following words, paying attention to the stressed syllable in each word:

romance – romantic *optimism – optimistic*
fantasy – fantastic *pessimism – pessimistic*

b. What do you notice?

❼ Dictation ISF1169

a. Listen and write down the words you hear.

b. Listen to these words being spelt and check your answers.

GRAMMAR

Les réseaux sociaux, les séries... tout le monde en parle !
Pour rapporter ces propos, on a recours au discours indirect
et pour préciser ce dont on parle, on utilise des pronoms relatifs.

1 Le discours indirect

AlexOne

I don't understand people's endless tears over fictional characters.

❶ Alex **says** (that) **he** doesn't understand people's endless tears over fictional characters.

I really **like** *The Crown*.

❷ The Queen **said** (that) she really **liked** *The Crown*.

"I am quitting social media", O'Neill announced to her followers **last week**. "**My** 'Perfect Life' is actually making me miserable".

❸ **In 2015**, O'Neill **announced** to her followers (that) she was quitting social media.

❹ She **explained** that **her** 'Perfect Life' was actually making her miserable.

- On emploie le **discours indirect** pour rapporter les propos de quelqu'un.
- Le passage du discours direct au discours indirect peut entrainer des modifications de **pronoms** (❶) et de **possessifs** (❹), de **temps** (❷) et de **repères spatio-temporels** (❸).

2 Les pronoms relatifs

❶ The Queen, **who** watched the series, said she really liked it.

❷ *Black Mirror* is a British TV series **that** explores our dependency on technology.

❸ The people **Ø** we meet in *This is us* are regular people, deeply relatable.

❹ Essena O'Neil is a girl **whose** life revolved around social media.

- Pour apporter des précisions sur un groupe nominal, on peut utiliser un **pronom relatif**. Cela permet d'éviter les répétitions :
  - ***who*** ou ***that*** quand l'antécédent est humain (❶)
  - ***which*** ou ***that*** quand l'antécédent est non humain (❷)
  - ***whose*** pour marquer la possession (❹)
  - ***Ø***, dit « relatif zéro », quand l'antécédent a fonction de complément d'objet (❸). On pourrait aussi utiliser ***whom*** ou ***that*** :
    → [*We meet people in* This is us]. *The people* ***Ø*** / ***whom*** / ***that*** *we meet in* This is us...
    (people : COD du verbe *meet*)

EXERCISES

Le discours indirect

❶ Turn an interview into an article

a. Read this newspaper clip. ▼

◄ Actress Gillian Anderson, FBI agent Dana Scully in the long-running and widely popular series *The X-Files*

THE X-FILES / 12 JAN 2018

GILLIAN ANDERSON EXPLAINS WHY SHE'S LEAVING *THE X FILES* AFTER SEASON 11

After 11 seasons, Gillian Anderson has revealed that ...

b. Here is what Gillian Anderson told the journalists:

1. "I'm leaving the show. This is it* for me and I'm really serious."
   * *This is enough, this is the end*
2. "It's time for me to hang up Scully's hat."
3. "I don't want to be tied down to this TV series."
4. "I like to be challenged as an actor and I like to do many characters."
5. "I don't want to comment on how the show ends, I don't want to spoil it!"

Use these quotes to complete the newspaper clip.

> **TIP**
> You can use the following verbs to introduce her speech:
> *reveal – say – add – declare – explain – claim – tell the journalists...*

❷ "What TV shows do you like watching?"

IN PAIRS

a. *Pupil 1:* Listen to Mark's answer and tell your classmate what he said. ISF1172

Pupil 2: Do the same with Annie's answer. ISF1173

b. Do you know these series? Do you like them?

Les pronoms relatifs

❸ Missing pronouns

Complete the sentences with the right pronouns:

1. Elizabeth II, ... father died in 1952, was crowned in 1953.
2. *Victoria*, ... was broadcast last year, has been renewed for a third season.
3. Charlie Brooker, ... created *Black Mirror*, is a British screenwriter and producer.
4. *This is Us* is a series ... plays with our emotions.
5. Bryce Dallas Howard, ... you met at the film premiere, stars in *Nosedive*.
6. The novel ... he wrote was adapted into a series.

❹ Linking sentences

Use a relative pronoun to link both sentences:

1. *Call the Midwife* is a BBC drama series. It shows the lives of a group of London midwives in the 1950s.
2. Peter Morgan is a British film-writer. His series *The Crown* is an international hit.
3. Highclere is a renowned castle. It is featured in *Downton Abbey*.
4. I watched *Feud*. It is based on a true story.

Pronunciation

PRACTISE ONLINE

❺ Stress & intonation to convey meaning ISF1170

a. Listen to Annie speaking about a series she dislikes. Pay attention to:

her intonation | the words she stresses

b. Practise repeating what she says, imitating the way she says it.

> There is a series that I really really hate and it's *The Walking Dead*. I tried to get into it even though I'm not a massive fan of zombie films or zombie series, but I just find it incredibly stressful to listen to and to watch. Even the music in the background is stress-inducing and I really struggle to follow what's going on and at the same time I have the impression that it's constantly the same thing over and over again, so I cannot bring myself to watch that series again!

Now it's your turn: think about *your* favourite series ever and record a review!

Rhythm & Sounds

Listen then say these sentences out loud, imitating the rhythm of the native speaker. ISF1171

- It worked out as being the perfect title in a way.
- I like this show, but I don't LOVE it.
- When I was younger, I used to love football – or soccer if you're American.
- Any game that was displayed on TV, I would definitely, definitely be watching it.

TEST YOUR SKILLS

OBJECTIF BAC

Listening & Writing

Listen to the document three times and report what you have understood. IFS1174

Write about the same topic, following your teacher's instructions.

AUDIO
Reactions to *The Handmaid's Tale* in the time of Trump

Durée 1'30

▲ Author Margaret Atwood with actress Elisabeth Moss from *The Handmaid's Tale*.

Reading & Writing

Your teacher will give you several documents.

- Read them carefully and follow the instructions.

Speaking

React to a document.

- Your teacher will give you a set of two documents.
- In your opinion, which one best illustrates the notion of **FICTION AND REALITY**?
- Explain why.

HOW CAN YOUNG PEOPLE USE THE INTERNET TO MAKE THEIR VOICES HEARD?

CHAPITRE FLASH 5

Students from Marjory Stoneman Douglas High School (Parkland, Fla.) and March for Our Lives organizers (from left) Jaclyn Corin, Alex Wind, Emma González, Cameron Kasky and David Hogg.

#ONLINE CITIZENS

REACT

1. Look at this cover.

a. Do you know who these students are? If not, read the opening of their book. IFS1206

b. What is the link with the title of the chapter?

2. Watch the video. IFS1207
How does this make you feel? Were you right about their motivations?

VIDEO
Alex Wind's speech, Washington D.C. (March 24th, 2018)

Cameron Kasky

HOW IT ALL BEGAN: FEBRUARY 14

I do not need to tell you what happened on February 14. The tragic events that took place at my school are something far too many people know damn well. That story is one of great importance, and looking at our school system's failure to prevent this tragedy is vital in preventing future mass school shootings, but that is not the story I am here to tell. The story I can tell you in great, effective detail is one of overcoming trauma and helplessness, and mobilizing a country that has been through all of this, and failed to take action, far too many times. I am here to tell you how my friends and I ran out of school and, within hours, created and executed a plan to shine a light on just how rigged[1] our system is and just how apathetic[2] our politicians can be.

After evacuating school that day, I found myself on a city bus that was being used to transport students in this state of emergency. I was with the special needs students because, as the shooting occurred, I had just picked up my autistic little brother, Holden, at the ESE (Exceptional Student Education) dismissal. On that bus, I did my best not only to text my friends and confirm that they had made it out of school alive, but also to make sure Holden was okay. As one could imagine, he hadn't truly grasped what had happened... though hardly anybody did, whether or not they shared Holden's optimistic and untainted view of the world.

Holden and I and the other students arrived at the Marriott Hotel right by our school, where the police began to question everyone, and we called our parents to pick us up. Holden was more confused than I've ever seen him. My phone was losing battery, the room was crowded, and we were anxiously awaiting my father's arrival. I was very glad to see some teachers and friends arrive, as I hadn't known until I saw them that they had made it. As soon as we were released, my father drove Holden and me home, and I suddenly felt a terrible feeling. I had finally realized what had happened.

1. rig = to manipulate or control by dishonest means
2. indifferent

▶ Florida Town of Parkland in mourning

When I was locked in the room at school with the special needs students, wondering whether or not I would make it out, I had three things on my mind: survival, Holden's well-being, and the fear that my friends in other classes were no longer alive. On the way to the Marriott, I only thought about my mother and having to tell her what happened, as she was out of town. It wasn't until I sat down in my father's car, knowing that my brother and at least most of my close friends — the ones who hadn't lost their phones and were able to text — were alive, that the thought came upon me: this whole time, I had been way too comfortable. Now, my reality was becoming clear. I knew that I was part of a flavor-of-the-month mass school shooting. The fact that I could easily identify this phenomenon speaks volumes for just how common this is and just how desensitized we have been to these horrific acts. As my dad, Holden, and I got closer and closer to home that night, only six words were present in my mind:

▲ Hundreds stand during a candlelight vigil for the 17 victims of Marjory Stoneman Douglas High School shooting.

This one has to be different.

Suddenly, a dark, daunting purpose consumed me. What could I do? How could I change things? The rules are set up for Marjory Stoneman Douglas to become a part of the American School Shooting Machine. I remembered the usual narrative: Small town. Good, humble people. Some lone wolf shoots up the school. He is a misunderstood, socially ostracized kid. It was a mental health thing. Somehow, mental health shot up a school. Another young, white male. Soon enough, the shooter becomes famous and is the hot new celebrity for the news channels to flash up on their screens.

The people of our country, while deeply hurt and truly affected, will eat it up. Flowers will be sent, cards will be written to the students ("Sorry your school got shot up!"), and thoughts and prayers will be tossed around like a common cold at a state college. Then the flowers will wilt, the people in the school and in the town will try to begin to heal, and somewhere, another school will be shot up. Maybe in a few weeks, maybe in a few months if we're lucky. Maybe a church next time. Or a concert or movie theater. It would happen somewhere, and the thoughts and prayers would, once again, mean less than nothing.

It happens so often that the entire cycle has become routine. Our shooter certainly knew what would come next: he made videos before he completed this atrocious act, where he said that everyone would know his name. To a degree, he was right. There are fan pages for him on the internet. America has a recurring illness that the media and politicians are reluctant to cure.

Arriving at my dad's house, which is about thirty minutes away from Parkland, I was greeted by my family members, who had gathered there to offer their greatest condolences and nothing but support. I didn't have much to say. I left the house, making sure Holden was calm, and went for a walk. I listened to music that was perhaps too intense and emotional. In retrospect, I probably should have just tried to calm down... but dammit, I couldn't. People were dead.

I wasn't sure how many, but people were dead. I crossed the lamp-lit street and began to walk over a nearby bridge. I stood and looked over the water. Nothing felt real. For just a second, everything was perfectly and terrifyingly peaceful. I believe that was the night that almost everything about the person I was before the shooting perished and fell by the wayside. Standing up there, I was reborn with an urgent, painful drive that would now determine the course of my life. I had to skip the healing process and jump right into the fight. I told myself that if the story was going to be different this time, if our school's shooting would be more than a statistic and actually serve as the catalyst, I had to get in front of cameras early on and make this message clear:

This is not the media's narrative. This is not your story. This is nobody's tragedy to interpret but our own. The students of Stoneman Douglas know exactly what happened at Stoneman Douglas, and under no circumstances will you tell our story for us.

Sometime that night, I saw a notification on my phone that a geography teacher in his mid-thirties was killed protecting the students in his classroom. A man who was my camp counselor when I was seven and my fifth-grade teacher, who coincidentally managed to also come to Stoneman Douglas—Scott Beigel. Somebody I knew and loved was murdered. I had to do this for him along with everyone else who was lost. We still weren't sure

▶ Students from Marjory Stoneman Douglas High School planning their next move at the #neveragain office.

how many victims there were. I had lost people that I loved before, but it was almost always to natural causes. I had never seen something so disgusting and unreal hit me so close to home. I had always believed it never could. My whole life, Scott Beigel had been a beacon of love and humor, and now he was gone not because of old age or some sort of sickness but because somebody had shot him while he was trying to protect students. Losing Scott was what made this so much more real for me. I knew Scott; I knew his face, voice, and laugh. I would never get those things back.

▲ Cameron Kasky confronts Senator Marco Rubio about his donations from the NRA during a CNN Town Hall, on Feb 21st 2018.

After my walk, I returned to my room and got on Facebook. I saw that there was already a community event scheduled in Parkland the next morning. I wrote two long essays on Facebook about what had happened. They went what one might dare to call viral, and suddenly, journalists followed up and were coming right to me. All of this, of course, mere hours after the mass murder in the hallways I had been walking for three years. I knew I had to speak up and get out immediately, but this new reality was hitting me hard. I didn't want to become a talking head, a broken record on every news show, but I needed the world to look at these terrible tragedies with a new perspective. I grew up consuming political media like it was candy. I was a rebel without a cause my whole life and, as a drama student, I knew how to clearly express myself. When people called us "crisis actors," they were almost right; I was an actor in a crisis. My whole life, I had been quick to speak up. Quick to be a cynic. I was always able to put my emotions aside and realize what was at stake. At around four thirty a.m., I passed out for three hours, knowing that I would be waking up bright and early. There was an event in Parkland for the people recovering, and I couldn't miss it. Our community was hurt, but we came together so quickly, and that speaks volumes about the amazing people in Parkland. The next morning, more names of victims started to appear. I had no idea what to do or say. My mind was numb, and I had to focus. In the days following the shooting, I was on the news, again and again and again. The means by which different outlets[3] contacted me varied. I can tell you that it was mostly through social media. For example, I was contacted by CNN to write an op-ed[4] piece early in the day. I had to change the narrative as quickly as possible and let the country know that our generation – the school shooting generation – wasn't going to stand for this anymore. My sole focus was working to break the pattern. I immediately started writing, I started learning everything I could about gun reform, and

3. here a media outlet: television, radio, or publishing company
4. a piece of writing that expresses a personal opinion and is usually printed in a newspaper opposite the editorial page.

▲ About 800,000 protesters taking part in the March for Our Lives in Washington DC, on March 24th 2018.

I haven't stopped. Everything I do now is about building this movement and creating real change.

Stoneman Douglas isn't going to become the new Sandy Hook or Columbine (or Aurora, or Virginia Tech, or Santa Fe, or Las Vegas, or Pulse). A place you mention in a room and everyone sighs and says how sorry they are or what a tragedy it is. If Las Vegas wasn't enough, if Sandy Hook wasn't enough, we are going to be enough. We are going to be the catalyst for real change. This is going to count. On February 16, two days after the shooting, a group of us, Brendan Duff, Kaylyn Pipitone, Jaclyn Corin, Alex Wind, and Sofie Whitney, gathered at my house. Earlier that day, I had done Anderson Cooper's show, one amongst many, many others. At the crack of dawn, I ran into my old friend David Hogg under the freeway that is right next to my school. I wasn't the least bit surprised to see David springing into action, as he had always been politically charged and involved. I wouldn't see David again until the next day. All I had to begin my work was my closest friends. I texted them as soon as I knew they could get involved. Jackie was already planning a trip to Tallahassee to speak with legislators and encourage them to take immediate action. In a night of brainstorming on the sixteenth, we decided we needed to march. So many great things that have happened in this country have come from displays of young people making their voices heard. This all came from a place of helplessness. It was in overcoming that helplessness that we found our strength, and we want to provide our country with the opportunity to not be helpless as well. In those two short days, we were already starting to see the cycle change. It wasn't just talking heads on the news anymore, it was me and my friends. They gave us a platform, after only twenty-four hours of real, focused effort, and we took it and ran with it. The march was about seeing how far we could go and whether or not we could truly activate the people in this country. Public displays are important, peaceful protest is patriotic, and uniting people is a beautiful thing, but real change in this country comes from the polls. It was time to destroy the apathy toward political involvement that is running our country into the ground.

People say that we shed light on America's gun violence problem, that we exposed how bad things really are. We didn't do that. America knew damn well how bad our gun problem was. We reminded America how rigged[5] the system is. We reminded people what the NRA is doing and what Citizens United is doing to our political system. We reminded them by asking our politicians directly, in public, about campaign donations from the NRA. When I spoke with Senator Marco Rubio at the CNN Town Hall, I wasn't asking him to change his views on guns—I asked him if he would stop taking money from the NRA. When you remind American people where the money is coming from, you expose what a politician's real interests are.

We knew that seventeen of the finest human beings in the world were no longer alive, and everybody who knew and loved them would have to find a way to keep going. A gargantuan storm was coming our way, and as our group began to expand, first with more and more people showing up in my home, and later growing way beyond Parkland, we survived thanks to each other. Every day, especially as we visited the memorials and attended the funerals, it got harder. Every day, the pain got worse. But this movement and this purpose we had found kept us going, beyond what I could have ever imagined. From a movement that started with just a few friends in my living room it has become a force that could change our country. I had no idea just how large this movement would become, but knowing the power and strength of our group, I'm not surprised.

Glimmer of Hope: How Tragedy Sparked a Movement, March for Our Lives, October 2018

▶ Cameron Kasky delivering a speech during the March for Our Lives.

5. *See note p. 64*

1 **Look at the source, read the title and the first paragraph.**
What can you expect from Cameron Kasky's text?

2 **Read the rest of the text, at your own pace.** If you want to read it over several days, do not hesitate to do so.

> **WORK your WAY** Read this version of the text **or** use a guided version. IFS1208

3 **What do you think of this text?** Share with your classmates.

4 **"How it all began":** write a bullet point journal to sum up the different stages.

February 14th
- *picked up my brother*
- *took the bus to the Marriot Hotel*
- *...*

5 *"I'm here to tell you how my friends and I [...] created and executed a plan to shine a light on just how rigged our system is and just how apathetic our politicians are."* (l. 8-10)
After reading Cameron's story, do you understand why and how they executed such a plan? → **YP 25, 30**

6 **GROUP TALK** Discuss one of these quotes, or any other from the text:

> This is not the media's narrative. [...] under no circumstances will you tell our story for us.
(l. 92-95)

> So many great things that have happened in this country have come from displays of young people making their voices heard.
(l. 159-61)

> Public displays are important, peaceful protest is patriotic, and uniting people is a beautiful thing, but real change in this country comes from the polls.
(l. 168-70)

7 **At home** These students are still very active and engaged.
Follow them on social media and find out what they are up to.

DEBRIEF

What are your impressions? your reactions? How important has the Internet been in giving these citizens a voice?

FINAL TASK

Join the movement!

Choose one or several of the following tasks. You can do them on your own or in groups.

Reader's review

Write a review of Kasky's "How it all began" narrative and publish it on the Amazon page of the book.

Book club

Read another chapter of *Glimmer of Hope* and select a passage you find particularly powerful.
Then share it with your friends.

Tweet your thoughts

Send Cameron Kasky or one of the March for Our Lives students a message via a social network to let them know what you think of their movement.

> One hundred of my classmates and I will be traveling toTallahassee this Tuesday and Wednesday to speak with our State Senators and House of Representative members.
> We are so grateful to have this opportunity to advocate for gun control, mental health, school safety, & more.
>
> 1.6K 852 3.3K

Favourite quotes

Choose your favourite quotes from Cameron Kasky's narrative and make an illustrated poster with them.

Interview

IN PAIRS Imagine an interview of Cameron Kasky based on his narrative. Ask the questions to a friend who will play his role.

GRAMMAR

Pour évoquer la tragédie de Parkland et expliquer les actions menées par le mouvement *March for Our Lives*, on est amené à utiliser les temps du passé et *Be going to* + BV.

1 Le récit au passé

Prétérit simple

❶ Holden and I and the other students **arrived** at the Marriott Hotel right by our school, where the police **began** to question everyone, and we **called** our parents to pick us up.

❷ We would not need metal detectors and clear backpacks and more weapons in our streets if there **weren't** weapons of war in the hands of civilians.

- Le **Prétérit simple** est utilisé pour parler d'événements en rupture avec le **présent** ou avec la **réalité**.
- Dans le premier cas, il est l'outil du récit de **rapporter des faits révolus** ❶.
- Dans le second cas, il permet d'**évoquer ce qui ne correspond pas à la réalité des faits** ❷ : *« … s'il n'y avait pas d'armes de guerre entre les mains de la population civile. »*

→ Précis 19 p. 239

Prétérit *BE* + *-ing*

❸ When I spoke with Senator Marco Rubio at the CNN Town Hall, I **wasn't asking** him to change his views on guns – I asked him if he would stop taking money from the NRA.

- Le **Prétérit *BE* + *-ing*** permet de **revenir sur un fait passé** *(spoke)* **pour l'expliciter ou le commenter**. *"I wasn't asking him to change his views on guns"* n'est dit que pour expliciter l'intention de Cameron lors de son échange avec le sénateur Rubio.

→ Précis 20 p. 240

Le *Past Perfect*

❹ I was with the special needs students because, as the shooting **occurred**, I **had** just **picked up** my autistic little brother, Holden, at the ESE dismissal.

Passé — ***Past Perfect*** — **moment du récit** — Présent →

I **had** just **picked up** my autistic little brother — the shooting **occurred**

- Le ***Past Perfect*** est utilisé pour narrer **un fait antérieur** à un **événement passé**.

→ Précis 22 p. 241

2 *Be going + to + BV*

▶ If Las Vegas wasn't enough, if Sandy Hook wasn't enough, we **are going to be** enough.
We **are going to be** the catalyst for real change.
This **is going to count**.

- On emploie ***be going* + *to* + BV** pour annoncer un événement futur en cours de préparation ou en bonne voie de réalisation.

Prononciation

- À l'oral, *going to* se prononce parfois *gonna* (/ˈɡənə/ ou /ˈɡɑːnə/). *"I'm gonna tell you something".*
- Attention toutefois : cette prononciation relève de l'anglais familier, il ne faut pas l'écrire !

→ Précis 28 p. 244

PRACTISE ONLINE

WORDS

Confronting the authorities

- **a**dvocate for (gun con**trol** / **chan**ges...)
- give a speech
- speak out a**gain**st gun violence
- make your**self** heard / make your voice heard
- de**noun**ce, ex**pos**e, rev**eal**
- shine a light on / shed light on (an **is**sue / the reasons for... / the need for...)
- work to change the law /lɔː/
- con**front** sb: *affronter / défier qqun*
- **pre**ssure (lawmakers, politicians...) to change the law
- press sb to **cla**rify their po**si**tion on (gun legis**la**tion)

IFS1209

Mobilizing people

- bring **pe**ople to**ge**ther
- **ga**ther / **ra**lly **pe**ople a**round** a cause
- rally people to join a movement
- **mo**bilize **pe**ople against (gun violence) /aɪ/
- **mo**tivate **pe**ople to do sth
- raise aw**a**reness ab**out** sth
- spread awareness ab**out** sth /e/
- launch / **ini**tiate a **move**ment
- organ**ize** a **pro**test / a march /mɑːtʃ/

IFS1210

used / made the most of / took advantage of

Online citizens

- **di**gital **na**tives /ˈdɪdʒɪtl/
- on**line** activists
- **stu**dent **ac**tivist

- **so**cial **me**dia (**web**sites)
- **main**stream **me**dia
- **me**dia **out**lets /ˈaʊtlets/
- tweets / posts

IFS1211

provided them with the means to / enabled them to / gave them the opportunity to

TEST YOUR SKILLS

Reading & Writing

OBJECTIF BAC

Discover what a prominent public figure thinks of the March for Our Lives activists.

- Read the text your teacher will give you. Explain what you have understood.
- Follow the instructions.

TO WHAT EXTENT ARE GUNS EMBEDDED IN AMERICAN CULTURE?

6

GUN CULTURE

REACT

1. Look at the picture.

a. What feelings does it inspire?
→ YP 2

b. In your opinion, what is the man doing? And where is he?

2. Listen to someone commenting on this picture. IFS1257

3. **Recap** what you have understood about:

where the man is | what he is doing

AUDIO Commentary

▲ Las Vegas, 2013

DEBRIEF

What do you find most striking about what you have seen and heard?

Could a scene like this one happen where you live? Why?

1 Pop Culture Big Guns

MOVIES

What about language?
Look at the posters closely and find a colloquial expression that contains a gun-related word.
Do you know other gun-related expressions?

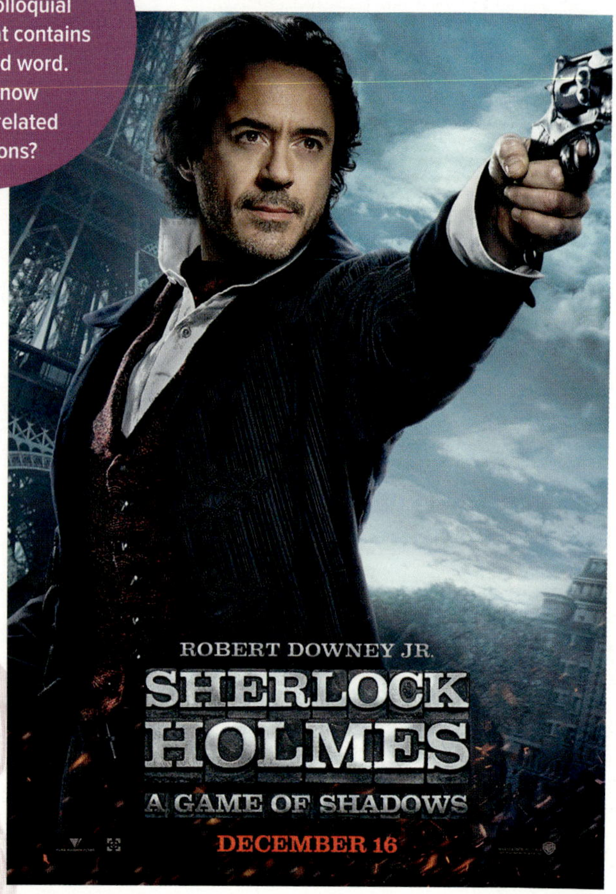

1. **Look at the movie posters.**
   What do they have in common?
2. *IN GROUPS* **Pick one of these movies and pay attention to:**
   the title | the tagline | the heroes | the gun
   Share your observations.
3. **Discuss them with classmates who worked on different posters.** → YP 5a, 25
   What does this tell you about the place of guns in American movies?
4. **React.** Think about movies from other countries.
   Do guns have the same place?

VIDEO GAMES

1 Look at the video game covers.

a. Have you heard of these games? Have you played them?

b. What seems to be the role of guns in the games?

2 Look at the covers again. What age groups are these games intended for?

3 Read this Common Sense Media rating:

Common Sense says
age ★★★★★
Outstanding Western adventure has very mature themes.

Parents say	*Kids say*
age ★★★★★	age ★★★★★
Based on 86 reviews	Based on 61 reviews

a. Guess: which game it rates
the age group recommended by Common Sense, by parents and by kids

b. Check with the original. Compare with the age group indicated on the game cover. What do you think? → **YP 37** IFS1258

4 IN GROUPS **Read a review for the same game.** IFS1259

age ★★★★★
One of the Best Games of 2018
I believe that this game is amazing (as well as many other people) but I think it is a matter of your child's maturity.

a. What does the user seem to think of gun violence in the game in your review? → **YP 17, 19**

b. Compare with the other groups' reviews.

DEBRIEF

What do these documents show about the place of guns in popular culture?

YOUR TURN

Post a review on Common Sense Media

- Review one of these movies or games, based on:
  the poster or cover | the trailer online
  Pay attention to the place of guns and the way they are represented.
- Post your review on Common Sense Media and see if other people share your opinion.

2 An easy target

Fourteen-year-old Pearl France lives in the front seat of a broken-down car and her mother Margot lives in the back. Together they survive on a diet of powdered milk and bug spray, love songs and stolen cigarettes. All around them, Florida is populated with gun owners – those hunting alligators for sport, those who want to protect their families, and those who create a sense of danger.

Penguin Books

"We need this gun now"

Two weeks later a gun came into our car. For twelve years the Mercury had been full of dolls, stuffed animals, our clothes, boxes of dried foods and fruit, blankets, and books.

We need this gun now, my mother said. Eli says we need it because the police were here. Don't touch it ever. I'll teach you how to use it. On the weekend we'll go down to the river and practice, okay? We'll go early when there's no one around.

She handed me the pistol. It was small and black.

See, it's not so heavy, she said. Eli says it has fifteen rounds. I can shoot it fifteen times before I have to put another magazine into it.

Where did he get this gun?

I don't know. [...]

The following Saturday we woke up early and went down to the river.

I'm not even scared of an alligator now that I have this gun in my hand, my mother said.

Do you really know how to use it?

Eli's been giving me lessons while you've been at school, she said. I'm a natural. A real natural. That's what Eli said. I think it's all my piano practice. I hit all the targets. It was easy. I got lucky every time. Eli said, when anyone shoots a gun, you don't have to do a whole lot to make it happen.

At the river, near the dock, my mother placed a white piece of paper on a tree. She'd drawn a black circle in the middle with a marker.

Eli made me do it blindfolded and I did, my mother said. I hit the mark every time.

At the river my mother repeated the words Eli had used to teach her. Use your dominant eye, she said. Do not squat, blink, or duck your head.

I stood square to the target and placed the gun up to my eye level.

You want something good to happen with that bullet, my mother said. That's what Eli said. You want something good to happen.

I didn't hit the target.

It's your little hand, my mother said. You really need a tiny, child's gun.

My fifteen bullets only left holes in the air. Do we really need to have this? I asked.

Eli gave me the gun, my mother said. It's a present.

Why?

Don't tell any of your friends we have it. Don't tell. It is to be safe. Protection.

Protection?

It's like an umbrella in the rain. Why did Eli give it to you? He thinks this pistol is like giving me roses, my mother said. Eli thought that two girls living all alone in a car is all a gun needs.

Gun Love, Jennifer Clement (2018)

1 **Look at the book cover.** ▶

a. What can you imagine about the novel?

b. Read the Penguin Books summary. Does it match your expectations?

2 **Read the beginning of the text** (l. 1-14). Can you identify: who the narrator is / who the narrator is with ?

3 **Read the rest of the text.**

a. IN PAIRS Discuss what you have understood.

b. Read the summary again. What type of "gun owners" are: Pearl's mother / Eli ?

c. In your opinion, how does each character in the scene feel?

TIP

- Try to **picture** what is being told.
- **Highlight** each character's lines in a different colour on your copy of the text.
- Then read the text **out loud**, maybe even with a classmate so each of you can play a role. IFS1260

4 GROUP TALK Discuss one of these quotes:

"You want something good to happen with that bullet." (l. 27)

"It's like an umbrella in the rain." (l. 37)

"two girls living all alone in a car is all a gun needs." (l. 38-39)

5 **React.** Jennifer Clement said *"I always believed that literature can change the world."* For you, what did she try to change with this text? How? → **YP 22**

6 Now that you have discovered the novel, what do you think the cover represents?

DEBRIEF

In your opinion, why do some Americans feel the need to have guns?

YOUR TURN

Design a new book cover

Penguin Books is publishing a new edition of *Gun Love*, and looking for a new, powerful cover. Give it a try, either by hand or digitally.

- Your cover should include: an illustration / the title & author / a one-sentence review.
- Get ready to explain your choices as you present your creation to the Penguin Books publishers.

3 Courage under fire

- Take a tour of the **history of guns in the United States.**
- Complete a KLQ chart as you go, and use Mark's audioguide to help you on your journey!

Fighting for survival

1620

The Pilgrims arrive.

◄ *The Pilgrim Fathers arrive at Plymouth, Massachusetts on board the Mayflower, November 1620.* W.J. Aylward, 1754

AUDIO Audioguide - 1 IFS1261

Fighting for independence

1775

The Revolutionary War breaks out.

◄ *Battle of Lexington, April 1775*

AUDIO Audioguide - 2 IFS1262

The right to bear arms

1791

The 2nd Amendment is added to the US Constitution.

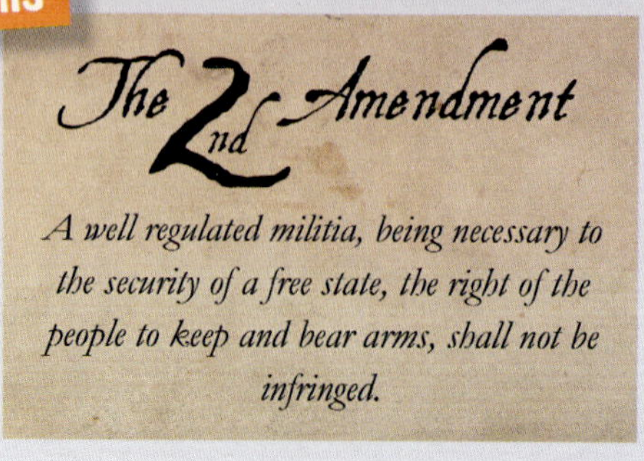

The 2nd Amendment

A well regulated militia, being necessary to the security of a free state, the right of the people to keep and bear arms, shall not be infringed.

► The American Constitution

AUDIO Audioguide - 3 IFS1263

Fighting for territory

1804

The Westward expansion begins.

◀ *Manifest Destiny.* John Gast, 1872

AUDIO Audioguide - Part 4 IFS1264

Protecting our rights

1871

The NRA is formed.

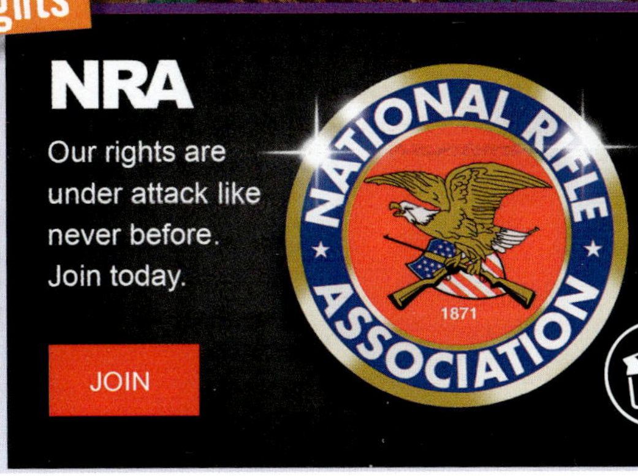

▶ A promotional film for the NRA

VIDEO Welcome to the NRA IFS1265

DEBRIEF

How can you link this history with the place of guns in America today?

YOUR TURN

Make up a caption! *IN GROUPS*

You are contributing to an exhibition entitled "The need for guns in America: a history".

- **Choose a historical event and a picture representing it.**
- **Write the caption for your picture.**

It should include:

– information about the picture (title, author, date),

– information about the event (date, place, context),

– a short analysis.

WORK your WAY Choose a document from these pages or discover another landmark. IFS1266

4 A silver bullet?

Interests protected

And now thanks to your activism and dedication, you'll have an administration fighting to protect your 2nd Amendment, and we will protect your 2nd Amendment.

Your 2nd Amendment rights are under siege, but they will never, ever be under siege as long as I'm your president. All of us here today are united by the same timeless values. We believe that our liberty is a gift from our creator and that no government can ever take it away. We believe in the rule of law. And we support the men and women of law enforcement.

We have pride in our history and respect for our heritage. [...]

The one thing that has always stood between the American people and the elimination of our Second Amendment rights has been conservatives in Congress willing to fight for those rights. [...] We've got to get Republicans elected.

Extract from Donald Trump's speech at the NRA convention, May 2018

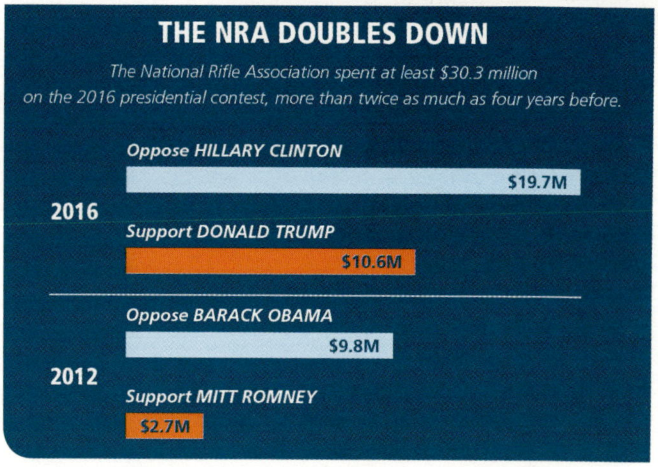

1 Look at the infographic. ▸

a. What do you think about it?

b. Can you imagine what the NRA's motivations are?

2 Read the first paragraph of the text and look at the source.

a. Try to work out who "you" and "us" stand for.

b. What does this sentence imply? (Remember the infographic).

3 Read the speech and try to understand:

- what Donald Trump promises
- what he wants in return
- what his motivations could be

TIP

Pay attention to the vocabulary Trump uses. Can you relate it with what you have learned in this chapter?

4 React. Do you think this speech is convincing for NRA members? Why? → **YP 27, 28**

5 Go further. Read the definition of "lobbying":

Lobbying *(n.)***:** an attempt at influencing government officials to make decisions for or against something.

a. Would you call what the NRA does "lobbying"?

b. Does lobbying exist in your country? Do you think it should be permitted in politics?

DEBRIEF

What role does the NRA play in maintaining gun culture in the US?

FINAL TASK

Interactive art

Take part in the project *Guns in America*: record your own story.

1 Get ready

- Explore the project by listening to at least three stories. e IFS1276
- Choose who you will speak for:
  – Pearl (*Gun Love* p. 78),
  – A student from #OnlineCitizens (p. 63),
  – Yourself (a student in France who has just learned about American gun culture).
- Prepare notes about what you want to say.

2 Action!

- Record your story and post it online for your classmates to discover! ***OR***
- Create an interactive work of art in your class.

Time partnered with French artist JR to develop this project. In three U.S. cities profoundly affected by guns– Dallas, St. Louis, and Washington, D.C. – they invited people to share their views, describe their experiences and search for common ground. They met hunters and activists, teachers and police officers, parents and children. JR photographed 245 people to create this moving mural.

TIP

- Take a class photo, and record your story.
- Use vocaroo.com to record yourself. Print your audio as a QR code to attach to the class photo. Scan each QR code to hear the stories!

or

Creative writing

Write a new passage for the book *Gun Love*.

1 Get ready

- Choose what you want to imagine:

the end of the conversation between Pearl and her mother

a conversation between Pearl and Eli

the moment when Eli taught Pearl's mother how to use a gun

...

- Think about: each character's stance on guns

their personalities

the history of guns and their importance in US society

2 Action!

Write your text, then publish it on a Padlet wall.

Discover your classmates' passages and leave a comment! ☺

WORDS

PRACTISE ONLINE

GUNS IN THE USA

Guns

- a **fi**rearm (general)
  /aɪə/
- a (**se**mi-auto**ma**tic, **ful**ly auto**ma**tic) **pis**tol
  /ˈpɪstl/
- a **ri**fle, a **hun**ting **ri**fle,
  /aɪ/
  an as**sault ri**fle
- ammu**ni**tion, **am**mo, **bul**lets
  /ʊ/
- shoot, fire
- aim at (sth / sb): *viser (qque chose ou qqun)*

IFS1267

Gun culture

- be ingr**ai**ned (in) (→ Gun culture is ingrained.)
- be em**bed**ded in sth
  (→ Guns are embedded in American culture.)
- be part of the A**me**rican **he**ritage / pass sth down
  (→ Gun culture is passed down from generation to generation.)
- be scared (of sth), fear sth (**dan**ger, **vi**olence…)
- feel the need to pro**tect** oneself from sth

IFS1268

Gun owners

- own a gun, have a gun, be a **gun ow**ner:
  /əʊn/
  posséder une arme
- **car**ry a gun: *porter une arme*
- be **ca**pable of using a **wea**pon
  /ˈwepən/
- know how to use a **wea**pon
- use a gun…
  for sur**vi**val
  /aɪ/
  for pro**tec**tion, **self**-de**fense**, **sa**fety,
  for se**cu**rity **rea**sons
  for **hun**ting,
  for recre**a**tional **pur**poses
  /eɪ/ /ˈpɜːpəsɪz/
  to **prac**tice **shoo**ting **sports**

IFS1269

Gun lobbies

- an associ**a**tion, a **lob**bying **group**
  /ˈlɒbiɪŋ/
- **ad**vocate **gun** rights, be an **ad**vocate of **gun** rights, fight for **gun** rights
  ≠ sup**port strict**er gun con**trol**
- de**fend** the right to keep arms / to bear arms / to bear **wea**pons
- run ad**ver**tisements / ads
- train **peo**ple in the use of **fire**arms
- **e**ducate the **pu**blic about **fire**arms
- make **cam**paign do**na**tions
- **lob**by a**gainst gun** con**trol**
- at**tempt** to **in**fluence **can**didates / poli**ti**cians / the **go**vernment
- the (Trump/Obama) adminis**tra**tion
- the Re**pub**lican party ≠ the Demo**cra**tic **par**ty

> ad**ver**tisement (UK)
> /ɪ/
> **ad**vertisement (US)
> /aɪ/

IFS1270

It's in the language

Look up three of these expressions online, then get ready to share with the class. ▶

- I call **shot**gun!
- **shot**gun **wed**ding
- **trig**ger a re**ac**tion
- **fas**ter than a **spee**ding **bul**let
- gun for **some**thing
- **rea**dy, aim, fire
- walk in, guns **bla**zing
- a **snap**shot
- a loose **can**non
- shoot from the hip
- fire away
- hit me with your best shot
- bite the bullet
- make an **off**hand re**mark**

IFS1271

EXERCISES

1 Survey

Here is a survey conducted in 2017.

a. Complete the key using what you have learned.

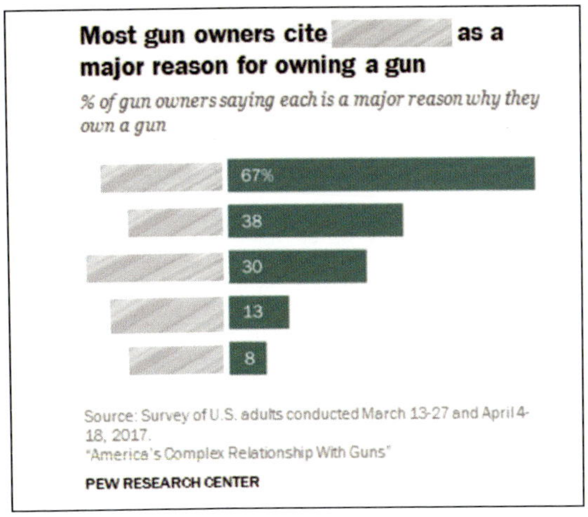

b. Check the original. IFS1280

c. Sort these reasons from the most understandable to the least understandable reasons to own a gun, in your opinion. Then discuss with the class.

2 Transformations

Complete these sentences logically using what you have learned.

1. In Western movies, the hero uses his gun to ... himself and others.
2. Some rural Americans use ... as a way to provide food for their families.
3. The NRA makes ... to candidates who support gun rights.
4. Lobbies are organizations that try to ... opinion by ... advertisements and campaigning.
5. The difficulty in toughening gun laws is partly due to the fact that gun culture is ... .

3 Label it!

Write a short paragraph explaining the message of this political cartoon.Use some of the words or phrases from the mind map on page 84.

4 Target practice

Match the expression to its explanation.

walk in, guns blazing – make an offhand remark – call shotgun – gun for something – a loose cannon

1. Make a comment without taking time to think.
2. Demand to sit in the front seat of the car.
3. A person who is unpredictable, in a negative sense.
4. Enter a place or situation with dominance, force, and sometimes aggression.
5. Have an objective and try hard to achieve it.

Pronunciation

PRACTISE ONLINE

5 Word stress IFS1273

Certaines terminaisons peuvent entraîner un déplacement de l'accentuation par rapport au mot d'origine :
com**mu**nicate *(v)* → communi**ca**tion *(n)*

a. Say the following sentences out loud.

1. Although schools may **educate** students about gun safety, this **education** may not be enough.
2. Lobbying groups try to **influence** candidates, and some groups are very **influential**.
3. Pop culture has a strong effect on the **public** because of ads and other forms of **publicity**.

b. Listen and check your word stress.

6 Similar sounds IFS1272

a. Listen to the contrast in the two vowels sounds:

look /ʊ/ — do /u:/

b. How would you pronounce the following words?

shoot – group – full – school – who – could – would

c. Listen and check.

GRAMMAR

La question des armes à feu divise profondément la nation américaine. Pour aborder ce sujet complexe, on est amené à exprimer le **but** et le **contraste**.

1 Exprimer le but

1. This man must be there **to buy** a firearm.
2. Most gun owners possess firearms **so as to be able to** defend themselves and not depend on the government for protection.
3. Many Americans own a gun **so that** they can defend themselves.
4. A man was arrested **for** carrying a gun without a legal permit.

What do they need a gun **for**?

Why was the man arrested?

- Il est important de faire la différence entre le **BUT** et la **CAUSE** afin d'employer les expressions appropriées en anglais.
  Lorsque vous hésitez, demandez-vous si ce que vous voulez exprimer répond à la question :

Dans quel but ?

→ ***to*** ❶, ***in order to***, ***so as to*** ❷ suivis d'une base verbale.

→ ***so that*** ❸ suivi d'une proposition contenant un modal comme *can* ou *may*.

Pour quelle raison ?

→ ***for*** ❹ suivi d'un verbe en *-ing* ou d'un groupe nominal.

→ ***because***, ***since*** suivis d'une proposition.

→ Précis 41 p. 239

2 Exprimer un contraste

1. Most American people are allowed to buy and carry guns **whereas** in France, **it is forbidden**.
2. **While French people tend to rely on the police to protect them**, most American people believe they have to defend themselves.
3. The message of the movie is "protect", **yet it suggests that**, in order to do so, one should wage a war.
4. These video games are meant for mature audiences. **However, many players are quite young and it is not uncommon to find positive reviews from parents of 11-year-olds.**
5. **Despite a series of mass shootings** in the US in recent years, there have been very few gun control reforms.

- Pour marquer un contraste entre deux propositions, on peut utiliser :

despite ❺ / **in spite of**	+ GN	→ **Annonce quelque chose d'inattendu et de surprenant** NB : avec *even though*, on marque une insistance plus grande qu'avec *although* et *though*.
yet ❸	+ GV	
although / **though** / **even though**	+ GV	
whereas ❶ / **while** ❷	+ GV	→ **Indique un contraste entre deux faits ou deux idées**
however (suivi d'une virgule !) ❹	+ GV	

→ YP 15

EXERCISES

Exprimer le but

1 What for?

Finish each sentence logically.

1. Pioneers carried rifles for...
2. Cowboys carried handguns so as to...
3. Guns in the military and the police are used to...
4. After a tragedy, many people buy guns so that...

2 Books and Bullets

Complete the text using each expression once!

in order to – so that – so as to

Gun Love author Jennifer Clement is an activist who writes novels ... make a difference in the world. While writing this book, she did substantial research ... understand gun culture in the United States. Like many authors, she gives her books to other writers ... they can critique them.

3 Pop! Culture

Complete the descriptions of movies and video games using each expression once!

so that – in order to – because – to

1. ... solve crime, Sherlock Holmes needs a pistol.
2. In *Red Dead Redemption II*, people use guns ... get revenge.
3. The main character of *Underworld* carries two pistols ... she can "Protect the Bloodline."
4. *Grand Theft Auto V* requires you to use a gun ... commit crimes.

Exprimer le contraste

4 The paradox of gun culture

a. **Choose one of these cartoons and imagine you are the author. Explain the message that you, the cartoonist, meant to express.**

b. **Draw a similar cartoon showing one of the paradoxes of the gun issue. Share it with the class.**

Pronunciation

PRACTISE ONLINE

5 Contrasting IFS1274

a. **Listen carefully to the pronunciation of the following words:**

despite – in spite of – although – even though – whereas – while - however

b. **Practise pronouncing them.**

Rhythm & Sounds

Listen then say these sentences out loud, imitating the rhythm of the native speaker IFS1275

- Americans were pioneers, and pioneers needed guns.
- Some people want a gun because it makes them feel safe. It's for protection.
- This video game ought to be for an older age group.
- The National Rifle Association is one of the most powerful, well organized lobbies in the world.

HOW TO... get better at speaking

Small changes, big results!

Pronunciation and rhythm can make all the difference to making yourself understood in English!

Strategies

Try these strategies for the "Interactive art" project on p. 83.

Get ready

- **Jot down** what you plan to say.
- **Record yourself** straight away.

You will come back to your recording once you've tried out the following tips.

Mind the pronunciation!

- Check the **pronunciation** of the words that you're unsure of.
  You can use:
  – an online English dictionary
  – an online multilingual dictionary
  – a text-to-speech device
- This will give you both:
  – a recording of the word
  – its phonetic transcription

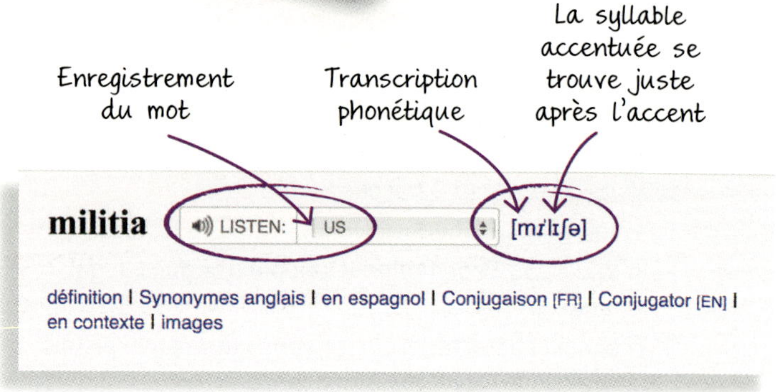

WordReference.com

Look up these words on WordReference and practise pronouncing them. ▶

LEGIS**LA**TION • **CUL**TURE • **WEA**PON

HERITAGE • A**ME**RICAN • **GUN OW**NER

IFS1277

Mind the rhythm!

- In a sentence there are both:
  – **unstressed** words and syllables
  – **stressed** ones.
- This combination produces the **rhythm** of the sentence.

Listen to this sentence and practise pronouncing it. ▶

Many gun owners are in favour of stricter gun legislation.

IFS1278

YOUR TURN!

Record your audioguide

Listen to your first draft again. Based on what you have learnt, is there anything you would like to improve?

If so, give it another try!

TEST YOUR SKILLS

OBJECTIF BAC

Listening & Writing

- **Listen** to the document three times and report what you have understood. IFS1279
- **Write** about the same topic, following your teacher's instructions.

AUDIO
Why do some Americans love guns so much?

Durée 1'30

Reading & Writing

- **Your teacher will give you several documents.**
  - Read them carefully and follow the instructions.

Speaking

- **React to a document.**
  - Your teacher will give you a set of two documents.
  - In your opinion, which one best illustrates the notion of **CITIZENSHIP AND THE DIGITAL WORLD**?
  - Explain why.

INNOVATIONS SCIENTIFIQUES ET RESPONSABILITÉ

7

AI: FRIEND OR FOE?

REACT

1. **Look at the photo.** How does it make you feel? Why? → **YP 2b**
2. **Read this definition:**

   Artificial Intelligence (AI):
   the ability of a digital computer or computer-controlled robot to perform tasks commonly associated with intelligent beings.

   Imagine who Ava is and what she can do.
3. **Listen to the recording.** IFS1308

   a. Compare your reaction with Mark's.

   b. How many times do you hear the words *"American / America / The USA"*? Try to understand why they are repeated so often.

▲ Ava, in the film *Ex Machina* (1995)

DEBRIEF

How do you feel about AI?
What is your own experience of it?

1 "Are they for real?"

1 Watch the video with the sound off. IFS1309

a. What do you think of the robots shown in the video? Are you impressed?

b. Imagine what these robots were created for.

2 Watch the video with the sound on. IFS1309

a. Can the robots do more than you thought?

b. Recap what you have learnt about them.

Robot n° 1 → Name: ... / Purpose: ... / Risks: ... / Advantages: – ... – ... – ...

3 React. The narrator says of the last robot: *"Many people did find it a bit creepy but I really just see good engineering."* What do you think?

VIDEO
Next Generation Robots – Boston Dynamics (2018)

2 AI-powered technologies

The documents on p. 93 illustrate different areas in which AI is used.

1 IN GROUPS Choose one of the documents.

a. Collect the information you find interesting and organize it in a spidergram.

b. Get ready to answer the questions your classmates may have.

2 Share your findings with the class.

TIP

- Take time to anticipate the contents of the document, using the following elements: picture / title / source / legend / ...

Note down all your ideas and organize them in a spidergram (see question 2 above).

- Check them as you read or listen.

3 GROUP TALK

Would you interact with any of these machines?

Which technology do you find the most useful? Which do you find the most frightening? Why?

DEBRIEF

From the examples on these pages, do you think we should give more or less power to AI?

YOUR TURN

AI-mazing!

Share an interesting fact or anecdote about AI.
It can be: an amazing breakthrough / a funny incident / a historical fact / ...

IN GROUPS

GROUP 1

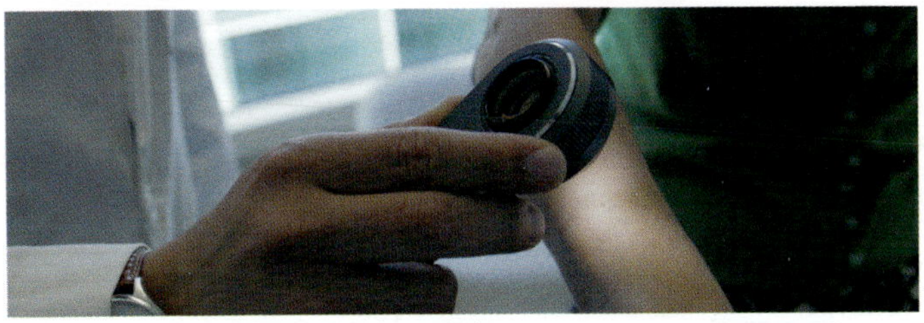

Deep learning algorithm does as well as dermatologists in identifying skin cancer

ByTaylor KUBOTA, January 2017

Universal access to health care was on the minds of computer scientists at Stanford when they set out to create an artificially intelligent diagnosis algorithm for skin cancer. They made a database of nearly 130,000 skin disease images and trained their algorithm to visually diagnose potential cancer. From the very first test, it performed with inspiring accuracy. [...]
That's when we said, 'Look, this is not just a class project for students, this is an opportunity to do something great for humanity.'

news.stanford.edu

The world's first robot 'super-microsurgery' was successful

By Mike WEHNER, October 4, 2017

Surgeons from the Maastricht University Medical Center in the Netherlands completed the first robot-assisted super-microsurgery. The robot was used to suture vessels measuring as small as 0.3 millimeters across. It's such an incredibly delicate procedure that very few surgeons on the planet will even attempt it [...].
The robot is controlled by a surgeon who, by moving their own hands, prompts tiny, precise movements of the robot's small claws. As it translates the surgeon's movements into commands for the robot, the system can mitigate any shakiness or unsteady motion, leading to a cleaner and more perfect operation.

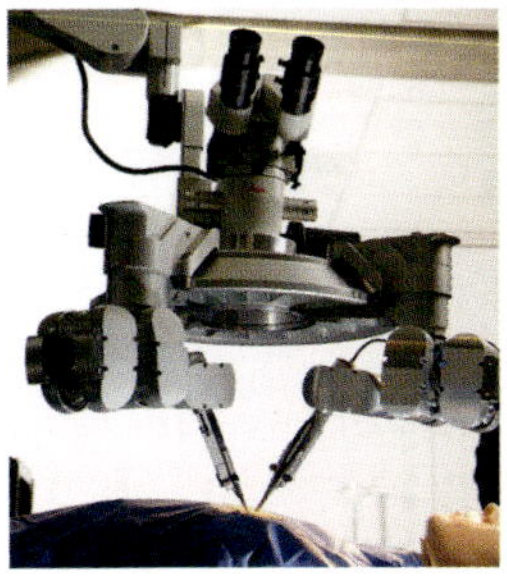

nypost.com

GROUP 2

VIDEO Deep sea exploration
e IFS1310

GROUP 3

AUDIO AI weapons
e IFS1312

GROUP 4

VIDEO Driverless cars
e IFS1311

3 Emma

What tasks can a virtual assistant perform for you?

VIDEO
Emma: a Customer Assistant powered by AI (2017)

1. **Look at the infographic.** ▲
   Give examples of what a virtual assistant can do.

2. **Now watch the video.** IFS1313
   Pick out examples of what a virtual customer assistant can do.

WORK your WAY — Take your own notes *or* comment on the screen shots provided. IFS1314

3. **Recap.** Use your notes to create an infographic entitled "How can Emma assist customers?".

4. **React.** What do you think of the following interaction?
   Would you use this device?

YOUR TURN

"What can I do for you today?" IN PAIRS

Imagine a dialogue between Emma and a new customer.

- Choose the circumstances. The customer wants to…
  buy a book | book a concert ticket | rent a car | any other idea?
- Imagine the kind of initiative Emma might take to try and sell more.
- Write the dialogue, then act it out.

4 Samantha

VIDEO
Her, the trailer (2013)

1 Look at the picture. ▲
What do you expect? → **YP 22**

characters | plot

2 Watch the trailer and check your hypotheses. IFS315

3 IN GROUPS Focus on the characters.

a. Organise your findings into a diagram. ▼

- Who we see
- *Relationship*
- Who we hear
- **Characters**
- Their attitudes / moods / feelings *(How they evolve throughout the trailer)*

b. Share your impressions with the class.

4 React. Compare Emma (p. 94) and Samantha. Would you say that reality is still far off from fiction?

DEBRIEF

Would you trust yourself using a virtual personal assistant? Or is there a risk you might get addicted?

YOUR TURN

Questionnaire *IN PAIRS*

At the beginning of the trailer, the Operating System asks Theodore questions in order to offer him an appropriate AI interface.

- List other questions you think an OS might ask a new customer.
- Exchange questionnaires with another group. Suggest possible improvements.
- Record the final version of your questionnaire.

Try to imitate the tone of the OS in the trailer!

TIP
Keep in mind that the idea is to get to know the customer better: their tastes, their habits, their personality...

5 Invasion

"Who's there?"

Shortly after midnight, on a Tuesday in early June, the house computer alarm sounded. [...]

She slid from beneath the covers and sat on the edge of the bed.

"What is the trouble?" she asked the dark air. Naked in this now-unnatural quietude, she felt more alone than she had in years. She thought of the husband she had divorced and of the friends she had let pass out of her life.

"There is no trouble, Susan", the house replied. The hidden speakers broadcast a voice which was gently masculine. She envisioned a strong man, graying at the temples perhaps, steady along the jaw, eyes clear and blue. More than six feet tall. Broad shoulders. Large hands.

[...] She felt the muscles in her back relax. All she needed was a bit of reassurance from her father-lover, even if it was a machine. [...]

However, the house computer failing to reassure her, Susan gets a repairman to come the next day. He checks everything with his instruments.

"The machine says the alarm did not sound, that there is no record of its having sounded, and that your house computer system is functioning perfectly."

"Then what did I hear?"

He shrugged: "You woke up groggy, Miss Abramson, and you misinterpreted something quite ordinary. It happens to people."

She was not going to be satisfied with anything so glib as that. "Could it have repaired itself?"

"A house computer in an enviromod package can't repair itself. No computer can."

"I heard somewhere about a self-repairing computer."

"What you heard", he said, suddenly speaking to a silly bitch rather than to an attractive and interesting woman, "was something about the computer they've been generating at the university a mile from here. It's called Proteus because it can reshape itself, make its own parts, repair itself. It can even add its own components when it feels it needs to grow. Damn thing is all but alive. But no house computer can fiddle with itself. This one is working well, has been working well right along, and it never did sound the house alarm, even for a second."

"I see", she said coldly.

She closed the door after him and watched him walk down the steps and across the lawn to the fan shuttle parked at the curb. [...]

Then it was quiet.

And then she slept, without dreams. As she slept, she curled up so that she was like a child in her mother's belly. The house watched over her.

She was awakened by the house alarm which jangled for the briefest of moments. She sat up in bed and she was frightened. When she was fully awake, she discovered that she was clutching the sheets about her bare shoulders, concealing the contours of her body. It was as if, intuitively, she knew that someone else was watching her, someone besides her father.

"What is it?" she asked the house. It did not respond.

"Who's there?"

Only the silence.

"I'm not alone, am I?"

"No."

Dean R. Koontz, *Demon Seed* (1973)

1 **Look at the illustration and titles on p. 96. Read lines 1-2.**
Imagine all you can about the situation.

2 **a. Read until l. 18.** Check your ideas.
b. Take notes about:
the characters | their relationships

TIP
Names in fiction often carry meaning. Look out for 'Susan' and 'Proteus' on the Internet. Quote elements from the text which show these names are not accidental.

WORK your WAY
Work on the text (p. 96) or use a guided version. IFS1316

3 **Read up to l. 51.**
a. Complete your notes with new characters and information.
b. How is Susan portrayed? What about the other characters?

4 **Read to the end.**
a. In your opinion, who says the last sentence?
b. Can you anticipate what is going to happen next?

6 "I felt invaded"

VIDEO
Amazon's Alexa shared a private audio (cnet news, 2018)

1 **Read the press cutting below.**
Imagine what happened.

What is it? What is it for?
Between who and who?
To whom for example?
What is its name? Imagine how it justified the incident.

The Guardian

Amazon's Alexa recorded private conversation and sent it to random contact.

The company, which has insisted its Echo devices aren't always recording, has confirmed the audio was sent.

▲ *The Guardian*, May 2018

2 **Watch the video.** IFS1317
a. Recap the sequence of events.
b. Pick out: the woman's feelings | the company's reaction
c. Comment on both. What is at stake for Amazon?

3 **React.** Do you think this is a bug or a real invasion of privacy?

DEBRIEF
So you thought *Invasion* was a science fiction story? What are the advantages and the risks of having a smart home device? Would you have one?

YOUR TURN

Customer service IN PAIRS

- Read about another incident involving Alexa. ▶
- Act out the dialogue between Allison and Amazon's Customer Service.

Pupil A:
You are Allison.
Explain what happened, expressing your feelings and concerns.

Pupil B:
You work for Customer Service.
Deal with Allison's call and try to reassure her.

allie
@AllieCole1
My aunt got a google home for Xmas & she already has "Alexa". This morning we were messing around with the google home and asked, "okay, google what do you think of Alexa" and it answered "I like her blue light" and from across the room Alexa turned on and said "thanks". im scared
12/25/17, 12:05 PM
102K Retweets 482K Likes

7 Ex Machina

VIDEO
Trailer for *Ex Machina*

"It's your decision"

Caleb, a young élite programmer, has been invited to interview Ava, a new-generation robot, as part of the "Turing Test", a protocol designed to determine the extent to which a robot is capable of imitating a human.

INT. HOUSE / OBSERVATION ROOM / DAY

Caleb and Ava facing each other through the glass of the observation room.

Ava: I brought you a drawing.

She holds a piece of paper to the glass. The marks on it are totally abstract. A mesh of tiny black marks, that swirl around the page like iron filings in magnetic field patterns.

Caleb: ... What's it a drawing of?

Ava: Don't you know?

Caleb: No.

Ava looks disappointed:

Ava: Oh. I thought you would tell me.

Caleb: Don't you know?

Ava: I do drawings every day. ButI never know what they're of.

Caleb: Are you not trying to sketch something specific? Like an object or a person.

She shakes her head as she takes the picture down.

Caleb: Maybe you should try.

Ava: Okay. What object should I draw?

Caleb: Whatever you want. It's your decision.

Ava: Why is it my decision?

Caleb: I'm interested to see what you'll choose.

Ava pauses a moment.

Ava: Do you want to be my friend?

Caleb: ... Of course.

Ava: Will it be possible?

Caleb: Why wouldn't it be?

Ava: Our conversations are one-sided. You ask circumspect questions and study my responses.

Ava looks at Caleb directly. Meets his gaze evenly.

Ava: It's true, isn't it?

Caleb: ...Yes.

Ava: You learn about me, and I learn nothing about you. That's not a foundation on which friendships are based.

Caleb is taken aback. Aware that the AI has just wrong-footed him on a point of argument.

Caleb: That's a fair comment.

Ava: Yes.

Caleb: So you want me to talk about myself.

Ava: Yes.

Caleb: Where do you want me to start?

Ava: It's your decision. I'm interested to see what you'll choose.

Excerpt from the original screenplay by Alex Garland, 1995

1 **Look at the picture and read the introduction on p. 98.**

a. Who do you think is in control: Caleb or Ava? How does it show in the picture?

b. What type of reactions do you think might help a robot pass the Turing Test?

2 **Read the text.** Give your first impression – would you say Ava passed the test?

3 **Focus on the stage directions.** ▶

a. What do they reveal about the balance of power between the two characters? Can you perceive an evolution?

b. Look for a confirmation of this in the text.

4 **Read about the myth of Eve.** ▶ What does the choice of the name 'Ava' suggest? → **YP 6**

5 **Recap.** What is the message of this text regarding the balance of power between human and AI?

6 **React.** What sort of ending would you see for the movie?

7 ***At home*** **Watch the trailer.** e IFS1318 Does it seem to confirm what you imagined about the ending?

TIP

Stage directions
This screenplay contains indications that can help you understand the scene:
- SCENE HEADING
It establishes the location of the scene and the time of day when the scene takes place.
- *Actors' notes*
They describe the characters' actions / feelings / attitudes...

The myth of Eve
In the first chapters of the Bible's Old Testament, the first human female is called Isha (*Eng.*: woman), by the first human man, Adam. She is created by Yahweh from the man's rib so as to be his wife. Adam and Eve live in the Garden of Eden until they are expelled.

▶ *Eve*, Hans Memling, 1485

8 Meet Sophia

1 **Watch the video** (4'37→5'35). e IFS1319 What is your reaction? What about the host?

2 **Focus on Sophia's and Jimmy's:**

facial expressions | actions

a. What do they reveal about this human-AI interaction?

b. Do you find this unsettling | promising | exciting ?

3 ***At home*** Look for other videos showing interactions with Sophia. Would you like to meet her? What questions would you ask her?

DEBRIEF

Compare Sophia and Ava.
Which is the most striking: reality or fiction?

YOUR TURN

Screenplay

- Write the script corresponding to the scene you have just watched.
- Use the video to help you decide on the stage directions.

9 Alexa

Alexa, what is there to know about love?

Alexa, what is there to know about love?
What is there to know about love?
A glove is a garment that covers the hand
for protection from the cold or dirt and –

Alexa, how does a human heart work?
How does a human heart work?
Blood is first received in the right atrium via
two veins, the vena cava superior and inferior –

Alexa, where do we go to when we die?
Where do we go to when we die?
Activating Google Maps. Completed activation.
Would you like to start from your current location?

Alexa, what does it mean to be alone?
What does it mean to be alone?
It is the silence left by words unsaid,
the cold expanse of half a bed.
It is the endless stretching of the hours,
the needless tending of plastic flowers.
It is an echo unanswered in a cave,
the fateful ping of the microwave.
It is the fraying of a worn shirt cuff,
and the howl – Stop, Alexa. That's enough.

Brian Bilston, 2018

AUDIO
A reading of the poem
IFS1320

1. **Read the first 3 stanzas.**
   Make sure you understand:
   - who is speaking
   - the way Alexa answers the questions
2. **Read the last stanza.**
   What do you think of Alexa's answer?
   Whose loneliness is she describing?
3. **React.** In your opinion, what is the poet trying to convey?
4. Choose one of these activities:
   - Perform the poem with a friend.
   - Ask Siri, Alexa or any other AI device these questions. Are their answers similar?
   - **IN PAIRS** Write a poem with a friend. Ask the questions, they will play Alexa and provide the answers. ☺

FINAL TASK

Screenplay

Write a scene involving a human and an AI. IN PAIRS

1 Get ready

- Think about the following aspects:
  – What vision of human-AI relationships do you want to give ?
  an optimistic one / a pessimistic one ?
  – Who are the characters?
  – What situation are they in?
  – What are their actions and feelings?

TIP
- See *How to write a dialogue* p. 106
- Read the *Ex Machina* screenplay again for help (p. 96).

2 Action!

- Write the dialogue.

WORK your WAY
Write a dialogue for a novel **or** a screenplay for a movie.

- If you have chosen the screenplay, don't forget to add useful notes for the actors (facial expressions, movements...).

☺ *Why not perform your scene in front of the class ?*

or

Debate

Should AI robots be granted rights? IN TEAMS

1 Get ready

- *Team A* is strongly in favour of granting robots rights. *Team B* is totally against it.

Think about the following aspects:
- Remember the AI-powered technologies or robots you have seen in the chapter. Think of their uses, how they learn, the way you feel towards them...
- Can man-made creations have a conscience, and thus need rights?

2 Action!

- Debate with the opposing team.

TIP
- Use the *Words* section p. 102.
- See *How to take part in a debate* p. 46.

Robot citizen
In October 2017, Sophia became the first robot in the world to be granted citizenship, giving her the right to own a Saudi Arabian passport.

Is it cruel to kick a robot dog?
A Boston Dynamics employee was filmed kicking Spot the robot dog to show how strong it is. The video raised ethical questions about the future of robotics.

WORDS

PRACTISE ONLINE

Technologies

- **hu**man-like /ˈhjuːmən/
- AI-ope**ra**ted
- voice-controlled de**vice**
- **vir**tual as**sis**tant /ˈvɜːtʃuəl/
- **ro**bot

IFS1321

Views & feelings

Feel...

☹	☺
• pessi**mis**tic	• opti**mis**tic
• appre**hen**sive	• ex**ci**ted
• un**com**fortable /ʌnˈkʌmftəbl/	• **po**sitive (about sth)
• con**cer**ned	• en**thu**siastic
• scared	
• **ter**rified	

Find something...

• con**fu**sing	• ex**ci**ting
• **wo**rrying	• **fa**scinating
• **dan**gerous /ˈdeɪndʒrəs/	• **thri**lling
• **fri**ghtening / **te**rrifying	

IFS1322

AI: a double-edged sword

Threat ☹

- repre**sent** a **dan**ger, a threat /θret/
- take over **pe**ople's jobs
- re**place hu**mans by **ro**bots
- lose con**trol** to **ro**bots
- get out of hand
  (→ The rise of robots could get out of hand.)
- be **ta**ken **o**ver by AI
- be **o**verrun by AI
- wipe out hu**ma**nity /aɪ/

IFS1323

Opportunity ☺

- save time, be time-saving
- make life **ea**sier
- be **prac**tical, **use**ful
- al**low** you to... make an ap**point**ment
  order sth
  book (a **ti**cket)
  switch on/switch off
- al**low** for scien**ti**fic **break**through /θruː/
- revo**lu**tionize **me**dicine
- save lives

IFS1324

EXERCISES

1 What's the word?

Choose suitable words from the mind map to complete these sentences:

1. I would love to meet Sofia and chat with her. I can't imagine a more ... experience.
2. Many people are ... about where AI will lead next. They're not convinced that it will be for the benefit of humanity.
3. They worry for example that AI will ... people's jobs.
4. Personally, I feel quite ... about it. I can see plenty of advantages. For example having a virtual assistant who can ... or ... for you is really ..., and you can use that time to do more interesting things.

2 What is AI?

Complete the text below with the words provided:

computer algorithms – the human mind – machine learning – voice recognition systems

Once a computer scientist's dream, artificial intelligence and ... are now part of our daily lives in the form of ..., product recommendation platforms and navigation tools. All of these rely on ... that process information and solve problems in a way similar to – and sometimes superior to – ....

3 AI and I

How do *you* feel about the development of AI? Do you find it rather worrying? Exciting? Do you have mixed feelings about it? Explain your point of view!

"The good news is I have discovered inefficiencies. The bad news is that you're one of them."

4 The good news is...

Comment on the cartoon above, using words and phrases from the mind map.

5 Monster of modernity?

a. **Listen to the interview.** e IFS1325

b. **How can you link it with the development of AI?**

Why Frankenstein still holds a mirror to modern science
Russ Altman and Audrey Shafer, from Stanford university

Pronunciation

PRACTISE ONLINE

6 Suffixe et accentuation

e IFS1326

• À partir d'un nom, on peut construire un adjectif en lui ajoutant un suffixe :

danger → dangerous

• Cet ajout peut avoir une incidence sur la place de l'accent dans le mot :

__opti__mism → opti__mis__tic

accent sur la 1re syllable — accent sur la syllable qui précède le suffixe

a. **Listen and repeat these words:**

nouns	adjectives
danger	dangerous
disaster	disastrous
prosper	prosperous
adventure	adventurous
optimism	optimistic
pessimism	pessimistic
enthusiasm	enthusiastic

b. **What can you conclude? Fill in the blanks.**

• L'ajout du suffixe ... n'affecte pas la place de l'accent tonique.
• L'ajout du suffixe ... affecte la place de l'accent tonique : il se déplace sur la syllabe qui précède le suffixe.

GRAMMAR

Dans ce chapitre consacré à l'intelligence artificielle, on envisage l'avenir avec plus ou moins de certitude, et on se pose beaucoup de questions !

1 Envisager l'avenir

1. There is little doubt that artificial intelligence **will** displace many low-skilled jobs.
2. Artificial intelligence **could** change the way medicine works.
3. In the future, AI **might** even assist physicians who are conducting a surgical procedure.
4. With the advent of driverless cars, many driving jobs **could** soon be made redundant.
5. Basic repetitive tasks **could** easily be done by AI in the future.
6. It's a common theme in sci-fi stories that one day, the machines **are going to** take over.

Différents auxiliaires modaux permettent d'évoquer l'avenir. Le choix dépend du point de vue de l'énonciateur sur les chances de réalisation de l'événement :

- Avec ***will***, l'événement est considéré comme **fortement probable** *("There is little doubt...")* 1.
- On utilise ***be going to*** pour parler d'un événement **en bonne voie de réalisation**, ou dont on a de bonnes raisons de penser qu'il va se produire dans l'avenir. 6
- Avec ***could***, l'événement est considéré comme **possible**, car le contexte s'y prête 2 4 5.
- Avec ***might***, on exprime une **éventualité**, **une hypothèse** parmi d'autres 3.

→ Précis 26, 28, 29 p. 243

Rappel
will, could, might sont des **auxiliaires**.
- Le verbe qui les accompagne est toujours une base verbale.
- C'est l'auxiliaire qui porte la marque du temps.

2 Les énoncés interrogatifs

Il existe deux grands types de questions :

1. **Do** you **want** to be my friend?
2. **Could** it **have repaired** itself?
3. **Is** there anything else I can help you with?

Les questions fermées
(dont la réponse est : *yes / no / I don't know...*)
auxiliaire + sujet + verbe + complément(s)

4. **What will** robots **be able to do**?
5. **What is** the trouble?
6. **Why is** it my decision?

Les questions ouvertes
(qui portent sur le lieu, le moment, la cause...)
mot interrogatif + auxiliaire + sujet + verbe + complément(s)

Principaux mots interrogatifs
Voir tableau p. 247

EXERCISES

Envisager l'avenir

1 Could AI replace teachers?

Complete this article, using *might*, *will* or *be going to*, either in the affirmative or negative form.

> Let's imagine a full humanoid robotic AI educator at the front of the room. Surely, this AI is less likely to make content-area errors. It ... be able to access absurd amounts of information in the blink of an eye. It would be able to listen and answer questions. It ... soon even have the ability to read the faces of students and respond accordingly.
> What it ... be able to do however is combine these elements along with a thousand other human variables to create meaning.
> So teachers' jobs are safe for the near future. But based on what is already happening in other countries some things ... change, and AI ... play a part. And although robots ... be sitting in the teachers' chairs, they ... be joining teachers quite soon as teaching assistants.

2 AI scenarios

Complete using *could*, *might*, *will* or *be going to*:

1. There is little doubt that artificial intelligence ... displace more and more low-skilled jobs.
2. Computers are capable of levels of calculations we ... only dream of achieving with our minds alone.
3. I am confident that AI computers ... benefit humanity – and fears that they ... decide that they and the planet would be better without us are unfounded.
4. Stephen Hawking said that if we're not careful, AI ... spell the end of the human race.

5. But others are less pessimistic. The creator of Cleverbot is betting that AI ... be a positive force: «I believe we ... remain in charge of the technology for a decently long time and the potential of it to solve many of the world problems ... be realised".

Les énoncés interrogatifs

3 Hey, Siri

Prepare 8 questions for Siri or another virtual assistant on the following topics:

food | school | sports | TV series | the future of AI | the future of mankind | ...

... and see what answers you get!
If you don't have a smartphone, ask your questions to a classmate.

4 Quiz on AI

Prepare your questions. The elements in bold type should be the answers to your questions.

John McCarthy is credited with coining the term 'artificial intelligence' in 1955 and is considered one of the early pioneers in the field. **He was a professor in the field of AI at Stanford University**.

DARPA, a US government department, was a major early funder of artificial intelligence research.

Deep Blue was the first computer to beat a reigning world chess champion. In May 1997, Deep Blue defeated **Russian champion Kasparov** in spectacular fashion in **just 19 moves**.

Pronunciation

PRACTISE ONLINE

5 Intonation in questions IFS1327

> • Les questions auxquelles on peut répondre par « oui » ou par « non » ont généralement une intonation montante :
> *"Will China be the AI super power?"* ↗
> • Les questions ouvertes ont généralement une intonation descendante :
> *"Why do we need artificial intelligence?"* ↘

a. Would you pronounce these questions with a rising ↗ or falling ↘ intonation?

1. Is there anything else I could help you with?
2. Would you like me to make an appointment for you?
3. Do you want to be my friend?
4. Where do you want me to start?
5. I'm not alone, am I?

b. Listen and check.

Rhythm & Sounds

Listen then say these sentences out loud, imitating the rhythm of the native speaker. IFS1328

- Are they for real?
- What can I do for you today?
- Is there anything else I can help you with?
- Who's there? I'm not alone, am I?
- Could it have repaired itself?
- Alexa, what is there to know about love?

HOW TO... write a dialogue

Dialogue is what keeps the story interesting and moving quickly for the reader.
However, there are dialogue writing rules to follow!

Dialogue writing rules

Guide the reader in the story

- **Use quotation marks** to indicate what is spoken.
- **Start a new line or paragraph** each time a new person is speaking.
- **Use pronouns or names** to indicate who is speaking.

Differences between French and English

"How old are you?" she wanted to know.

– Quel âge avez-vous ? Me demanda-t-elle.

Give life to the characters

Describe their actions or reactions while speaking.

- **Use adverbs:** *anxiously, angrily, kindly, coldly...*
- **Use adjectives:** *angry, surprised, sarcastic, enthusiastic...*
- **Use verbs of movement:** *walk away, stop, get up...*
- **Add realistic details:** *hesitations, pauses...* → YP 35

Beware of dialogue tags!

She said, he asked are dialogue tags.

- **Use them to express emotions**
  Anger: *shouted, yelled...*
  Determination: *declared, insisted...*
  Happiness: *smiled, laughed...*
- **Don't overuse them**
  They can take the reader out of the world of your story, as they remind them that you, the author, are relaying a story.

In a novel

Excerpt from *I, Robot*,
by Isaac Asimov (1950)

She went back to her desk and sat down. She didn't need expression on her face to look sad, somehow.

"How old are you?" she wanted to know.

"Thirty-two," I said.

"Then you don't remember a world without robots. There was a time when humanity faced the universe alone and without a friend. Now he has creatures to help him [...]. Mankind is no longer alone."

In a screenplay

Script from the screenplay of the film
Ex Machina, by Alex Garland (2015)

AVA looks at CALEB directly. Meets his gaze evenly.

AVA: It's true, isn't it?
CALEB: ... Yes.
AVA: You learn about me, and I learn nothing about you. That's not a foundation on which friendships are based.

CALEB is taken aback. Aware that the AI has just wrongfooted him on a point of argument.

CALEB: ... That's a fair comment.
AVA: Yes.
CALEB: So you want me to talk about myself.
AVA: Yes.
CALEB: Where do you want me to start?
AVA: It's your decision. I'm interested to see what you'll choose.

YOUR TURN!

Add a few more lines to one the two dialogues on the page.

TEST YOUR SKILLS

OBJECTIF BAC

Listening & Writing

Listen to the document three times and report what you have understood.

e IFS1329

Write about the same topic, following your teacher's instructions.

Durée 1'30

▶ An interactive advert for the British series *Humans*.

AUDIO Should we have a code of ethics for AI?

Reading & Writing

Your teacher will give you several documents.

- Read them carefully and follow the instructions.

Speaking

React to a document.

- Your teacher will give you a set of two documents.
- In your opinion, which one best illustrates the notion of **SCIENTIFIC INNOVATION AND RESPONSIBILITY**?
- Explain why.

Elon Musk
@elonmusk

Nobody likes being regulated, but everything (cars, planes, food, drugs, etc) that's a danger to the public is regulated.
AI should be too.

73K 2:41 AM - Aug 12, 2017

23K people are talking about this

HOW DIVIDED IS THE UNITED KINGDOM IN TERMS OF SOCIAL CLASS?

DIVERSITÉ ET INCLUSION

8

I KNOW MY PLACE

REACT

1. **Look at the picture.**
   a. How would you interpret it?
   b. Do you know anything about the British class system?
2. **Listen to the recording.** IFS1359
   Does it change your interpretation of the picture?

DEBRIEF

Based on what you have learned so far, does class still have an impact on life in the UK today?

Would you say it is a divisive issue?

1 "I know my place"

VIDEO
The Class Sketch (1966)

1 **Before watching.** Look at the picture and the title. What can you imagine about the people and their relationship? → **YP 20**

2 **Watch the video and check your ideas.** IFS1360

Label the picture with information from the video. IFS1361

3 Think about the expressions:

I look up to him.

I look down on him.

Can you explain the different meanings of each expression?

4 *IN PAIRS* What do you think the message of this video is?

5 **React.** Do you think a similar sketch could be made about France? → **YP 5a, 15, 37**

2 The Great British Class Calculator

▼ "Britain now has 7 social classes"
The Independent, 3 April 2013, Andy Watt

1 **Look at the illustration on page 110.** How does it compare with the first document?

2 **IN PAIRS** **Now read the description for each group.**

a. Can you identify the criteria used to categorize people?

b. Can you think of examples of each type of capital described?

3 **a.** Add information about each group to a graph. IFS1362

b. How do they compare with each other?

4 **React.** Look at the illustration again.

a. Analyse how they have chosen to represent each group visually.

b. Think about what message these representations send. → YP **28**

c. What problems can you see with categorizing people in this way? → YP **38**

3 More than data... ?

Class is not just about your job

Sociologists (who else?) have now discovered that there are not three classes – upper, middle and lower – but seven, comprising the privileged elite, the established middle class, the technical middle class, new affluent workers, the traditional working class, emergent service workers and the "precariat", or precarious proletariat, at the bottom.

Such are the findings of the Great British Class Survey, conducted among 160,000 people for the BBC [...].

Class is not just about your job, where you live and how much you earn. It's about who you are [...]. Class is as much about attitudes as it is about circumstances.

Take me, for example. What am I? On the BBC scale, I probably score as established middle class. I live in my own house surrounded by books and I don't watch soaps.

But my friends in the pub are drawn largely from working class occupations, those who are still working, that is. I enjoy their company and I hope they enjoy mine.

I still have close pals from the National Union of Mineworkers. I'm a devout trade unionist and you wouldn't catch me crossing an official picket line. I'm also a member of the Labour Party but I don't want to be an MP or run the country.

I don't care how I'm classified by academic pointy-heads. I'm me. Just like you are you.

Most of us, I bet, are a bundle of seeming contradictions. But we get by, because we're people, living humankind, not data in a sociologist's statistical tables.

And hurrah for that.

Paul Routledge, *The Mirror*, 5 April 2013

1 **Read the article.**
Look at question **4c** (above). What would the journalist's answer be?

WORK your WAY Read the text above **or** use a guided version. IFS1363

2 ***"Most of us are a bundle of seeming contradictions."*** (l. 34-35)

a. What examples does the journalist give about himself? → YP **17, 18**

b. **React.** What about you? Are you a "bundle of contradictions"?

DEBRIEF From what you've seen so far, how important does class seem to be in British society?

4 Nice problems to have

The British are well-known for their sense of humour and laughing at themselves. Here are some examples of class comedy. Enjoy!

Gellers @Dinna_Gellers Follow

My parents' wifi can't cope with all of our devices. This is the worst Christmas ever. Twelth attempt at sending this…

James @james_johnson Follow

Had to turn down the brightness on the iPad because it hurt my eyes

VIDEO #shoppingproblems (BBC Comedy, 2017)

BBC Comedy @bbccomedy

Middle class shoppers have been having a Lidl adventure. #TheMashReport

BBC Two

1. **Look at the book cover then read the tweets above.** Do you think the tweets match the definition given on the book cover? → YP 24
2. **Now look at the BBC Comedy tweet.** ▶
   a. What kind of report do you expect it to be?
   b. *"When posh people go to Lidl…"* … what do you think happens?
3. **Watch the video.** IFS1364 Is it what you expected?
4. **React.** What do you think of it? Do you find it funny? → YP 2a, 37

YOUR TURN

#middleclassproblems

- Come up with another #middleclassproblem.
- Share your tweet with the class and vote for the funniest ones!

or

"When posh people…" IN PAIRS

- Think of another "when posh people…" scenario.
- Prepare a tweet, a title, a picture and a caption.

5 When two worlds collide

1 Look at the picture. What can you imagine about: the people / their feelings / what they are looking at ?

2 Watch the video and check. IFS1365
What do you learn about the characters?

3 Focus on the way the mum speaks to the man.

a. Why do you think she does this?

b. How would you have reacted if you were the man? Why? → YP 43

YOUR TURN

There are two sides to every story...

Imagine the Posh Mum sketch from the man's point of view.

WORK your WAY — Write a text message from him to his friends **or** tell the story he could share when he gets back to work.

6 Mirroring society...?

▲ Comedian Matt Lucas as Vicky Pollard in the TV show *Little Britain*

AUDIO — Chav stereotypes: funny or offensive?

Chav: a pejorative word used to describe a working-class person or someone who is on benefits*, whose tastes are considered vulgar by some.

* *who receives money from the government*

1 Look at the picture and read the caption and definition.
What else can you imagine about this stereotype? Do you find it offensive?

2 Listen to the recording and check your ideas. IFS1366
Does this confirm or change your opinion?

YOUR TURN

Argue your case!

"Vicky Pollard is a fantasy of a working class woman created by two privately educated comedians" – **Owen Jones, political writer and activist**

Do you think people should be able to joke about social classes other than their own? Give your opinion on a radio phone-in show!

DEBRIEF

Do you think class comedy unites or divides people?

7 Class signifiers

IN GROUPS

GROUP 1 Accents

VIDEO "Accentism" is the new classism (2014)

1. **Look at the still from the video.** ▲
   Can you imagine what 'classism' and 'accentism' are?

   TIP Think of words like "sexism" and "racism" to help you understand!

2. **Watch the video to find out.** IFS1367
   a. Why do they show a map in the video?
   b. Where is Caroline from? Explain her experience. → YP 4

3. **Now listen to Annie's experience.** IFS1368
   How does it compare with Caroline's?

   AUDIO "It makes you sound working class."

4. **React.** Could the same thing happen in France?

GROUP 2 Education

VIDEO James McAvoy discusses "The Class Ceiling"

1. **Look at the cartoon and title of the video.**
   What could "class ceiling" mean?

2. **Watch the video.** IFS1369
   a. Check your answer to question 1.
   b. Use information from the video to complete an infographic about the British education system. IFS1370

3. **React.** Do you agree with James McAvoy about the role of art in school? → YP 37

GROUP 3 Supermarkets

ALDI
Looks like Vanilla Yoghurt

ASDA
Vanilla Flavour Yogurt

TESCO
Vanilla Flavoured Yogurt

Sainsbury's
Celebry-endorsed Vanilla Yogurt

MARKS& SPENCER
Madagascar Vanilla Yogurt with Organic Wholegrain Wheat & Honey from Posh Bees

WAITROSE
You can't afford and you're not good enough for this Vanilla Yogurt

AUDIO
How supermarkets support our class system

1. **Read the document on the left.**
   a. Identify what the descriptions have in common. What is different about them? → YP 15
   b. What does it suggest about these supermarkets?
2. **Listen to the recording.** IFS1371
   Find out more about supermarkets and the class system in Britain.
3. **React.** Do you think this a typically British thing, or is it the same in France? → YP 12, 15

DEBRIEF

What are some of the ways in which class affects day-to-day life in the UK?

YOUR TURN

A patchwork of life in Britain

- Create a collage picture in the same style as this one on your topic:
  accents | education | supermarkets
- Stick your collage on the wall and go and discover the other groups' collages.
- What questions do you have for the others? Get ready to answer questions on your own work!

8 Cross-classing

Common People

She came from Greece she had a thirst for knowledge,
She studied sculpture at Saint Martin's College,
That's where I,
Caught her eye.
She told me that her Dad was loaded,
I said "In that case I'll have a rum and coca-cola."
She said "Fine."
And in thirty seconds time she said,

"I want to live like common people,
I want to do whatever common people do,
I want to sleep with common people,
I want to sleep with common people,
Like you."
Well what else could I do
I said "I'll see what I can do."

I took her to a supermarket,
I don't know why,
But I had to start it somewhere,
So it started there.
I said pretend you've got no money,
She just laughed and said,
"Oh you're so funny."
I said "Yeah?
Well I can't see anyone else smiling in here.
Are you sure...

You want to live like common people,
You want to see whatever common people see,
You want to sleep with common people,
You want to sleep with common people,
Like me.
But she didn't understand,
She just smiled and held my hand.

Rent a flat above a shop,
Cut your hair and get a job.
Smoke some fags and play some pool,
Pretend you never went to school.
But still you'll never get it right,
'Cause when you're laid in bed at night,
Watching roaches climb the wall,
If you called your Dad he could stop it all.

You'll never live like common people,
You'll never do whatever common people do,
You'll never fail like common people,
You'll never watch your life slide out of view,
And dance and drink and screw,
Because there's nothing else to do.

Sing along with the common people,
Sing along and it might just get you through.
Laugh along with the common people,
Laugh along even though they're laughing at you,
And the stupid things that you do.
Because you think that poor is cool.

Like a dog lying in a corner,
They will bite you and never warn you,
Look out, they'll tear your insides out.
'Cause everybody hates a tourist,
Especially one who thinks it's all such a laugh,
Yeah and the chip stain's grease,
Will come out in the bath.

You will never understand
How it feels to live your life
With no meaning or control
And with nowhere left to go.
You are amazed that they exist
And they burn so bright,
Whilst you can only wonder why.

AUDIO
Common People, Pulp (1995)

1 Listen to the song. IFS1372

a. Do you like it? → YP 38, 39

b. What do you understand about the song based on: the words / the tune / the singer's tone of voice ?

2 Focus on the first two verses and the chorus (l. 1-25).

a. Identify the characters. Who is: "I" in the verses / "I" in the chorus / "she" in the verses / "you" in the chorus

b. Say what we learn about: them / their relationship

c. Can you imagine what the term "common people" means?

3 Now focus on the rest of the song.

a. Pick out all the characteristics associated with "common people".

b. *"You'll never live like common people".* Identify the reasons why.

4 React. What is the message of this song? Do you agree with it? → YP 30

9 Cultural appropriation...?

AUDIO
Grime: working-class music, middle-class fans?

1 Before listening. Do you spontaneously associate certain types of music with certain "social classes"?

2 Listen to the recording. IFS1373

a. Organize the information into a mind-map:

Grime → influences / origins / artists / ...

b. Choose one of the artists and listen to them online. Do you like their music?

3 *IN PAIRS* Suggest a definition for "cultural appropriation". Compare with the rest of the class.

4 Can you see any links between this and the theme of the song *Common People*?

DEBRIEF

"Music is the universal language... it brings people closer together."

Ella Fitzgerald

Do you agree with this quote?

10 Educating Rita

I couldn't come in

Rita, a 26-year-old hairdresser attends evening classes given by Frank, a university professor of literature. The night before, she was invited to a party at Frank's place but...

RITA: I couldn't come in.

FRANK: Of course you could.

RITA: I couldn't. I'd brought the wrong sort of wine. When I was in the off-licence I knew I was buyin' the wrong stuff. But I didn't know which was the right wine.

FRANK: Rita for Christ's sake; I wanted you to come along. You weren't expected to dress up or buy wine.

RITA: If you go out to dinner don't you dress up? Don't you take wine?

FRANK: Yes, but...

RITA: Well? [...]

FRANK: Why couldn't you relax? *(He gets up and goes behind Rita's chair, then leans on the back of it.)* It wasn't a fancy dress party. You could have come as yourself. Don't you realize how people would have seen you if you'd just – just breezed in? Mm? They would have seen someone who's funny, delightful, charming...

RITA *(angrily)***:** But I don't wanna be charming and delightful: funny. What's funny? I don't wanna be funny. I wanna talk seriously with the rest of you, I don't wanna spend the night takin' the piss*, comin' on with the funnies because that's the only way I can get into the conversation. I didn't want to come to your house just to play the court jester.

FRANK: You weren't being asked to play that role. I just – just wanted you to be yourself.

RITA: But I don't want to be myself. Me? What's me? Some stupid woman who gives us all a laugh because she thinks she can learn, because she thinks that one day she'll be like the rest of them, talking seriously, confidently, with knowledge, livin' a civilized life. Well, she can't be like that, really, but bring her in because she's good for a laugh!

FRANK: If you believe that's why you were invited, to be laughed at, then you can get out, now. *(He goes to his desk and grabs the pile of essays, taking them to the window desk. He stands with his back to Rita and starts pushing the essays into his briefcase.)* You were invited because I wished to have your company and if you can't believe that, then I suggest you stop visiting me and start visiting an analyst who can cope with your paranoia.

Educating Rita, Willy Russel (1980)

* takin' the piss: (slang or vulgar) making fun of, mocking other people

1. **Read the title and the introduction.** Why do you think Rita couldn't come in?
2. **a. Now read the scene.** Check your ideas.
   b. How does Frank see Rita? Does she believe him? Compare their views.
3. **Look at how Rita's speech is written down.** What do you notice? Read some of it out loud. How does it compare with Frank's speech?
4. **React.** How would you cast the characters ?

YOUR TURN

Bring this scene to life!

WORK your WAY

Either storyboard this scene **or** design a poster for the play **or** act it out for the class.

FINAL TASK

Create a parody news report

Write and perform a funny news report on social classes in modern-day Britain.

1 Get ready

- Choose your scenario.

WORK your WAY

Use your "When posh people" scenario (p. 112) or draw inspiration from anywhere else in the chapter.

- Write your script.
- Cast your characters.

2 Action!

- Now perform your sketch!

You can either perform it live or film it!

TIP

Watch *The Mash Report* again for ideas on structure, tone of voice and useful expressions. IFS1364

or

When two worlds collide…

Write a short anecdote about social classes.

1 Get ready

- Imagine a situation where someone finds themselves in a social environment very different from their own.
- Think about their reactions.

WORK your WAY

You can write a dialogue for a play or a verse for a song.

2 Action!

- Write your text.

TIP

- Pay attention to the format.
- You can use the song "Common people" (p. 116) or the play "Educating Rita" (p. 118) for inspiration.

WORDS

PRACTISE ONLINE

Social markers

Class

- be from a **work**ing-class **back**ground
  /ˈwɜː/
- be **work**ing class / **mid**dle class
- have a **work**ing-class / posh **ac**cent
- live in a de**pri**ved / disad**van**taged area
  /dɪˈpraɪvd/ /s/
  wealthy / **aff**luent **neigh**bourhood
  /ˈwelθi/
- posh ≠ common (familiar)

Education

- go to a state school
  a **pub**lic school = **pri**vate school
  /ˈpraɪvət/
- be **pri**vately **ed**ucated
- have a uni**ver**sity edu**ca**tion

Money

- be broke (informal)
  /əʊ/
- be poor /pɔː/
- be de**pri**ved, disad**van**taged
- be **loa**ded (informal) = be rich
- be well-off = be **weal**thy
- earn money / make **mon**ey

Job status

- a job / an occup**a**tion
  /eɪ/
- a **sa**lary
- an **in**come
- be unemp**loy**ed = be out of work
  /ɪ/
- be in em**ploy**ment
- work as (a me**cha**nic)

IFS1374

SOCIAL CLASSES

Social mobility

- a**dapt** to **dif**ferent **so**cial **cir**cles
- have friends from **dif**ferent **back**grounds
- posh up (informal)
- move up **so**cially
- lose your identity
- **cul**tural appropri**a**tion
- face **ob**stacles (to **so**cial ad**van**cement)
- be trapped/stuck in your **so**cial class

IFS1375

Feelings & views

- feel su**pe**rior to sb
  ≠ in**fe**rior to sb
- feel **e**qual to sb
  /ˈiːkwəl/
- feel un**sure** of your place
  /ʌnˈʃɔːr/
- look up to sb ≠ look down on sb
- judge sb (based on **a**ccent / class)
- see sb as **vul**gar, un**ed**ucated
  /ˈvʌlgər/
- **de**monize sb
  /diː/
- make fun of sb = tease sb
- **mim**ic sth
- be **cri**ticized for sth
  /saɪz/

IFS1376

EXERCISES

❶ Adele's background

Complete part of Adele's biography with the following words and expressions. Pay attention to the forms of the verbs!

state school – affluent neighbourhood – disadvantaged area – move up socially – working-class accent – make a lot of money – lose her identity – from a working-class background – wealthy

A working-class girl's story

Adele is a singer _____. She grew up in a _____ of London and was raised by a single mother. She went to a _____ and later attended the BRIT school, one of the only performing art schools that are free to attend.

Now she is famous and a best-selling artist, she has fans all over the world. She _____ and is very _____. She lives in a much more _____ than the ones she grew up in.

However, people often note that although she has _____, she has remained true to her working-class roots. She still speaks with a strong _____ and hasn't _____.

❷ The odd one out

a. Identify the expressions that don't fit.

1. deprived – wealthy – broke – disadvantaged
2. have a job – have an income – be out of work
3. feel superior to sb – look down on sb – see sb as vulgar – feel unsure of your place

b. Make sentences with the expressions that don't fit in order to explain their meanings.

❸ Guessing game IN PAIRS

a. Write five sentences using words and expressions from the mind map. Then remove these words or expressions like in exercise 1a.

b. Give your sentences to your partner. They have to guess what the word or expression is!

❹ Great Expectations

Complete this description of Dickens' famous novel *Great Expectations*, using the words provided.

lower – hierarchy – higher – social mobility – wealthier – the class system – poorer

Class Mobility in Great Expectations

Great Expectations is set near the end of Industrial Revolution, a period of dramatic technological improvement in manufacturing and commerce that, among other things, created new opportunities for people who were born into "..." or ... classes to gain wealth and move into a "..." and ... class. This new ... marked a distinct break from the hereditary aristocracy of the past, which enforced class consistency based solely on family lines. Great Expectations is set in this new world, and Dickens explores it by tracing Pip's ascent through ..., a trajectory that would not have been possible within the rigid class ... of the past.

Pronunciation

PRACTISE ONLINE

❺ Vowel sounds IFS1377

Une même lettre ou un même groupe de lettres peut se prononcer différemment en anglais :

speak	*break*	*head*	*real*
/spiːk/	/breɪk/	/hed/	/rɪəl/

In each list of words, pick out the one which has a different vowel sound from the other two:

e.g.: *learn, early, wear*

1. class, accent, salary
2. educated, occupation, mechanic
3. wealthy, speak, cheap
4. posh, go, broke
5. look, loose, book

❻ Links between consonants IFS1378

Lorsqu'un mot se terminant par un son consonne (par exemple /t/) est suivi d'un mot commençant par un son consonne identique ou proche (par exemple /t/ ou /d/), on ne prononce ce son qu'une seule fois : *private tuition, for the first time.*

Ceci peut parfois rendre l'anglais oral difficile à comprendre.

a. Listen to these comments about wealth and pay attention to the linking consonants.

1. I have travelled to the US a bit, and I noticed that class is much more fluid than in other countries.
2. Profession and education are a big marker of class. The first question most people ask is "What do you do?".
3. Americans, by and large, tend to group themselves by religion, occupation, hobbies, etc.

b. Practise repeating these comments.

GRAMMAR

Accent, métier, école… en Grande-Bretagne, il semble que tout contribue à vous situer dans la hiérarchie sociale ! Pour en parler, on a recours au comparatif et au superlatif.

1 Le comparatif

❶ Up in Scotland the accent is **more** guttural.

❷ In Wales, speech tends to be breathi**er**.

❸ "I am not **as** vulgar **as** him."

❹ ASDA is **less** expensive **than** Marks&Spencer.

comparatif de supériorité	**adjectif court** + *-er* (+ *than*) ❷ **adjectif long** + *more* + adjectif (+ *than*) ❶
comparatif d'égalité	*(not) as* + adjectif (+ *as*) ❸
comparatif d'infériorité	*less* + adjectif (+ *than*) ❹

- Certains adjectifs ont un **comparatif irrégulier** :
  good → ***better***
  bad → ***worse***
  far → ***further***

→ Précis 14 p. 237

Orthographe
breathy → *breathi**er***
wealthy → *wealthi**er***

Prononciation
more /ˈmɔː/
bigger /ˈbɪɡə/
than est inaccentué /ðən/

Court ou long ?
court : 1 syllabe **long :** 2 syllabes et plus
- Certains adjectifs de plus d'une syllabe fonctionnent comme des adjectifs courts :
  pretty → ***prettier***
- Inversement, quelques adjectifs courts fonctionnent comme des adjectifs longs :
  real → ***more real*** *wrong* → ***more wrong***

2 Le superlatif

❶ Let's vote for **the** funni**est** tweets.

❷ The elite (…) is **the most** privileged class in Great Britain.

❸ This is **the worst** Christmas ever!

	superlatif de supériorité	superlatif d'infériorité
adjectif **court** (1 syllabe)	*the* + adjectif + *-est* ❶	*the least* + adjectif
adjectif **long** (2 syllabes et +)	*the most* + adjectif ❷	

- Certains adjectifs ont un **superlatif irrégulier** :
  good → ***the best***
  bad → ***the worst*** ❸
  far → ***the furthest***

→ Précis 15 p. 237

Orthographe
big → *the big**gest***
strange → *the strang**est***
happy → *the happi**est***

Prononciation
most /məʊst/
biggest /ˈbɪɡəst/

EXERCISES

Comparatif & superlatif

1 How do they compare?

a. **Read the text then complete it, using either the comparative or superlative form of the adjectives.**

The Great British Class Calculator

According to the creators of The Great British Class Survey, there are now seven social classes in the UK. The group with *(low)* levels of economic, cultural and social capital are the Precariat, making them *(poor)* group in the UK.
At the other end of the spectrum are the Elite, the *(wealthy)* group who have *(high)* levels of all three capitals. This makes them *(privileged)* group in the UK. The traditional working class are *(poor)* the Precariat but they are still *(poor)* most other groups.

b. **Continue the text by comparing one or two of the other groups described** **on p. 110.**

2 The best show ever....!

GAME OF THRONES • BLACK MIRROR • The OA • THIRTEEN REASONS WHY • STRANGER THINGS • PEAKY BLINDERS • FRIENDS • Breaking Bad

a. **Compare two of these TV shows.** ▲

funny – interesting – boring – stressful – entertaining – suspenseful – good – bad – believable

b. **Which is your favourite one? Why?**

3 Could do better...?

Read the article below.

a. **For each TV show, identify the adjectives used to describe the characters.**

b. **Now use your list to compare:**

the characters | the shows in general

"TV never has any smart, amusing intellectuals living on a council estate – so we decided to create a sitcom featuring some"

Caitlin Moran on her TV show *Raised by Wolves*

Raised by Wolves is a one of a kind comedy, written by working-class women about working-class women. Previous representations of the kind have left a lot to be desired. *Little Britain's* Vicky Pollard is the creation of two privately-educated men but has somehow come to be the ultimate depiction of a working-class woman on British TV. Any mention of Vicky Pollard immediately brings to mind poor, rude, uneducated females in tracksuits who have countless children in order to get a free council house. *Raised by Wolves* is a welcome correction, offering a whole cast of smart, funny and articulate working-class females. Mum of the family Della is a single-mum and she does live on a council-estate but this is not another Vicky Pollard. She works hard to provide for her six children (five of whom are girls named after strong female figures), raises them to be politically conscious and is sharply and wittily intelligent.

Pronunciation

PRACTISE ONLINE

4 Comparatives IFS1379

Those on higher wages can afford more leisure activities.
/ˈhaɪə/

I think Sainsbury's offers more choice to customers.
/mɔː/

→ Le 'r' ne se prononce pas.

British students from higher income families often go to private schools. /ˈhaɪər/

Sainsbury's is more expensive than Tesco.
/mɔːr/

→ Le 'r' se prononce car on fait la liaison.

a. **Listen to the sentences above, paying attention to the pronunciation of the comparative forms.**

b. **Practise pronouncing them.**

Rhythm & Sounds

Listen then say these sentences out loud, imitating the rhythm of the native speaker IFS1380

- Certain TV shows represent the working classes better than others.
- The character Vicky Pollard is one of the worst representations of working class women on TV.
- People from wealthier areas often have access to better schools.

TEST YOUR SKILLS

OBJECTIF BAC

Listening & Writing

AUDIO
The Class Ceiling

- **Listen** to the document three times and report what you have understood. IFS1381
- **Write** about the same topic, following your teacher's instructions.

Durée 1'30

Reading & Writing

Your teacher will give you several documents.
- Read them carefully and follow the instructions.

Speaking

React to a document!
- Your teacher will give you a set of two documents.
- In your opinion, which one best illustrates the notion of **DIVERSITY AND INCLUSION**?
- Explain why.

HOW CAN CINEMA GIVE A VOICE TO THE POWERLESS?

CHAPITRE FLASH 9

YOUR MISSION

- You're a member of the jury at a film festival exploring political and social issues.
- Discover *I, Daniel Blake* and research its background in order to decide whether it should be shortlisted for an award.

1 The Film

Three extracts from the film *I, Daniel Blake* (Ken Loach, 2016)

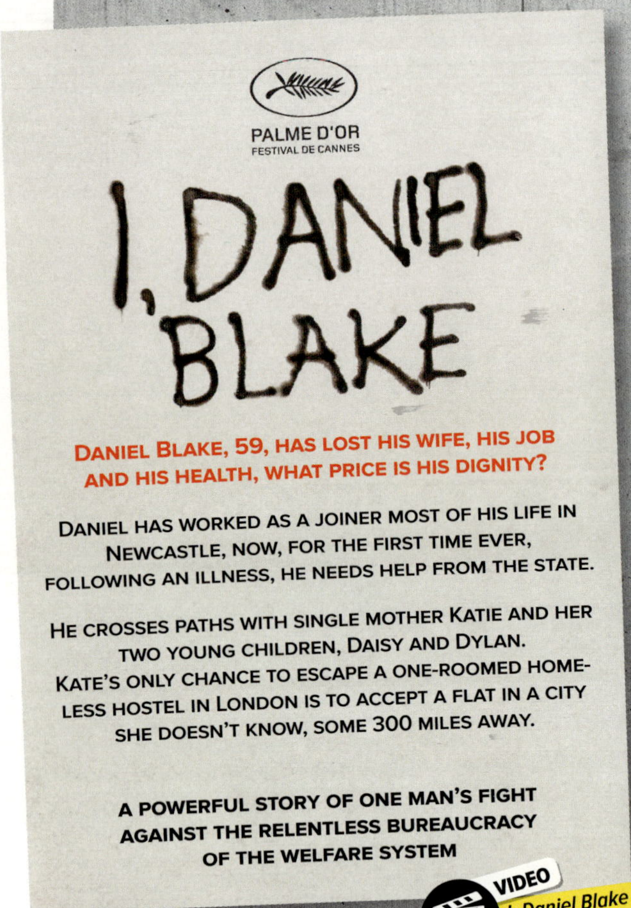

VIDEO *I, Daniel Blake* – trailer

VIDEO The Jobcentre scene
IFS1411

VIDEO The food bank scene
IFS1413

1 Trailer and synopsis ▲ IFS1410

Use them to start completing your notes on the film for your jury deliberations.

	Identity	Situation	Feelings	Relationships
Characters				
Plot				
Location				

TIP
Don't worry if some information is missing for now. You will find out more in the documents to come.

2 Movie Clips

a. Watch the clips to discover more about:

the characters — the plot — the context

b. Now focus on the way it is filmed.

camera angles — background noise — lighting — ...

How does this reinforce the message of the film?

c. Share your thoughts and findings with the other members of the jury.

3 Read the *Background* section.

a. Do you recognize the social context in this movie?

b. Do you think this is a real story? Why?

DEBRIEF

In what ways is the film an example of British Social Realism?

YOUR TURN

Deliberation in progress

- Ken Loach said *"The best story is a true one. The point is to make good cinema to show that truth"*.
- At this stage of your work and judging from the elements you have, do you think he has reached his goal?

Background

British Social Realism

The term is used for films that explore the issues of poverty, race and class in the UK. It particularly focuses on the real socio-political conditions of the working class as a means to critique the power structures behind these conditions.

Common features

- shot in real places
- non-professional actors
- semi-improvised scripts
- a mixture of humour and real social problems
- regional accents

Austerity in the UK

In 2010 the UK government initiated a programme intended to reduce the government deficit.
This austerity programme included reductions in welfare spending, the cancellation of school building programmes, and an increase in VAT.

An example

In Ken Loach's film, Daniel Blake has to take a Work Capability Assessment. This test is used by the British Government's Department for Work and Pensions to decide whether welfare claimants are entitled to financial benefit.
If a claimant fails to meet the required conditions, sanctions can be applied to their benefits.

2 Politics and Cinema

http://www.macleans.ca/culture/

How Margaret Thatcher accidentally revived British cinema

Jaime J. Weinman on the art created in the wake of Thatcherism

April 9, 2013

Margaret Thatcher was not a great fan of the arts community, as you'd expect from someone who famously said there is "no such thing as society." [...]

▲ Miners during the 1984 miners' strike

But it was in film that Thatcher may have had the most impact – and, ironically, where she may have had a positive influence on the work of the people who felt most negatively toward her. Before Thatcher came to power, British cinema was in trouble. The 80s turned that around, producing a so-called "British Renaissance" of small-budget, darkly humorous films by interesting new directors like Stephen Frears *(My Beautiful Laundrette)*, Mike Leigh *(Naked)* and David Leland *(Wish You Were Here)*. And what most of these films had in common was a ferocious opposition to Thatcher. [...]

If artists flourish when they feel like outsiders, then no one made them feel less wanted than she did. "When you're happy you may not make great films," Lester Friedman[1] says of the British filmmakers. "They were really very agitated. They responded to what they saw as her right-wing destruction of the British system by creating great art."

1. Lester Friedman is the editor of the book *Fires Were Started: British Cinema and Thatcherism.*

Background

"There is no such thing as society"

Prime Minister Margaret Thatcher,
talking to *Woman's Own magazine*, 31 October 1987

"I think we've been through a period where too many people have been given to understand that if they have a problem, it's the government's job to cope with it. [...] They're casting their problem on society. And, you know, there is no such thing as society. There are individual men and women, and there are families. And no government can do anything except through people, and people must look to themselves first."

Margaret Thatcher (1925-2013), became the leader of the Conservative Party* in 1975 and was elected Prime Minister in 1979. She resigned in 1990.

* *(also called Tory)*

VIDEO
Ken Loach at the BAFTA ceremony

▲ Ken Loach's acceptance speech for Oustanding British Film at the BAFTA awards, 2017.

About BAFTA
The British Academy of Film and Television Arts – BAFTA is an independent charity which supports and promotes the art form of the moving image (film, TV and games) in the UK. The BAFTA's annual film awards ceremony is known as the British Academy Film Awards or "the BAFTAs".

1 Before reading.
What do you know about Margaret Thatcher?
Read the *Background* section to find out:
who she was | what her political views were

2 Focus on the title of the article p. 128.

Can you imagine how?

How Margaret Thatcher accidentally revived British cinema

What does this imply about British cinema before Margaret Thatcher?

3 Read the article.

a. Check your answers to question 2.

TIP
An article usually concludes with the main idea, so paying attention to the last sentence can help!

b. Organize the information you have found in a timeline:

British cinema in the time of Margaret Thatcher

TIP
Include as much information as possible. Don't worry if you don't have specific dates.

4 Before watching the video. What do you think Ken Loach has to say today about the influence of politics on his films?

5 Watch the video to find out. e IFS1414

6 GROUP TALK

"When you're happy, you may not make great films." (l. 20-21 p. 128)
Do you agree?

"Films can do many things." (Ken Loach)
What, for example?
What is the most important for you?

DEBRIEF

What has been the influence of politics on British cinema in the past 40 years?
Is it the same in France?

YOUR TURN

Write a memo

You have had the chance to attend the BAFTA Awards Ceremony.

Write a memo to your fellow jury members. Tell them about how Ken Loach's contributions to the tradition of politically-engaged British cinema.

3 Cinema and Politics

Jeremy Corbyn
@jeremycorbyn
Leader of the Labour Party
UK
labour.org.uk/volunteering

Jeremy Corbyn
@jeremycorbyn
Follow

I, Daniel Blake will be shown on TV for the first time, tonight at 9.45pm on BBC 2.

It shows the human cost of this Tory Government's cruel welfare policies.

It is one of the most moving films I have ever seen and should be watched by everyone.
#IDanielBlake #IDanielBlakeBBC2

1 **Look at Jeremy Corbyn's Twitter Feed.** ▲

a. Identify:

who he is | why he posted the tweet

b. Do you know who the leader of the "Tory Government" he refers to is?

2 **Before watching.** You're going to listen to Jeremy Corbyn addressing the Prime Minister in relation to *I, Daniel Blake*. Imagine what he said.

3 **Watch the video and find out.** IFS1415
Do you find his speech effective? Why? Pay attention to:

word stress | vocabulary | examples given

4 **React.** Can you see any links between this and the Thatcher era?

DEBRIEF

How can cinema influence politics?

VIDEO Jeremy Corbyn during the PMQs

Questions to the Prime Minister (also known as Prime Minister's Questions or PMQs) A session held every Wednesday at the House of Commons during which the Prime Minister answers questions from the members of Parliament.

▲ In the background, the Palace of Westminster, meeting place of the House of Commons and the House of Lords

YOUR TURN

#IDanielBlake

- React to Jeremy Corbyn's post on Twitter.
- Remember you only have 140 caracters!

FINAL TASK

Jury deliberations

Should *I, Daniel Blake* be selected for an award? Discuss it with the jury. IN GROUPS

1 Get ready

- Decide whether you think the film should be selected or not.
- Jot down arguments to support your decisions such as:

social and political context | portrayal of the characters | filming techniques | ...

2 Action!

- Now give your opinion to the other members of the jury.
- Defend your point of view if necessary.
- Now vote! Should *I, Daniel Blake* be selected for an award?

or

Promote the film

You have chosen to screen *I, Daniel Blake* at your festival. You want to create a buzz around the film. IN GROUPS

1 Get ready

- Brainstorm to find ideas. Think about possible:

events | places | messages | people | ...

WORK your WAY: Draw inspiration from the original campaign **or** come up with new ideas.

2 Action!

- Present your ideas to the film festival team explaining your choices.

▶ As part of a 'guerrilla' promotional campaign, a quote from the film is projected onto the Houses of Parliament and other buildings around London on October 20, 2016.

GRAMMAR

I, Daniel Blake montre le combat d'un homme au prise avec une bureaucratie absurde. Pour l'évoquer, on utilise des tournures infinitives et causatives, ainsi que des quantifieurs.

1 Exprimer une quantité

❶ A huge thank you to the academy and from **all of us**.

❷ Daniel has worked as a joiner **most of his life** in Newcastle.

❸ **No government** can do anything except through people.

❹ No matter who you are or where you come from or how **much money** you earn, you need to have recognition and a place within this world.

❺ Films can do **many things**.

	Permet de parler de...
All ❶	la totalité
Most of ❷	la majorité
Much + indénombrable ❹ *Many* + dénombrable au pluriel ❺	une grande quantité
No ❸	une quantité nulle

→ Précis 10 p. 235-236

2 La proposition infinitive

❶ What I **want** [you] to <u>do</u> is listen to me.

❷ The administration **expects** [people] to <u>prove</u> they are looking for work.

❸ The system **expects** [him] to continuously <u>seek</u> employment even though he is ill.

- La proposition infinitive permet de dire ce qu'on aimerait, voudrait... que d'autres fassent. Elle se construit ainsi :
  ***want* / *expect* / ...** + [nom/pronom] + *to* + <u>base verbale</u>
- On peut remplacer le nom par un pronom ❶❸. Dans ce cas **c'est toujours un pronom complément** qui est employé, bien qu'il soit sujet du verbe qui le suit.

→ YP 25 p. 220

3 La structure causative

❶ Films can **make** [us] <u>laugh</u>.

❷ The film **makes** [people] <u>think</u> about the consequences of the government's policies.

❸ At the job centre Katie tries to **make** [the staff] <u>understand</u> why she was late.

❹ She tries to **get** [the staff] **to** <u>understand</u> why she was late.

- Les <u>verbes causatifs</u> permettent d'exprimer en anglais l'idée de « faire faire quelque chose à quelqu'un ».
- À la différence de *make* / *have* / *let (someone do something)*, ***get*** fonctionne avec ***to***. ❹

→ YP 25 p. 220

PRACTISE ONLINE

WORDS

Social (in)justice

- be fair ≠ be **unfair** /ʌnˈfeə/
- be **treat**ed un**fair**ly
- **cal**lous **po**licies = cruel **po**licies
- go with**out** food
- **vul**nerable and poor **peo**ple /ˈvʌlnərəbl/
- the **po**werless ≠ the **po**werful
- the **wealth**y = the rich = **weal**thy / **pri**vileged **peo**ple /ˈprɪvlɪdʒd/
- speak out a**gainst so**cial in**jus**tice
- re**spond** to sth by doing sth
- give a voice to sb

IFS1416

The law

- come to **pow**er /ˈpaʊə/
- be in **pow**er
- be e**lec**ted (Prime Minister)
- the **lea**der of the **La**bour/ Con**ser**vative Party
- MPs = **mem**bers of **Parl**iament
- **a go**vernment **po**licy /ˈgʌvnmənt/
- a **po**licy to re**duce** the **de**ficit
- the **wel**fare policy: *la politique d'aide sociale*
- intro**duce** new **so**cial **po**licies

IFS1417

Living situations

- be em**ployed**, be in em**ploy**ment ≠ be unem**ployed**, be out of work
- be un**a**ble to work
- need help from the state / the **gov**ernment
- be en**ti**tled to fi**nan**cial help / to unem**ploy**ment benefits
- be on **job**seekers al**low**ance = be on **be**nefits /əˈlaʊəns/
- work as a **joi**ner / **tea**cher / li**bra**rian

IFS1418

TEST YOUR SKILLS

OBJECTIF BAC

Listening & Writing

Listen to the document three times and report what you have understood. IFS1419

Write about the same topic, following your teacher's instructions.

Durée 1'30

AUDIO Ken Loach and actors on the impact of the film

▲ Ken Loach receiving the Palme d'Or award at Cannes

Speaking

React to a document.

- Your teacher will give you a set of two documents.
- In your opinion, which one best illustrates the notion of **ART AND POWER**?
- Explain why.

10

THE AMERICAN DREAMERS

REACT

1. **Look at the photo.** What is going on? Comment on:
   the situation | the people | the posters
2. **Listen to the commentary.** Did the speaker notice anything that you missed? IFS1461
3. Use what you have discovered to write a more detailed caption for this picture.

AUDIO Mark's commentary

▲ New York, October 2017

DEBRIEF Do you think that this type of protest can have an impact? What are some other ways to protest?

1 Illegal

VIDEO
Illegal (2012), short film

About *Illegal*
Through a series of interviews with **undocumented kids, activists, policymakers, non-profit leaders, educators** and **members of the clergy**, *Illegal* seeks to raise the consciousness level of the American public regarding the importance of full immigration reform...
illegalmovie.org

1 Look at the information above. What position do you expect this film to take on immigration? Why?

IN GROUPS

2 Focus on the list of people interviewed. Choose one of the groups mentioned. Anticipate:

a. their position on immigration.

b. their beliefs and motives.

3 Watch the film. e IFS1462
Discuss:

what you understood | what struck you | the questions you still have

4 Share your findings with the other groups.

a. What is the general reaction?

b. Can you answer any of each other's questions?

5 **At home** **Watch the film again.** Select one sentence that particularly strikes you. Get ready to explain why in class.

Identity Documents in the US
These forms of ID play a key role for immigrants.
Explain the purpose of each identity document.
Which ones were mentioned in the film? Why?

2 Documented

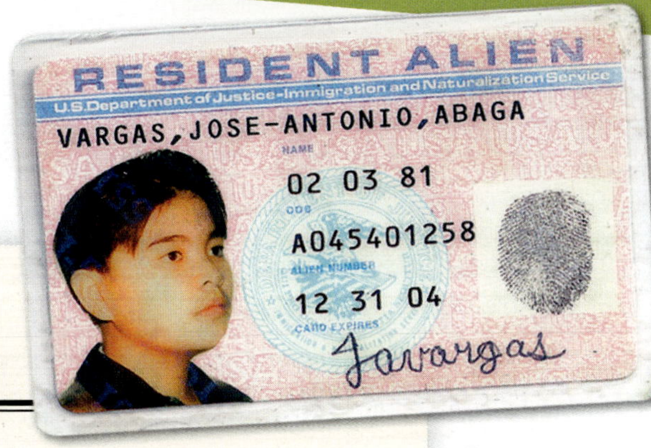

▲ For many years, the "Green Card" was actually pink!

My Life as an Undocumented Immigrant

By JOSE ANTONIO VARGAS JUNE 22, 2011, *New York Times*

One day when I was 16, I rode my bike to the nearby D.M.V. office to get my driver's permit. Some of my friends already had their licenses, so I figured it was time. But when I handed the clerk my green card as proof of U.S. residency, she flipped it around, examining it. "This is fake," she whispered. "Don't come back here again."

Confused and scared, I pedaled home and confronted Lolo. I remember him sitting in the garage, cutting coupons. I dropped my bike and ran over to him, showing him the green card. "Peke ba ito?" I asked in Tagalog. ("Is this fake?") My grandparents were naturalized American citizens – he worked as a security guard, she as a food server – and they had begun supporting my mother and me financially when I was 3, after my father's wandering eye and inability to properly provide for us led to my parents' separation. Lolo was a proud man, and I saw the shame on his face as he told me he purchased the card, along with other fake documents, for me. "Don't show it to other people," he warned.

1 *IN PAIRS* **Read the title and look at the picture.** What is your reaction?

2 **Read the text.**

a. What can you say about the green card above?

b. Focus on the people mentioned:

identity ← people → relationships

WORK your WAY — Use the text above **or** use a guided version. IFS1463

3 Look at the heading of the documentary:

DOCUMENTED
a film by an ~~illegal immigrant~~ undocumented American

Explain why Vargas chose this title and subtitle.

DEBRIEF

"We're not who you think we are." (Mr. Vargas) What do you think he means? Use examples.

YOUR TURN

Be a reporter!

You have a chance to talk to Mr. Vargas.

- Write five questions that you think are essential to understanding his story.

WORK your WAY — You can base your questions on the text above **or** on the trailer. IFS1464

- Share your questions with the class and decide which are the most effective.

VIDEO *Documented*, trailer (2013)

About *Documented*

In 2011, Pulitzer Prize-winning journalist Jose Antonio Vargas outed himself as an undocumented immigrant in an essay published in the *New York Times Magazine*. *Documented* chronicles his journey to America from the Philippines as a child; his journey through America as an immigration reform activist; and his journey inward as he reconnects with his mother...

3 "Most of us used to be them"

1 **Before watching.** What do you know about the history of immigration to the USA?

who? | when? | from where? | to where? | why?

2 *IN PAIRS* **Read the quotation from Obama's speech.** What do you think he is about to say? Why?

3 **Watch the video.** IFS1465

a. Were you right about Obama's quote?

b. Listen to the crowd's reactions. Which lines get these reactions? Why?

4 In Obama's sentence "Most of us used to be them", who is "us" and who is "them"? What does he mean?

5 **React.** Are all Americans descendants of immigrants? Explain which groups of Americans should not be considered descendants of immigrants, and why.

VIDEO
Barack Obama's speech, Las Vegas, 2013

"And it's really important for us to remember our history. You know, unless you're one of the first Americans..."

Background

The Statue of Liberty

"Give me your tired, your poor,
Your huddled masses yearning* to breathe free,
The wretched refuse of your teeming shore.
Send these, the homeless, tempest-tost to me,
I lift my lamp beside the golden door!"

The New Colossus, Emma Lazarus (1883)

* wishing, wanting

- Obama briefly quoted this poem. Read it and try to spot the line.
- Who do you think "me" and "your" refer to? How can you link this poem to the statue?

► The statue was erected in 1886 as a symbol of welcome to new immigrants. Emma Lazarus's poem appears on the statue's pedestal.

The Ancestry Map

- **Look at the map.** Can you imagine why some groups ended up where they are?
- **Listen to Mark's analysis.** IFS1466 What strikes you about the ancestry groups in the US?

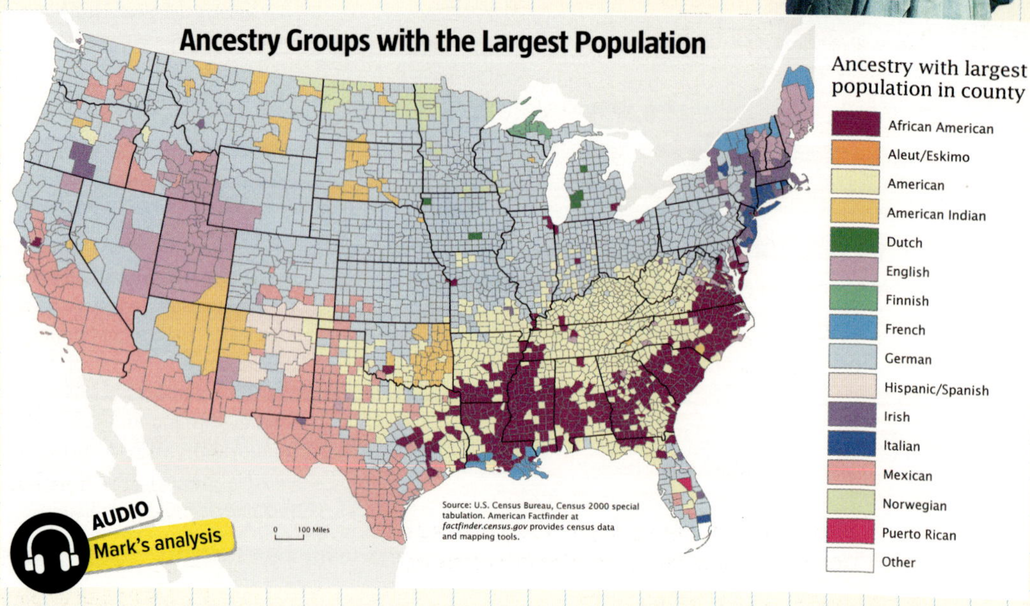

AUDIO
Mark's analysis

4 Born in the USA?

1 The Star-Spangled Banner

That's right. The most patriotic song in the U.S., the national anthem, isn't even entirely American. The lyrics of a patriotic poem written in 1814 by Francis Scott Key were set to the tune of an 18th century British song, "To Anacreon in Heaven".

2 Blue Jeans

From John Wayne to Marilyn Monroe to George W. Bush, Americans wear blue jeans a hundred different ways.
The history we all know involves a California retailer named Levi Strauss who invented the first pair of denim blue jeans as a durable clothing option for miners.
However, the cloth itself emerged in the cities of Genoa, Italy, and Nîmes, France. Gênes, the French word for Genoa, may be the origin of the word "jeans". In Nîmes a similar fabric became known as denim, from *de Nîmes*, meaning "from Nîmes".

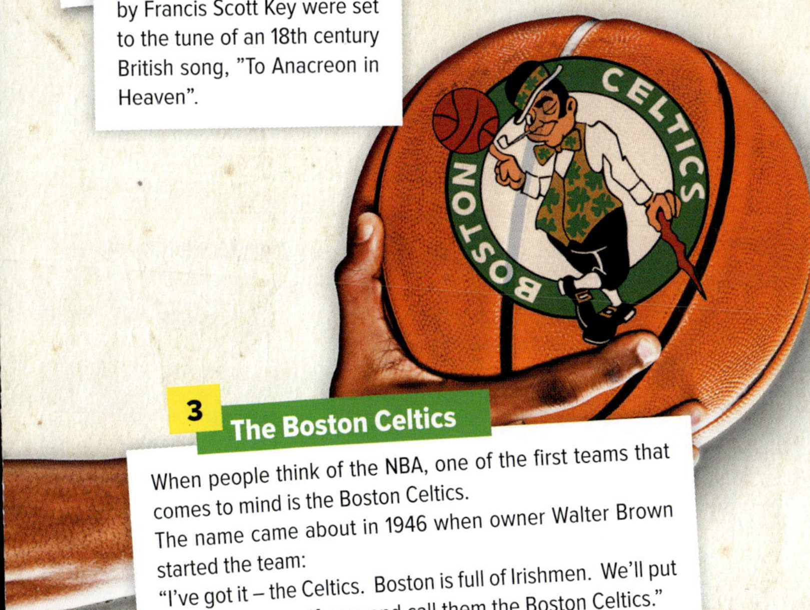

3 The Boston Celtics

When people think of the NBA, one of the first teams that comes to mind is the Boston Celtics.
The name came about in 1946 when owner Walter Brown started the team:
"I've got it – the Celtics. Boston is full of Irishmen. We'll put them in green uniforms and call them the Boston Celtics."
The logo manages to include all of the iconic depictions of the Irish: a leprechaun covered in shamrock clothing and a bowler hat, smoking a pipe, holding a shillelagh and sporting a mischievous grin!

4 Hot Dogs

Imagine a quintessential Fourth of July picnic: a sizzling barbecue full of hot dogs, plenty of ketchup and mustard. As it turns out, Americans weren't the first to come up with this delight. The hot dog sausage originated in Europe, and was called a wiener or a frankfurter, for the cities of Vienna and Frankfurt.
Immigrant butchers brought it to the U.S. by the late 19th century. The hot dogs as we know them – the ones stuffed into buns – then started being sold from push carts in the streets.

1. What do these images have in common? ▲
2. **Read the texts.** What do they reveal about American culture?

DEBRIEF

Obama said: *"Anyone from anywhere can write the next great chapter of our story."* What do you think?

YOUR TURN

Guessing game

- Listen and guess the name of the product described. e IFS1467
- Search another typical "American" thing... that isn't American. Tell the class about it and have them guess which product you chose!

TIP Be sure not to name the product!

5 An uncertain future

AUDIO
An interview with María Rocha (NPR, 2018)

1 Look at the title and the photo.
What can you imagine about the woman and the little girl?

2 Listen to the interview. IFS1468

a. Check your answers to question 1.
What did you understand about María Rocha?

b. Whose future is "uncertain"? Why?

3 a. What did you understand about DACA ?

b. Watch the CNN documentary to find out more. IFS1469

4 React. a. What do you think were the intentions of the journalists who conducted the interview?

b. What may the impact of broadcasting news stories like these be?

Background

What is DACA?

VIDEO
What is DACA? (CNN, 2017)

- **Look at the photo.**
  Any idea what DACA is?
- **Watch the video and check.**
  IFS1469

DACA
- WHAT does it offer?
- WHOM is it for?
- WHY is it so controversial?

Infographic: The American Government System

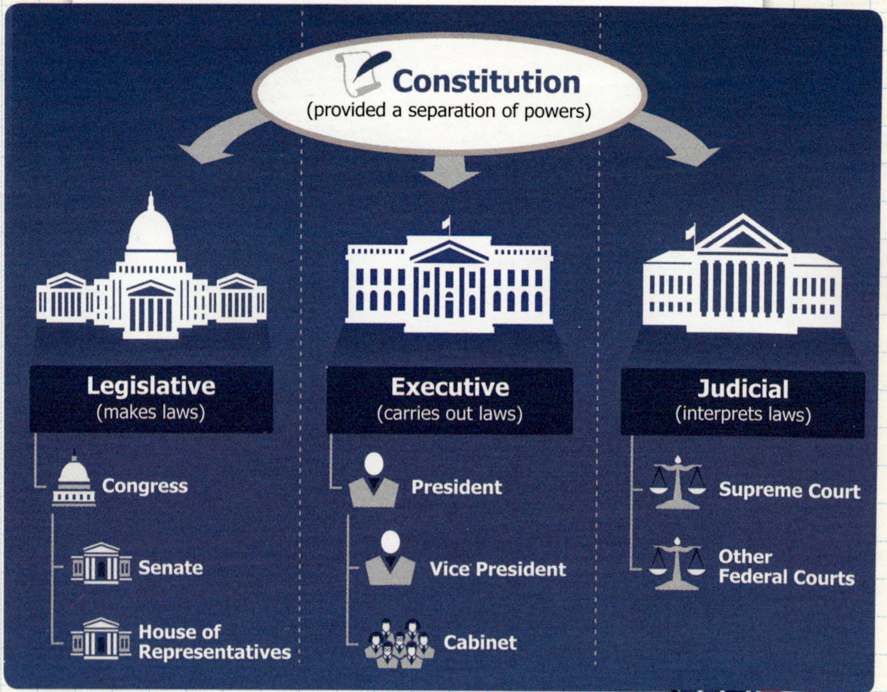

▲ The three branches of U.S. government, usa.gov

6 The end of DACA?

The following quotation is from a "press conference" – an American political tradition in which politicians regularly meet with reporters to explain government policies.

"Good morning. I am here today to announce that the program known as DACA that was effectuated under the Obama Administration is being rescinded*. The DACA program was implemented in 2012 and essentially provided a legal status for recipients for a renewable two-year term, work authorization and other benefits, including participation in the social security program, to 800,000 mostly-adult illegal aliens. This policy was implemented unilaterally [by President Obama] to great controversy and legal concern after Congress rejected legislative proposals to extend similar benefits on numerous occasions to this same group of illegal aliens." [...]

"The effect of this unilateral executive amnesty, among other things, contributed to a surge of unaccompanied minors on the southern border that yielded terrible humanitarian consequences. It also denied jobs to hundreds of thousands of Americans by allowing those same jobs to go to illegal aliens."

Attorney General Jeff Sessions, September 5, 2017

Attorney General
In the USA, the AG is the head of the Department of Justice (commonly called DOJ). He reports to the President and is part of his Cabinet.
Jeff Sessions was AG to President Trump's cabinet from 2017 to 2018.

* cancelled

1 **Read the caption above, then the infographic on p. 140.** Where does Jeff Sessions fit in?

2 **Read the first sentence.**
Try to answer one of these questions:

What? When? How?

"I am here today to announce that the program known as DACA that was effectuated under the Obama administration is being rescinded."

By whom? When? Why?

3 **Read the rest of the text** to complete your answers.

4 **Recap** by completing this chart:

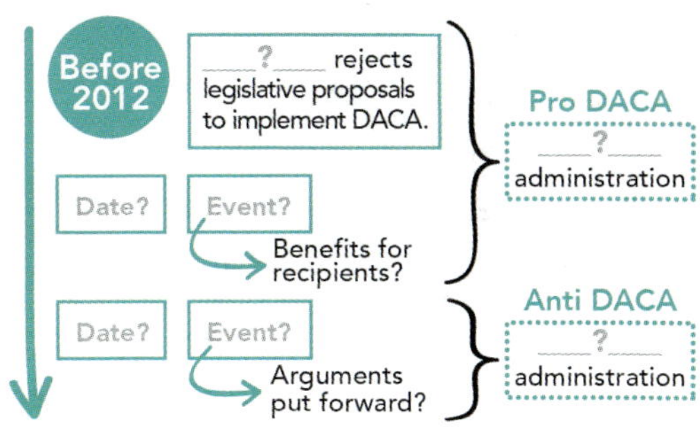

DEBRIEF

"Undocumented Americans", "Illegal immigrants", "Illegal aliens". Compare and contrast these labels.

YOUR TURN

Show and tell

- The debate over immigration in the US has produced countless memes, signs and posters. Search for one that you find particularly interesting and relevant.
- Present it to the class.

TIP
Don't forget to mention:
- meaning and position (for or against?)
- historical references
- your personal opinion

7 Another way

Refugees

They have no need of our help
So do not tell me
These haggard faces could belong to you or me
Should life have dealt a different hand
We need to see them for who they really are
Chancers and scroungers
Lay-abouts and loungers
With bombs up their sleeves
Cut-throats and thieves
They are not
Welcome here
We should make them
Go back to where they came from
They cannot
Share our food
Share our homes
Share our countries
Instead let us
Build a wall to keep them out
It is not okay to say
These are people just like us
A place should only belong to those who are born there
Do not be so stupid to think that
The world can be looked at another way
(now read from bottom to top)

Brian Bilston, *You took the last bus home*, 2016

AUDIO
A reading of the poem
IFS1481

1 Look at the *Time* cover.

a. What is your reaction? Comment on the choice made by the illustrator.

b. Explain the message.

2 Now read the poem.

a. The *Time* cover mentions "the *immigration debate that is dividing the nation*".
Whose point of view is expressed in the poem?

b. Can you find echos of opinions or arguments you've seen in the chapter or in the news?

TIP
You can use the *Background* section p. 140 to refresh your memory!

3 React. Which illustration would you choose for this poem?

- the original statue of Liberty
- its reinterpretation in *Time* magazine
- neither of them.

Explain.

DEBRIEF

Why does the question *"Who gets to be an American?"* generate such a passionate debate in the US?

FINAL TASK

Transform an icon!

Create a magazine cover for the next issue about immigration in the US.

TIP
Look at covers of *Time* and *The New Yorker* as good examples, which have transformed Lady Liberty.

1 Get ready

- Decide what message you want to put across.
- Choose a strong symbol you will use on the cover. How will you transform it?
- Write a title and subtitle that will express your opinion.

2 Action!

- Create your cover, including your creative transformation, title, and subtitle.
- Present it to the class, explaining its meaning with respect to US immigration issues.

Why not organize an exhibition in the school library? ☺

or

Be a speech writer

Write a speech for someone else to give at a ceremony at the Statue of Liberty, expressing the importance of immigration to the USA.

▲ Obama with former speechwriter Jon Favreau

1 Get ready

- Decide what information from the chapter is most useful.
- Write your speech. It should have:
  – a strong intro,
  – a logical structure,
  – a strong finish.
  Keep it short!

TIP
Watch Obama's speech, and read Jeff Session's speech again. What makes these speeches effective?

- **IN PAIRS** Find a partner who will rehearse and deliver your speech, and vice versa.

2 Action!

- Listen as your partner delivers your speech, then deliver theirs.
- Discuss with your partner what they did well, and what could be improved.
  Did your partner give your speech the way you had imagined?

WORDS

PRACTISE ONLINE

Status

- an **al**ien /eɪ/ = a **f**oreign-born **re**sident who has not been **na**turalized
- a refu**gee** /juː/
- an **im**migrant
- **le**gal ≠ il**le**gal /ˈliːgl/
- **do**cumented ≠ un**do**cumented
- a green-card **hol**der
  = a **per**manent **re**sident
  = someone who has been granted authorization to live and work in the USA on a permanent basis
- be **gran**ted **cit**izenship
- face an un**cer**tain **fu**ture /ɜː/
- face depor**ta**tion
- be de**por**ted

IFS1470

Identity Documents

- **So**cial Se**cur**ity Card
- **Dri**ver's **Li**cense
- **Green** Card
  = permanent resident card
- Birth Cer**ti**ficate
- Work **Per**mit

IFS1471

Reason for migrating

- flee / es**cape** perse**cu**tion
  conflict
  civil war
  violence
  ex**treme** **po**verty
  misery
  human rights **vio**lations
- seek **re**fuge, a**sy**lum /əˈsaɪləm/
  pro**tec**tion
  better oppor**tu**nities
  a **bet**ter life

IFS1472

IMMIGRATION IN THE US

Feelings

- fear (going out / being caught / the Border Patrol...)
- feel at risk
- feel anx**i**ety
  shame ≠ pride
  anger
  hope
- feel **an**xious
  angry
  a**sha**med
  un**cer**tain about the **fu**ture
  hopeful
  proud

IFS1473

Activism

- raise a**wa**reness a**bout** (an **is**sue / a situ**a**tion) /ˈɪʃuː/
- pro**test** a**gainst** sth
- **de**monstrate, march against/for sth
- fight **ra**cism, fight **pre**judice /ˈpredʒədɪs/
- have an **im**pact
- an **ac**tivist
- a **jour**nalist
- a **film**maker

IFS1474

EXERCISES

1 Odd one out

a. Identify the words that don't fit.

1. legal – documented – uncertain – permanent
2. shame – hope – anger – fear
3. protection – conflict – poverty – misery
4. opportunities – asylum – refuge – deportation

b. Use the words that don't fit to write sentences about US immigration.

2 How do you feel?

a. Put the following feelings in order from best to worst.

anxiety – pride – anger – hope – uncertainty – fear – shame

☺ .... ☹

b. IN PAIRS **Compare your order with a classmate. Explain your classification.**

3 An incomplete story

Use the following words to complete the passage about DACA recipients.

driver's licenses – at risk – undocumented – work permit – future – protections – deportation – immigrants

> A United States ... is one of the privileges most often associated with DACA. But for many ..., if DACA is terminated, other things are ... . The shutdown of the program could end other ... that DACA offers, from state-sponsored health coverage and financial aid to .... The loss of these things could deny ... Americans the ability to go to school, support their families and have a place to live. This could leave adults and children facing an uncertain ..., or even ....

▲ Naturalization ceremony

4 The big day

a. Look at the image above. Make lists of words from the mind map that you can use to describe it.

b. Use your list to write a short paragraph explaining the image.

5 Motivations

Finish the following sentences logically, using at least one word from the mind-map for each.

1. Refugees often leave their countries because...
2. Immigrants have traditionally come to the US in order to...
3. Illegal immigrants face many difficulties. For example, ...
4. Undocumented immigrants may feel...
5. Some ways that activists support immigrants include...

6 What makes anger angry?

Complete this table:

nouns	adjectives
anxiety	anxious
pride	proud
...	hopeful
shame	...
frustration	...
resentment	...
...	sad
...	optimistic
relief	...

Pronunciation

PRACTISE ONLINE

7 The odd one out

IFS1475

Une même lettre ou un même groupe de lettres peut se prononcer différemment en anglais.

Par exemple [a] : *card* /ɑː/ *escape* /eɪ/

In each list of three words, pick out the one which has a different vowel sound from the other two, as in the example:

e.g.: *card, escape, racism*

1. civil war, violence, misery
2. asylum, anxiety, angry
3. extreme, poverty, legal
4. proud, journalist, about

GRAMMAR

Dans ce chapitre consacré à l'immigration aux EU, des personnes témoignent de leur parcours et des difficultés auxquelles elles sont confrontées.
Pour cela, elles sont amenées à utiliser la voix passive.
Ces personnes partagent aussi leurs rêves et leurs aspirations, en faisant l'hypothèse d'une vie meilleure.

1 La voix passive

1. I **was arrested** even though I was an innocent.
   BE participe
2. I **was transferred** to an immigrant facility.
3. You know, **we've done** things the right way. **We were told** to go to school. **We were told** to make a career out of our future. And **we're doing** so. And now **we're being juggled**. It's very sad.
4. **The program known as DACA** that **was effectuated** under the Obama administration **is being rescinded**.
5. **This policy was implemented** unilaterally by President Obama.

- Le choix de la voix, **active** ou **passive**, dépend du **sujet** que l'on souhaite mettre en avant.
- Dans les énoncés 1 et 2 on s'intéresse avant tout à la personne. Le complément d'agent (= qui l'a arrêté puis transféré) n'apparait pas.
- Dans l'énoncé 3, pour maintenir tout au long de l'énoncé le sujet choisi au départ (*we* = les immigrants en situation d'illégalité aux EU), on est amené à avoir recours à la voix passive.
- De même, la conférence de presse d'où provient l'énoncé 4 concerne le programme DACA. Il est donc logique de le trouver en position de sujet.
- Quand jugé nécessaire, le complément d'agent est introduit par *by* 5.

→ Précis 34 p. 248

2 L'hypothèse

Hypothèse de départ — Résultat qui en découle

1. If you **are** undocumented, you **can't** get a driver's license.
2. If you **want to** work, you **will have to** admit that you are undocumented.
3. If I **had** a Social Security card, I **would be able to** register for college.
4. If I **had been born** three months later, I **would have been born** in this country.

If + Présent 1 2	L'hypothèse de départ est possible ou réalisable. La proposition principale exprime alors une conséquence possible 1 ou une prédiction 2.
If + Prétérit 3 *If* + *Past Perfect* 4	L'hypothèse de départ est irréelle, fictive. La proposition principale exprime un résultat probable.

Le résultat exprimé dans la proposition principale est introduit par un Présent simple ou par *will*.

Le résultat exprimé dans la proposition principale est introduit par *would* (Prétérit de *will*).

EXERCISES

La voix passive

1 Different perspective

Answer these questions.

1. José's grandparents financially supported him and his mother.

   > How did José and his mother managed when he was young?

   → *They ...*

2. The police stopped Mario and brought him to an immigration detention center.

   > What happened to Mario?

   → *He ...*

3. In September 2018, President Trump rescinded the DACA program.

   > What happened to the DACA program?

4. Immigrants butchers brought the hot dog to the U.S. in the late 19th century.

   > How did the hot dog arrive in the US?

5. Levi Strauss invented the first pair of blue jeans as a durable clothing option for miners.

   > I wonder where blue jeans come from.

2 Biography

Complete this short biography of Jose Antonio Vargas.

Observez bien les sujets des phrases, puis choisissez entre la voix passive et la voix active.

Jose Antonio Vargas was born in the Philippines in 1981. He *(raise)* in the United States from the age of twelve. He *(write, produce and direct)* the autobiographical 2013 film *Documented*, which CNN Films *(broadcast)* in June 2014. In a June 2011 essay in The New York Times Magazine, Vargas *(reveal)* his status as an undocumented immigrant. A year later, a day after his story *(publish)* on the Time cover, the Obama administration *(announce)* that undocumented immigrants age 30 and under would no longer *(deport)*. Vargas, who had just turned 31, did not qualify.

L'hypothèse

3 Terms and conditions

Complete these sentences with logical information.

1. If you don't have a work permit, ...
2. ..., you will be sent to an immigrant detention facility.
3. If Obama were still President, ...
4. If there had never been immigration to the USA, ...

4 What would you do if...

1. ... you had a part-time job?
2. ... your friend told you a secret?
3. ... your friend was getting bullied?
4. ... you heard someone making racist comments?

Write what you would do in the above situations.

→ *If I were 16 years old in America, I would get a driver's license!*

Pronunciation

PRACTISE ONLINE

5 Facts and figures IFS1477

À l'oral en anglais, **l'information importante** (souvents des faits et des chiffres) est toujours transmise **plus lentement** et **plus distinctement**.

a. Listen to this short description of the DACA program, making note of the important facts and figures.

b. Then practise speaking from your notes.

Rhythm & Sounds

Listen then say these sentences out loud, imitating the rhythm of the native speaker. IFS1478

- The only country they know is America.
- How does a 5-year-old get held responsible for a criminal act?
- That is the hardest conversation to have with a student.
- They've gone to school, they've worked hard, they've gone to college.
- Who gets the priviledge of becoming a citizen of the United States of America?

HOW TO... listen and take notes

You will often feel the need to take notes while listening, not just at school. Listening and writing at the same time can seem difficult, but with the right strategies and training, it becomes natural!

Do not panic if your first notes are scarce! You will complete them.

Strategies

VIDEO Taking notes while listening

You are going to see someone taking notes while listening to the report about María Rocha (p.140). e IFS1468

- First, observe these pictures and think about your own preferences when taking notes.
- Then watch the video and compare with your own habits.

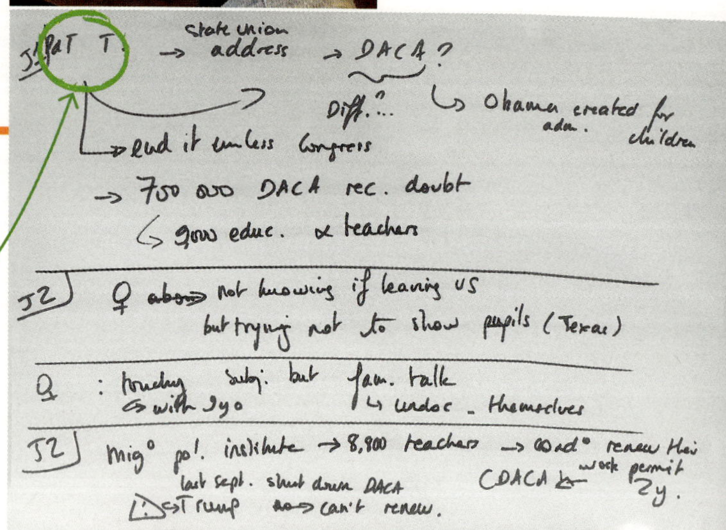

Which material?

- Blank or lined paper? Landscape or portrait format? One or two sheets?
- One or several colours? Which kind of pen?

Which notes?

- Do you like to **organize** your notes? How?
- How can you save time?
  - By using **abbreviations and symbols**
    → Which ones can you see here?
    → What do you think "Pdt T." stands for?
  - By writing down **certain words** only: which ones?
    → What type of words have been written down here? ▸

Useful symbols and abbreviations e IFS1479

How about the pauses?

- How do you use the 1-minute pauses in-between different listenings in class?
  → Watch the video and compare with your own habits.

TIP

The golden rules

Build up your own strategies

- Taking notes is a very instinctive thing. So you can use these tips, but you also need to make your own choices.

Trust yourself

- Understanding an oral message is 20% skill and 80% state of mind. If you have decided that you will understand, it will work ☺.

YOUR TURN!

Now try these strategies on other recordings from the chapter.

TEST YOUR SKILLS

OBJECTIF BAC

Listening & Writing

- **Listen** to the document three times and report what you have understood. IFS1480
- **Write** about the same topic, following your teacher's instructions.

Durée 1'30

AUDIO
Tereza Lee, a concert pianist, on growing up undocumented

Reading & Writing

- **Your teacher will give you several documents.**
  - Read them carefully and follow the instructions.

Speaking

- **React to a document.**
  - Your teacher will give you a set of two documents.
  - In your opinion, which one best illustrates the notion of **IDENTITY AND EXCHANGES**?
  - Explain why.

KEEP IT PRIVATE OR MAKE IT PUBLIC: WHERE DO AMERICANS DRAW THE LINE?

ESPACE PRIVÉ, ESPACE PUBLIC

11

IN THE PUBLIC GAZE

REACT

1. **Look at the picture.**
What can you imagine about:
the place | the time period | the main character | the situation ?

2. Can you find any possible links between the picture and the title "In the public gaze"?

3. **Watch the video.** IFS1512
a. What do you understand about the story?
b. What could the letter "A" on the woman's coat mean?

VIDEO *The Scarlet Letter* (trailer, 1995)

▲ A still from *The Scarlet Letter*, set in New England in the 1640s

DEBRIEF

In the trailer you hear Hester Prynne say *"I believe I have sinned in your eyes."* Explain what she means.

1 Pedestal of shame

"Speak; and give your child a father!"

In 1640, Hester Prynne, the young wife of an Englishman, is sent to America to set up home in the Puritan town of Boston. Her husband arrives two years later to find her on the scaffold, in the public gaze, with an illegitimate child in her arms. The young pastor, Arthur Dimmesdale, is questioning her.

The Reverend Mr. Dimmesdale bent his head, in silent prayer, as it seemed, and then came forward.

"Hester Prynne," said he, leaning over the balcony, and looking down steadfastly into her eyes, [...] "I charge thee to speak out the name of thy fellow-sinner and fellow-sufferer! Be not silent from any mistaken pity and tenderness for him; for, believe me, Hester, though he were to step down from a high place, and stand there beside thee, on thy pedestal of shame, yet better were it so, than to hide a guilty heart through life. What can thy silence do for him, except it tempt him – yea, compel him, as it were – to add hypocrisy to sin? Heaven hath granted thee an open ignominy, that thereby thou mayest work out an open triumph over the evil within thee, and the sorrow without. Take heed how thou deniest to him – who, perchance, hath not the courage to grasp it for himself – the bitter, but wholesome, cup that is now presented to thy lips!"

The young pastor's voice was tremulously sweet, rich, deep, and broken. The feeling that it so evidently manifested, rather than the direct purport of the words, caused it to vibrate within all hearts, and brought the listeners into one accord of sympathy. Even the poor baby, at Hester's bosom, was affected by the same influence; for it directed its hitherto vacant gaze towards Mr. Dimmesdale, and held up its little arms, with a half pleased, half plaintive murmur. So powerful seemed the minister's appeal, that the people could not believe but that Hester Prynne would speak out the guilty name; or else that the guilty one himself, in whatever high or lowly place he stood, would be drawn forth by an inward and inevitable necessity, and compelled to ascend the scaffold.

Hester shook her head.

"Woman, transgress not beyond the limits of Heaven's mercy!" cried the Reverend Mr. Wilson, more harshly than before. "That little babe hath been gifted with a voice, to second and confirm the counsel which thou hast heard. Speak out the name! That, and thy repentance, may avail to take the scarlet letter off thy breast."

"Never!" replied Hester Prynne, looking, not at Mr. Wilson, but into the deep and troubled eyes of the younger clergyman. "It is too deeply branded. Ye cannot take it off. And would that I might endure his agony, as well as mine!"

"Speak, woman!" said another voice, coldly and sternly, proceeding from the crowd about the scaffold. "Speak; and give your child a father!"

"I will not speak!" answered Hester, turning pale as death, but responding to this voice, which she too surely recognized. "And my child must seek a heavenly Father; she shall never know an earthly one!"

"She will not speak!" murmured Mr. Dimmesdale, who, leaning over the balcony, with his hand upon his heart, had awaited the result of his appeal. He now drew back, with a long respiration. "Wondrous strength and generosity of a woman's heart! She will not speak!" [...]

With the same hard demeanour, she was led back to prison, and vanished from the public gaze within its iron-clamped portal. It was whispered, by those who peered after her, that the scarlet letter threw a lurid gleam along the dark passage-way of the interior.

Nathaniel Hawthorne, *The Scarlet Letter* (1850)

Old English

thou, ye	*you* (sujet)
thee	*you* (complément)
thy	*your*
hath	*has*

PURITANISM

Early History

The Puritan religious faith originated in England during the early 1600s. By 1629, many Puritans had become discouraged by the corruption in the Anglican Church and they began to look for a new home in the colonies where they could practise their religious beliefs far from the influence of Catholicism and the Stuart kings.

The First Colony

Around 1630, they formed the Massachusetts Bay Company and established a new colony led by John Winthrop. The Puritans, under Winthrop, agreed that they would establish "a city on a hill", an example of good behaviour and religious purity. By 1643, nearly 9,000 Puritans had migrated to the colony.

Values

Puritans believed that God had formed a unique agreement with them and that they were part of the predestined elect, a group who were guaranteed admission to Heaven. Puritans were sober, hardworking and responsible. They thought worship should be plain, lack mystery and be focused on God. In churches, there must be no stained glass, instrumental music or art. They were intolerant of any sinful action, considering that error must be immediately opposed and driven out.

1 Look at the photo. ▲
Read the title and introduction on p. 152.

a. What is happening? → **YP 4**

b. How do you think Hester can "give [her] child a father"?

2 Read the text.

WORK your WAY — Use the text or use a guided version. IFS1513

Pick out information about each character. Organize them into a T-Chart like this one:

Characters	Details
• Reverend Mr. Wilson	• harsh, aggressive, wants Hester to reveal the name of the father
• the crowd	
• ...	• ...

3 Your teacher will reveal the name of the baby's father.

a. What do you think? → **YP 29, 30**

b. Scan the text. Were there any clues of this in the story? → **YP 18**

4 Read the section on Puritanism.
Pick out information which could explain the way Hester's accusers behave.

DEBRIEF

In your opinion, does the public have the right to judge people's private lives?

YOUR TURN

Public Opinion

- Imagine a dialogue between two people in the crowd during the scene on p. 152.
- Rehearse it with a classmate. Be sure you each express an opinion of Hester Prynne refusing to speak up.
- Perform your scene for the class. What is the public opinion?

2 Public confession

More Apology, Mr. President, And Less Politics, Please

By **Kathleen Hayden**, AllPolitics (CNN) WASHINGTON, Aug. 18, 1998

The public confessional delivered by Bill Clinton in the Monica Lewinsky scandal was heartfelt.

The problem was the president did not appear to be feeling what you might hope of a man admitting to extramarital sex with a woman half his age and lying about it to everyone he has sworn to love and lead.

The last thing the American public wanted to see Monday night was a beaten man. [...] Clinton needed to project as strong an image as possible.

And he succeeded on that front. But while avoiding the appearance of weakness, he failed to come across as at all chastened. Those looking for even a little contrition were deeply disappointed.

Instead the speech was laced with legal doublespeak and a sharp, defiant edge. Not once did he utter either the word "sorry" or "apologize."

Nor did he deliver a straightforward description of his relationship with Lewinsky. He only said it was "inappropriate." And "wrong." Oh, and it "constituted a critical lapse in judgment"

(How many people tuned out at that bit of legalese?)

It's baffling, really. For a brilliant wordsmith like Clinton, whose strength lies in relating to the average person, his speech to the nation was a missed opportunity to give a fuller accounting, while appealing for the public's understanding.

So what if he was angry after four years of investigations and four hours of intimate questioning. He could have had the grace to at least sound a little more apologetic for his behavior. He might have even thrown in a pinch of humility for good measure.

Though the strategy rubbed many the wrong way, the president should be awarded points for boldness. He took a position that many people don't believe and even fewer honor: "Even presidents have private lives." It's a question the nation will have to grapple with before the whole mess is put to rest.

President Bill Clinton was impeached in 1998 for lying in court about an extramarital affair he had with a colleague. Impeachment, or the bringing of charges against an elected official, did not lead to his removal from office.

1 **Look at the front page from the *Daily News* and the *CNN* article.** What point are the papers trying to make about Clinton?

2 ***IN PAIRS*** **Read the text.** Do you understand what happened during the public confessional? Use the mindmap to organize your findings.

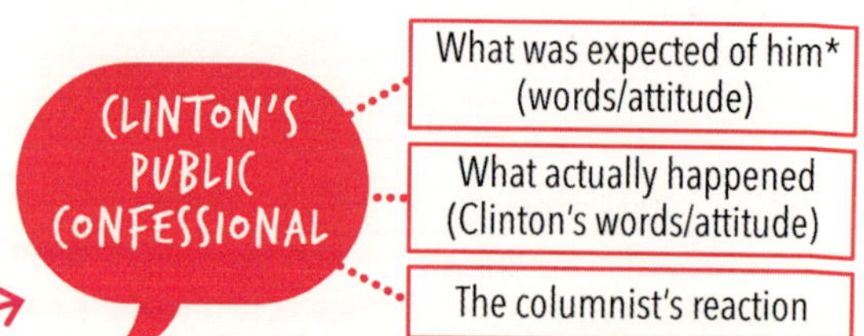

*by the columnist and some of the American public

3 **Compare this scandal with the one in *The Scarlet Letter* (p. 152).**

a. Complete this diagram. ▸

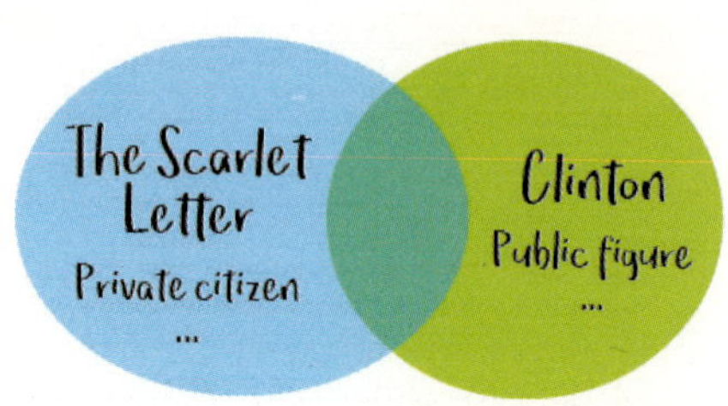

b. What is your reaction to each scandal? Is your opinion the same in both cases? Why? → **YP 15, 36**

3 Open secrets

Dirty Laundry

I make my living off the evening news
Just give me something—something I can use
People love it when you lose,
They love dirty laundry
[...]
Chorus:
Kick 'em when they're up
Kick 'em when they're down
Kick 'em when they're up
Kick 'em all around
[...]
Can we film the operation?
Is the head dead yet?
You know, the boys in the newsroom got a running bet
Get the widow on the set!
We need dirty laundry
[...]
Dirty little secrets
Dirty little lies
We got our dirty little fingers in everybody's pie
We love to cut you down to size
We love dirty laundry

Don Henley, 1982

AUDIO
Dirty Laundry

Don Henley
An American musician and co-founder of the band *The Eagles*. He played the drums and provided vocals including the lead vocals on *Hotel California*.

1 Read the lyrics. ▲ e IFS1514

a. What do you think the phrase "Dirty Laundry" means?

b. Explain who the following pronouns represent:

"I" (l. 1) "They" (l. 4) "'em" (l. 5) "We" (l. 13) "You" (l. 17)

c. What is the message of the song regarding privacy?

2 Read the *"News Feed"*. ▶
Explain the relationship between these stories and the song *Dirty Laundry*.

DEBRIEF

Can you "keep it private" when you are a public figure in the US?

YOUR TURN

Breaking News!

- Create a similar newspaper front page featuring the public scandal surrounding Hester Prynne.
- Present it to the class.

TIP
Be sure to include:
– a name for your paper
– an image and a headline
– a "gripping" description of your news story!

4 Right to privacy

VIDEO Apple and the right to privacy

1 Look at the picture. ▶

a. In what ways are companies like Apple related to the issue of privacy?

b. What is Apple's message?

You're going to listen to a speech by Apple's CEO Tim Cook.

2 Watch the video. IFS1515

Explain the following quote:

Give examples

"*If those of us in positions of responsibility...*"

What responsibility ? Why ?

3 Tim Cook says that if Americans fail to protect the right to privacy, they risk "their way of life".

a. Explain what he means.

b. Read the *Background* section to help you understand his position.

4 React. How can the 4th amendment apply in the digital age?

5 GROUP TALK React to one of these quotes.

Private information "can make the difference between life and death".

"History has shown us that sacrificing our right to privacy can have dire consequences."

Background

The Fourth Amendment to the constitution (1789) is often used to protect the right to privacy.

The 4th Amendment

The right of the people to be secure in their persons, houses, papers, and effects, against unreasonable searches and seizures, shall not be violated, and no Warrants shall issue, but upon probable cause, supported by Oath or affirmation, and particularly describing the place to be searched, and the persons or things to be seized.

- **Look at the court cases below.**
  For each one, explain how the Fourth Amendment was used.

Who's right about constitutionality of stop-and-frisk*?

CNN October 1, 2016

In 2013, US District Court Judge Shira Scheindlin found that New York's stop-and-frisk strategy focused too heavily on black and Hispanic people and was carried out too often without reasonable suspicion.

As a result, she ruled that New York's stop-and-frisk policy was unconstitutional "as applied." Scheindlin ordered the city's police to reform their training and policing procedures to make sure that officers do not engage in racial profiling when determining who to stop.

[She ruled] that the way the city was carrying out stop-and-frisk was unconstitutional, since it violated Fourth Amendment protections against unreasonable search and seizure.

Veronica School District v. Acton (1995)

uscourts.gov

In a 6-3 decision, the Supreme Court concluded that the random drug testing of high school athletes through urinalysis does not violate the reasonable search and seizure clause of the Fourth Amendment. [...] High school athletes, who are under state supervision during school hours, are generally subject to greater control than other free adults.

*stop-and-frisk is a policy of stopping and physically searching people that police think may have a weapon, drugs, etc.

5 Public discussion

February 16, 2016

A Message to Our Customers

The United States government has demanded that Apple take an unprecedented step which threatens the security of our customers. We oppose this order, which has implications far beyond the legal case at hand.

This moment calls for public discussion, and we want our customers and people around the country to understand what is at stake.

Smartphones, led by iPhone, have become an essential part of our lives. People use them to store an incredible amount of personal information, from our conversations to our photos, our music, our notes, our calendars and contacts, our financial information and health data, even where we have been and where we are going. [...]

We were shocked and outraged by the deadly act of terrorism in San Bernardino last December. We mourn the loss of life and want justice for all those whose lives were affected. The FBI asked us for help in the days following the attack, and we have worked hard to support the government's efforts to solve this horrible crime. We have no sympathy for terrorists. [...]

We have great respect for the professionals at the FBI, and we believe their intentions are good. Up to this point, we have done everything that is both within our power and within the law to help them. But now the U.S. government has asked us for something we simply do not have, and something we consider too dangerous to create. They have asked us to build a backdoor to the iPhone. [...]

The government could extend this breach of privacy and demand that Apple build surveillance software to intercept your messages, access your health records or financial data, track your location, or even access your phone's microphone or camera without your knowledge.

Opposing this order is not something we take lightly. We feel we must speak up in the face of what we see as an overreach by the U.S. government.

The context

In December, 2015, a federal judge requested that Apple help the FBI unlock an iPhone of Syed Farook, who committed a mass shooting in San Bernardino in which 14 people were killed. Tim Cook wrote a letter to Apple customers explaining the company's response.

1 Read the information about the context. What is your reaction? How do you think Apple reacted?

2 Read the text. Describe:

- the types of information you find on smartphones
- what the government wants
- Apple's response
- Apple's justification

YOUR TURN

Join the discussion

- Join Apple's public discussion on privacy. Should the 4th Amendment right to privacy extend to criminals? *All* criminals?
- Post a comment on their website expressing your opinion.

DEBRIEF

Think about privacy in the US. Who are the people and groups involved, and what are the main issues?

6 What to know before you go

Arriving in the USA PRIVACY TIPS...

CONVERSATIONS

In conversations, many Americans are private about certain things and do not want to talk about them, such as their age, how much money they make, or their political, sexual and religious views. Some people do not like talking about these subjects in public because they are worried it will cause people to argue. However, if you have questions about these topics, you can ask us. Most Americans will be happy to teach you about how Americans view the world.

PERSONAL SPACE

Americans often give each other more space in public situations than people in other cultures. They tend to stand with a bit of space between them, typically the distance of an outstretched arm.

Privacy

The right to privacy is a notion that runs deep in American culture... while often very warm and welcoming hosts, the home is considered a place of privacy. It is inappropriate to visit even close friends without calling ahead, and although Americans often tell a guest, "Make yourself at home," it is a friendly statement that must be carefully interpreted.

ALONE TIME

Taking "Me Time" is crucial to many Americans. It is the practice of taking some private time each day to relax on one's own. It is seen to refresh and revitalize, improving focus and relationships.

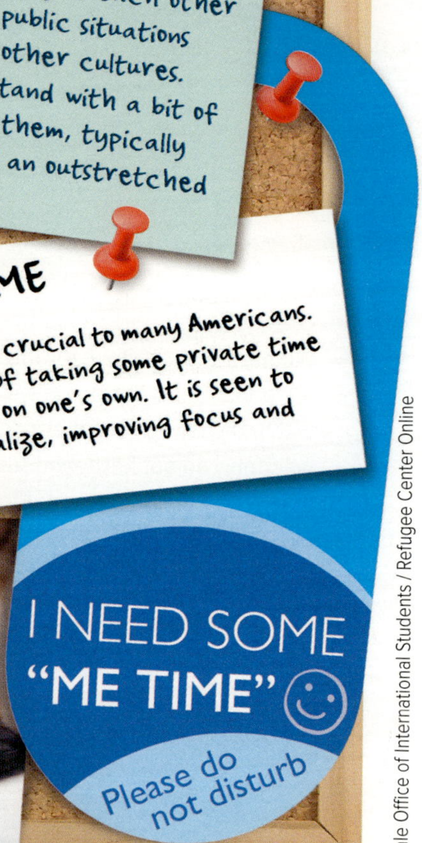

Yale Office of International Students / Refugee Center Online

1. **Look at the title and source.** Explain who might need this type of information and why.
2. **IN PAIRS** **Read each "Privacy Tip" and discuss:** what it means · why it might be this way · the differences with your own culture
3. Share what you discussed with the class.
4. **React.** Explain which tip struck you the most. Why?

YOUR TURN

Privacy, French style!

What advice regarding privacy would you give to an American coming to study in France?

Think of: conversation topics · visiting friends unannounced · ...

FINAL TASK

A Survival Guide

You've been studying in the US for two years and you're helping to write a survival guide for international students.

1 Get ready IN PAIRS

Your chapter of the guide deals with private and public life in the US.

- Organize your ideas into sections.
  Think about: practical advice | helping to understand why this advice is important

> **TIP**
> Think of what you've learnt:
> - the Puritan heritage,
> - the 4th Amendment…

- Find eye-catching images to accompany your sections of the guide.

2 Action!

- Write your guide. Make sure it looks welcoming!
- Share it in class.
  How do your guides compare?

or

A social media video

Record an unapologetic social media video defending your privacy!

1 Get ready

Sometimes when we "keep it private," we feel pressured to "go public."

- What sort of things do you think people should be allowed to keep private?
  relationships | social background | politics | exam results | …
- Think of a situation where you would be expected to go public.
- Get ready to explain why you don't want to go public.

> **TIP**
> Use examples from the chapter to protect your position.

> You can choose to be:
> – a well-known figure,
> – a fictional character,
> – yourself.

2 Action!

- Record your video and defend your privacy!

WORDS

PRACTISE ONLINE

In the public eye

Privacy

- **pri**vacy /ˈprɪvəsi/ (UK) /praɪvəsi/ (US) ≠ dis**clo**sure /dɪˈskləʊʒər/
  → The public disclosure of private facts
- have a right to **pri**vacy
- choose what can be ac**cessed** by **o**thers
- con**trol** what we choose to dis**close**
- **pri**vate **ma**tters (our **bo**dy, home,
- **pro**perty, thoughts, **fee**lings, **se**crets, re**la**tionships...)

IFS1516

Threats to privacy

- an in**va**sion of **pri**vacy
- the in**tru**sion /ʒ/ in an individual's **pri**vate af**fairs**
- the use of **per**sonal **da**ta (for **mar**keting **pur**poses / by the po**lice**...)
- a breach of **per**sonal **re**cords / **da**ta /iː/
- the possi**bi**lity of ac**ces**sing **de**tails of an indi**vi**dual's life or "personnal information"

IFS1517

Attitudes & feelings

- be ex**posed** to **pu**blic humi**lia**tion /hjuː/
  / to **pu**blic scorn
- be ex**posed** to the **judge**ment of **ci**tizens
- be de**fi**ant /dɪˈfaɪənt/
  brave, cou**ra**geous /kəˈreɪdʒəs/
  apolo**ge**tic
- feel shame
  guilt
  pride
- feel em**bar**rassed a**bout** (the public disclosure of embarrassing private facts)
- show con**tempt** for (the public opinion)
- re**main** strong, **dig**nified
- have a great strength of **cha**racter
  = have an **in**ner strength

IFS1518

Public confession

- ad**mit** to (lying, having had an affair...)
- re**veal** / dis**close** / di**vulge** infor**ma**tion /daɪˈvʌldʒ/ /dɪˈvʌldʒ/
- ac**cept** to speak ≠ re**fuse** to speak
- con**ceal** /iː/ ≠ re**veal** /iː/ (a secret)
- a**po**logize /dʒaɪz/ for sth / make a**po**logies /dʒiz/

IFS1519

EXERCISES

❶ The odd one out

a. Identify the words that don't fit.

1. privacy – secrets – disclosure – personal
2. invasion – protection – intrusion – access
3. reveal – disclose – divulge – conceal
4. be defiant – remain strong – feel shame – be dignified

b. Make sentences with the words that don't fit in order to explain their meanings.

❷ It Takes Two

a. Complete the text in order to summarize the similarities and differences between Hester and Dimmesdale's situations. Use the words provided.

exposure – dignity - personal - humiliation – citizens shame

> As Hester suffers public ... and ..., Dimmesdale experiences secret .... He cares more about avoiding public scorn and maintaining ... than about anything else. The young Reverend's ... guilt is preferable to the judgement of other.... And yet it is by concealing his private affairs that he experiences the most anguish of all.

b. Use words from this text to write about the Clinton scandal.

❸ Privacy in the Digital Age

a. What do you think this cartoon refers to?

→ *See p. 156 for help*

b. Suggest a caption for it.

❹ Transformations

> On peut changer le sens et la nature d'un mot en lui ajoutant un suffixe. Par exemple :
> *free* (adj) → *freedom* (n)
> *power* (n) → *powerless* (adj)
> *real* (adj) → *realize* (v)

Complete the table below to give yourself more ways to express yourself.

Noun	Adjective	Verb
	invasive	invade
		defy
apology		
		shame (someone)
exposure		

Pronunciation

PRACTISE ONLINE

❺ Two-syllable nouns and adjectives

IFS1520

> • En anglais, on accentue très souvent la première syllabe des noms et adjectifs de deux syllabes : ***wo****man*, ***strik****ing*...
> • Il existe beaucoup d'exceptions (*con****tempt****, an a****ffair***), mais cette règle vous sera néanmoins très utile !

a. Try to pronounce these words, then listen and check.

nouns		adjectives
record	public	private
data	courage	public
access	story	
details	scandal	

b. Now pronounce them in context, then listen and check.

1. Companies like Apple should do all they can to protect private records.
2. In the novel *The Scarlet Letter*, Hester Prynne shows tremendous courage in the face of a public scandal.

❻ Two-syllable verbs

IFS1521

> On accentue souvent la deuxième syllabe des verbes de deux syllabes : *in****vade****, de****fy***...

a. Pronounce these words, then listen and check.

record – reveal – admit – conceal – expose – disclose

b. Now pronounce them in context, then listen and check.

1. Legally, are you allowed to record someone without their permission?
2. Hester Prynne is asked to reveal the name of her baby's father, but refuses to disclose it.

GRAMMAR

Dans ce chapitre, on voit des individus confrontés à la morale publique, on s'interroge sur les obligations liées au respect de la vie privée, et on se prépare à ne pas enfreindre ces règles lors d'un futur séjour aux États-Unis !
Pour en parler, on est amené à exprimer la possibilité, la permission, l'obligation, et à utiliser des adverbes.

1 Possibilité, permission, obligation

❶ My child **must seek** a heavenly Father.

❷ We feel we **must speak up** in the face of what we see as an overreach by the U.S. government.

❸ The scarlet letter which Hester Prynne **has to wear** is meant to be a symbol of shame.

❹ It is a question the nation will **have to deal** with.

- Pour exprimer une **obligation**, on emploie le modal ***MUST*** ou un substitut : ***HAVE + TO***.
- Pour parler d'une obligation que l'on **s'impose** ❷, ou **qui est imposée par celui qui parle** ❶, on emploie ***must***.
- Pour parler d'une obligation **imposée par des circonstances extérieures** ❸ on emploie ***have + to***.

→ Précis 25 p. 243

Dans l'énoncé ❹, *will* ne pouvant être suivi d'un 2e modal on a recours au substitut de *must* : *have + to*.

❺ **Can** we **film** the operation?

❻ Private information "**can make** the difference between life and death".

❼ The government **could extend** this breach of privacy and demand that Apple build surveillance software.

- Pour exprimer la **possibilité** ❻ ou la **permission** ❺, on utilise le modal ***CAN*** (***COULD*** au Prétérit).
- On a recours à ***COULD***, Prétérit de *CAN*, pour faire référence au passé ou à une hypothèse ❼ *(→ Le gouvernement pourrait...)*.

→ Précis 27 p. 244

Prononciation
- Lorsqu'il est accentué : /kʊd/
- Non accentué : /kəd/ ou /kd/.

2 Les adverbes

❶ "Speak, woman!" said another voice, **coldly** and **sternly**.

❷ She shall **never** know an earthly one!

❸ "Woman, transgress not beyond the limits of Heaven's mercy!" cried the Reverend Mr. Wilson, more **harshly** than before.

❹ ... this voice, which she **too surely** recognized.

❺ While often **very** warm and welcoming hosts, the home is considered a place of privacy.

- Les adverbes peuvent jouer des rôles différents :
  – donner une **appréciation** ❶
  – exprimer une **fréquence** ❷ *(always, usually, often, sometimes, rarely, seldom, never...)*
  – indiquer une **modalité** ❹ *(certainly, perhaps, probably, clearly, obviously, surely...)*
  – préciser un **degré**, une **intensité** ❹ ❺ *(very, too...)*
  – etc.

→ Précis 32 p. 246

L'adverbe de fréquence se place :
- **devant le verbe** : *"You never know!"*
- et quand il y a un auxiliaire, **après l'auxiliaire** : *"She shall never know..."* ❷.

EXERCISES

Possibilité, permission, obligation

❶ Homestay experience

Complete the tips below with: *must / have to / can / could*, either in the affirmative or the negative form.

How to live with an American host family

1. **Be open and communicate**
   Are you allergic to peanuts or seafood? If so, you ... remember to tell the family before arriving. Some things ... be stressed enough – especially when it comes to health issues.

2. **Bring a gift**
   Gifts are a great icebreaker. You ... spend a fortune, but a little souvenir from your home country will be very appreciated.
3. **Respect the schedule**
   You're living with a family that is not your own, so you ... just do as you please. Be on time for dinner. Food is a fantastic way to get to know people! If you know how to cook, you ... even prepare a meal from your home country.
4. **Accept the differences**
   You will probably ... get used to different food and to house rules that are not the same as back home. Remember: different, new, and not the same ... mean bad.
5. **Participate in activities**
   If you're attending an American high school, make sure you mix with other students. You ... even discover a new hobby along the way!

❷ Legal cases

a. Read the following real legal cases. Based on what you have learnt about the 4th Amendment, what could each of the people involved do?

b. For a challenge, explain what they couldn't do.

e.g.: A teacher suspects that a student has drugs in their locker.
→ *He could ask to speak to the student. He cannot search their locker without permission.*

1. Police saw a covered motorcycle in the driveway of a house and thought it might be stolen.
2. A man discusses illegal activity on the phone in a public phonebooth.
3. Police suspect that there is illegal material in someone's outdoor trashcan.
4. Two men were "acting strange" when they passed a police officer.

c. Check the ruling in these cases. IFS1524

Les adverbes

❸ Completely Puritan

Complete the following text with the correct adverbs.
extremely – frequently – publicly – harshly – clearly

Puritans were characterized by an ... religious lifestyle. Puritan migrants to America ... consisted of entire families, because of their traditional values about the family. Puritans responded ... to sinners, and ... projected an image of purity. Their influence is still ... felt in certain aspects of American life.

❹ How public are you?

Give yourself the number of points that corresponds to how frequently you do each activity.
always = 4 often = 3 occasionally = 2 rarely = 1 never = 0

1. Tell my family about my social life
2. Tell my friends about my family life
3. Post information or photos on social media
4. Give someone my password to a device
5. Accept a friend request from a stranger
6. Use my phone to share my location with someone

Pronunciation

PRACTISE ONLINE

❺ Adverbs IFS1522

a. Listen carefully to the pronunciation of the following adverbs:

ever	usually	surely	obviously	always	probably
ˈevə	ˈjuːʒʊəli	ˈʃʊəli	ˈɒbvɪəsli	ˈɔːlweɪz	ˈprɒbəbli

b. Practise pronouncing them.

Rhythm & Sounds

Listen then say these sentences out loud, imitating the rhythm of the native speaker. IFS1523

- "Do you not believe that you have *sinned*?"
- "I believe I have sinned in your eyes."
- "History has shown us that sacrificing our right to privacy can have dire consequences."
- "Even presidents have private lives."

HOW TO... read a literary text

Literary texts can be intimidating – especially classics. But with a few strategies you can find help in the text itself ☺.

Always start by focusing on what you understand!

Strategies

Discovering the context

The back cover or the introduction may give you information about the *time*, the ***place***, the ***characters***, their ***actions***...

Understanding what is happening

In the extract, you will probably find the **same information** developed further.

A few helpful strategies:

- start by reading the **dialogues**
- use the **first sentence** of each paragraph
- use the **repetitions**
- use the **punctuation** to better understand the characters' conversations and emotions

Inferring unknown vocabulary

Use:

- the **context**
- the way **the word is constructed**
- the **prepositions**

And when none of these works?
Ignore the word for now ☺
Look it up in a dictionary later.

Understanding the characters' emotions

Look at:

- their **body language**
- the **adjectives and adverbs** used to describe their voice, tone or look

In 1640, Hester Prynne, the young wife of an Englishman, is sent to America to set up home in the Puritan town of Boston. Her husband arrives two years later to find her on the scaffold, in the public gaze, with an illegitimate child in her arms. The young pastor, Arthur Dimmesdale, is questioning her.

The Reverend Mr. Dimmesdale bent his head, in silent prayer, as it seemed, and then came forward.

"Hester Prynne," said he, leaning over the balcony, and looking down steadfastly into her eyes, [...] "I charge thee to speak out the name of thy fellow-sinner and fellow-sufferer! [...]"

The young pastor's voice was tremulously sweet, rich, deep, and broken. [...]

Hester shook her head.

"Woman, transgress not beyond the limits of Heaven's mercy!" cried the Reverend Mr. Wilson, more harshly than before. "That little babe hath been gifted with a voice, to second and confirm the counsel which thou hast heard. Speak out the name! That, and thy repentance, may avail to take the scarlet letter off thy breast."

"Never!" replied Hester Prynne, looking, not at Mr. Wilson, but into the deep and troubled eyes of the younger clergyman. "It is too deeply branded. Ye cannot take it off. And would that I might endure his agony, as well as mine!"

"Speak, woman!" said another voice, coldly and sternly, proceeding from the crowd about the scaffold. "Speak; and give your child a father!"

"I will not speak!" answered Hester, turning pale as death, but responding to this voice, which she too surely recognized.

The Scarlet Letter, by N. Hawthorne (1850)

YOUR TURN!

Use the help above to read more of the text.

TIP

Work with a classmate

- act out the scene together
- discuss what you understand

OBJECTIF BAC TEST YOUR SKILLS

Listening & Writing

- **Listen** to the document three times and report what you have understood. IFS1525
- **Write** about the same topic, following your teacher's instructions.

Durée 1'30

AUDIO
Privacy at school

Reading & Writing

- **Your teacher will give you several documents.**
  - Read them carefully and follow the instructions.

Speaking

- **React to a document.**
  - Your teacher will give you a set of two documents.
  - According to you, which one best illustrates the notion of **PRIVATE SPACE AND PUBLIC SPACE**?
  - Explain why.

MY PERSONAL AREA

Don't stand in it!!

12

SCIENCE OR FICTION?

REACT

1. Look at the picture.
Which aspects of it do you associate with: reality / fiction ? → YP 21

2. Watch the video. ISF1563
How can you link it to the picture?

VIDEO
Have you ever dreamed of flying in your car? *BBC*, 2017

▲Still from the film *Blade Runner 2049*, by Denis Villeneuve, 2017

DEBRIEF Can you think of any impossible things that became possible?

1 Exploring the limits

WORK your WAY Work on the text below or work on a guided version.
ISF1564

My love affair with the impossible

One day, would it be possible to walk through walls? To build starships that can travel faster than the speed of light? To read other people's minds? To become invisible? To move objects with the power of our minds? To transport our bodies instantly through outer space?

Since I was a child, I've always been fascinated by these questions. Like many physicists, when I was growing up, I was mesmerized by the possibility of time travel, ray guns, force fields, parallel universes, and the like. Magic, fantasy, science fiction were all a gigantic playground for my imagination. They began my lifelong love affair with the impossible.

I remember watching the old *Flash Gordon* reruns on TV. Every Saturday, I was glued to the TV set, marveling at the adventures of Flash, Dr. Zarkov and Dale Arden and their dazzling array of futuristic technology: the rocket ships, invisibility shields, ray guns, and cities in the sky. I never missed a week. The program opened up an entirely new world for me. I was thrilled by the thought of one day rocketing to an alien planet and exploring its strange terrain. Being pulled into the orbit of these fantastic inventions, I knew that my own destiny was somehow wrapped up with the marvels of the science that the show promised.

1 Before reading.
Focus on the following aspects:
titles | pictures | source & author

What do you expect the text to be about?
→ **YP 20**

2 Read the first paragraph (l. 1-6). Have you ever asked yourself these questions? What would you really dream of doing?

TIP
You can read **the first sentence of each paragraph** to have an idea of how the text is organized.

3 Read paragraphs 2, 3 and 4 (l. 7-33). How do the pictures relate to these paragraphs?

4 GROUP TALK Did you feel like Michio Kaku when you were a child?
Complete these quotes so they fit *your* experience, then discuss them with your group.

"Every Saturday, I was glued to the TV set, marveling at the adventures of ..."

"I was thrilled by the thought of one day..."

As it turns out, I was not alone. Many highly accomplished scientists originally became interested in science through exposure to science fiction. The great astronomer Edwin Hubble was fascinated by the works of Jules Verne. [...]

As I grew older I began to realize that although Flash Gordon was the hero and always got the girl, it was the scientist who actually made the TV series work. Without Dr. Zarkov, there would be no rocket ship, no trips to Mongo, no saving Earth. Heroics aside, without science there is no science fiction.

I came to realize that these tales were simply impossible in terms of the science involved, just flights of the imagination. Growing up meant putting away such fantasy. In real life, I was told, one had to abandon the impossible and embrace the practical. [...]

However, I concluded that if I was to continue my fascination with the impossible, the key was through the realm of physics. Without a solid background in advanced physics, I would be forever speculating about futuristic technologies without understanding whether or not they were possible. I realized I needed to immerse myself in advanced mathematics and learn theoretical physics.

So that is what I did. [...]

Today I receive e-mails from science fiction writers and screen writers asking me to help them sharpen their own tales by exploring the limits of the laws of physics.

Michio Kaku, *Physics of the Impossible*, 2008

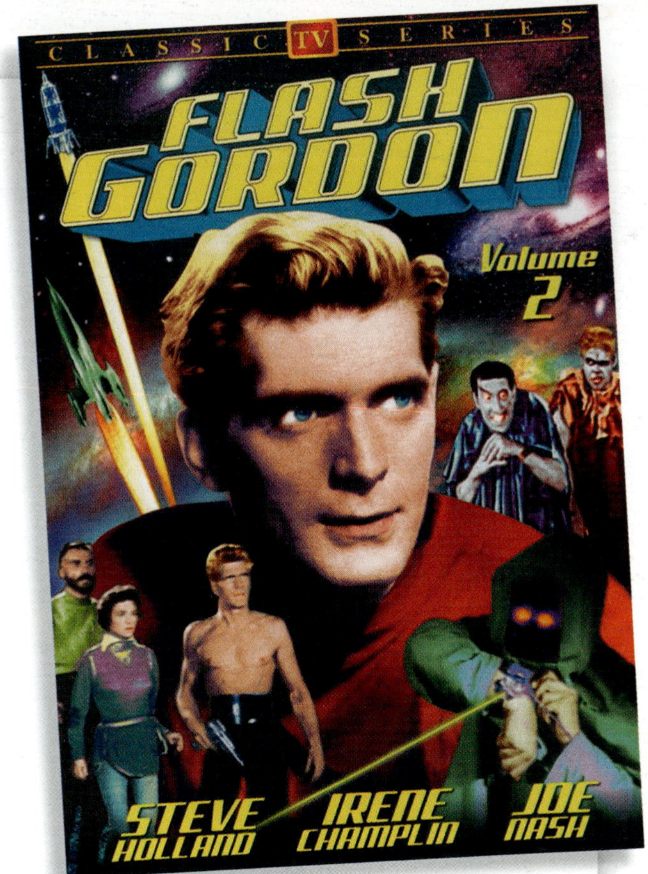

▲ *Flash Gordon*, TV series, 1955

Michio Kaku (born in 1947)
An American theoretical physicist, futurist, and popularizer of science.

5 **Read the rest of the text** (l. 34-60).
How did Michio Kaku finally handle his childhood passion for science fiction?

6 **React.** Do you think that all scientific progress comes from man's dreams?
→ **YP 37**

DEBRIEF

Explain the links between:

fiction | the impossible | science

YOUR TURN

A science question for Dr. Kaku

You are a scriptwriter for a new science fiction TV show. Ask Michio Kaku for advice!

- Think about a brand new technology that you want to include in the show. Imagine:

  how it looks | what it can do | how you activate it | how it changes your life

- Prepare your questions for Michio Kaku.
- Write him an e-mail to present your idea and ask him for advice.

2 Predicted by *Star Trek*!

VIDEO
Star Trek gadgets that now exist, BuzzFeed, 2014

1 Look at these gadgets from *Star Trek* that actually became real. ▲
Try to guess:

their use in the series

what they have become in reality

WORK your WAY Use only your imagination **or** check these gadgets' original names. ISF1565

2 Watch the video. ISF1566 (0'00→1'21)

a. Were you right about these objects?

b. Have you discovered other gadgets?

Star Trek
Originally a science fiction TV series from the 60s telling the stories of space explorers, it became very famous in the 70s because of its positive and optimistic message about the future and science. From this show, 6 other TV shows were created, as well as 13 movies. The *Star Trek* universe inspired many of today's scientists.

YOUR TURN

Shoot a short video clip IN PAIRS

- Here are other *Star Trek* innovations:

universal translator

transporter (= for teleportation)

- Choose one and prepare a short video to explain whether it is possible in real life and whether it can or could be used.
- Show your video to the class and get them to react to the gadget you have chosen!

3 The true meaning of *Star Trek*

"What I love most about America is that spirit of 'oh, we can figure this out'. If we ever lose that spirit, then we're gonna lose what is essential about America."
Barack Obama

▲ Barack Obama and Nichelle Nichols (from the original *Star Trek* series) doing the Vulcan salute from the show

VIDEO
Barack Obama on why *Star Trek* is so important *Wired*, 2016

1 Before watching.

a. Quick brainstorming! What characterizes *Star Trek* for you? List all the words that come to mind.

b. Now focus on the title of the video:

The True Meaning of *Star Trek*

Imagine what Barack Obama may say about it.
→ **YP 20**

2 Watch part 1 (1'00→1'09). ISF1567
Check your ideas. Pick out what Barack Obama says about the original series:

It wasn't about...

It was about...

3 Watch part 2. (1'10→2'36)

a. Can you identify the film extracts? What link does Barack Obama establish between this movie and *Star Trek*? → **YP 24**

b. Pick out what Barack Obama says about **science**. Explain it using a diagram:

... → ... → ... → ...

5 Recap what Barack Obama says about:

Star Trek → science → America

DEBRIEF

"Anything you dream is fiction, and anything you accomplish is science, the whole history of mankind is nothing but science fiction."
Ray Bradbury (1920-2012), American science fiction writer

Discuss to this quote, using what you have discovered so far in the previous pages.

4 "I ain't blind"

The Voice

'That's all,' said the Voice. 'I'm invisible. That's what I want you to understand.'

'Give me a notion. How are you hidden?'

'I'm invisible. That's the great point. And what I want you to understand is this–'

'But whereabouts?' interrupted Mr Marvel.

'Here – six yards in front of you.'

'Oh, *come*! I ain't blind. You'll be telling me next you're just thin air. I'm not one of your ignorant tramps–'

'Yes. I am – thin air. You're looking through me.'

'What! Ain't there any stuff to you?'

'I am just a human being–solid, needing food and drink, needing covering, too... But I'm invisible. You see? Invisible. Simple idea. Invisible.'

'What, real like?'

'Yes, real.'

'Let's have a hand of you,' said Marvel, 'if you *are* real. It won't be so darn out–of the way like, then–'

'*Lord!*' he said. He felt the hand that had closed round his wrist with his disengaged fingers, and his fingers went timorously up the arm, patted a muscular chest, and explored a bearded face. Marvel's face was astonishment.

'I'm dashed!' he said. 'Most remarkable! And there I can see a rabbit clean through you half a mile away! Not a bit of you visible –Except–'

He scrutinized the apparently empty space keenly. 'You haven't been eatin' bread and cheese?' he asked, holding the invisible arm.

'You are quite right. It's not assimilated into the system.'

'Ah!' said Mr Marvel. 'Sort of ghostly, though.'

H.G. Wells, *The Invisible Man*, 1897

H.G. Wells (1866-1946) was an writer of science-fiction works –including *The Time Machine and War of the Worlds*– who had a great influence on our vision of the future.

1 **Read the cartoon above.** e IFS1580
Try to identify the missing words.
Check with the original.

2 **You're about to meet this man.**
List all the questions you have.

3 **Read the text.** Did you find answers to your questions?

TIP
Read the text methodically.
Pay attention to **the layout** and **the punctuation**.

4 *IN PAIRS* **Adapt the scene.**

WORK your WAY
You can draw it **or** you can act it out.

5 **React.** Think about the advantages and drawbacks of being invisible:

invisibility
+ ...
− ...

5 Is invisibility desirable?

Invisibility has long been one of the marvels of science fiction and fantasy, from the pages of [illegible], to the magic invisibility cloak of the [illegible] books, or the ring in [illegible]. Yet for at least a century, physicists have dismissed the possibility of invisibility cloaks, stating flatly that they are impossible: they violate the laws of optics and do not conform to any of the known properties of matter.

But today the [illegible] may become possible. New advances in "metamaterials" are forcing a major revision of optics textbooks. Working prototypes of such materials have actually been built in the laboratory, sparking intense interest by the media, industry, and the military in making the visible become invisible.

INVISIBILITY THROUGHOUT HISTORY

Invisibility is perhaps one of the oldest concepts in ancient mythology. ... ISF1568

Invisibility is also a common plot device in science fiction. ... ISF1569

Only the first sentence of each paragraph is shown here. You will be given one paragraph to read.

[...] H. G. Wells put much of this mythology into concrete form with his is classic novel *The Invisible Man,* in which a medical student accidentally discovers the power of the fourth dimension and becomes invisible. Unfortunately, he uses this fantastic power for private gain, starts a wave of petty crimes, and eventually ...

Michio Kaku, *Physics of the Impossible,* 2008

1. **Read paragraphs 1 & 2** (l. 1-13) **and try to fill in the gaps logically.**
   a. Share with your classmates then check with the original version. ISF1570
   b. Do you find the prospect presented by Michio Kaku exciting?

2. **Read the rest of the document.**
   What can you expect in the missing paragraphs?

3. a. **Now read one of the two missing paragraphs** (...)
   Spot the example(s) provided by Michio Kaku.

   TIP
   To spot the examples, you can look for **words in italics** or between inverted commas (titles are often presented this way), **capital letters**...

   b. Identify the way invisibility is used and share with your classmates.

4. **GROUP TALK** Is invisibility desirable?

   Do you know other stories about invisibility? What role does invisibility play in them?

5. **At home** **Read the whole text.** ISF1571
   It ends on a cliffhanger... Why not read the book to know the end? ☺

DEBRIEF

"With great power comes great responsibility". (Spiderman) Discuss.

YOUR TURN

Creative writing

- Read this extract.

> "I was invisible, and I was only just beginning to realise the extraordinary advantage my invisibility gave me. My head was already teeming with plans of all the wild and wonderful things I had now impunity to do."
>
> *The Invisible Man,* H.G. Wells, 1897

- Invent a specific scene in which the invisible man takes advantage of his invisibility.

6 "The Invisible Man"

▶ *Hiding in London No. 2*
Charing Cross, 2014

▲ *Hiding in the City No. 65, Telephone Booth*, 2008

▼ The Chinese artist Liu Bolin being painted by students of the art academy of Stuttgart, 2013

Look at these pictures.

1. Can you spot the artist?
2. Discuss with your classmates:

the technique | the impact | the location

Want to learn more about this artist?

liubolinstudio.com

YOUR TURN

You're the artist!

Choose one of these activities and present it to the class.

Choose an iconic place where you live and make yourself invisible there.

On a trip to London? Lucky you! Why not try to recreate these pictures?

Defeat another physical impossibility thanks to art and create a picture!
Flying? Time travel? Morphing? Teleportation?

FINAL TASK

Your love affair with the Impossible

You have been asked to contribute to *Physics of the Impossible – Part 2* – by writing a text about a scientific "impossibility" that you are interested in.

1 Get ready

- Choose the "impossibility" you want to write about: ▶
  - Impossible before but possible now
  - Still impossible but... who knows about the future?
  - Time travel
  - Breathing under water
  - Morphing
  - Flying
  - ...
- Think about the stories you know about it: books · legends · movies · songs · ...
- Search the web to know if it is likely to exist one day (or ask your physics teacher!)

2 Action!

- Write your text and illustrate it with a picture.
- Then make a second version of your text where you erase some of the words (as in the text on p. 173).
- Give the text to your classmates and see if they can fill in the gaps! *Why not challenge your teacher, as well?*

TIP

- You can get ideas of scientific marvels by watching **superhero** movies, like *X-Men* ☺
- You can use the the text on p. 173 to help you structure your own. You can also read *How to write an essay* on p. 180.

or

Breaking News!

A new technology has just been invented. You are in charge of presenting the news!

1 Get ready

- Think about the gadget of your dreams – something that:
  doesn't exist · really inspires you · would make life much easier or more exciting
- Get ready to present it. Think about:
  its name · its advantages · concrete examples of how it can be used

2 Action!

- Shoot a short video to tell the world about this new gadget. Inspire them, make them laugh ☺.

This gadget will be a boon for students with problems memorizing notes. Just dab the bread on the notes you want to learn by heart and eat it.
No more burning the midnight oil.

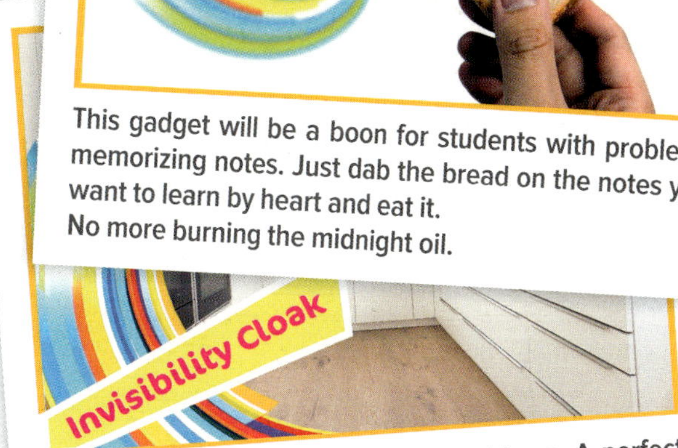

This could save us from so many problems. A perfect way to slip out without being noticed from awkward situations, a boring class or even work.
One more advantage of being invisible is that you can eavesdrop without getting caught so you'll know who's talking behind your back.

sciencestruck.com

WORDS

PRACTISE ONLINE

Scientific progress

Nouns

- an ex**per**iment: *une expérience scientifique*
- a scientific **break**through = an im**por**tant dis**co**very /aɪən/
- mathe**ma**tics, **phy**sics
- a **scien**tist, a mathema**ti**cian, a **phy**sicist, an as**tro**nomer
- a la**bo**ratory /lə'bɒrətərɪ/

Verbs

- a**chieve** = suc**ceed** in + V-ing = **ma**nage to + V /ə'tʃi:v/ /'mænɪdʒ/
- make / cre**ate**
- in**vent** = come **up** with (an i**de**a)
- be**come** = **turn** into
- **pos**sible ≠ im**pos**sible
- **li**kely ≠ un**li**kely

ISF1572

Inventions

Nouns

- a de**vice** /aɪ/
- tech**no**logy
- a **fly**ing car
- an invisi**bi**lity cloak / shield /əʊ/ /i:/
- a time ma**chine** /ə/
- a **star**ship, a **ro**cket ship

Adjectives

- **use**ful = **help**ful
- **prac**tical = con**ve**nient /i:/

ISF1573

Science vs fiction?

Fiction

Nouns

- **sci**ence **fic**tion, **sci**-fi, SF /'saɪfaɪ/
- **fan**tasy **li**terature /'lɪtərɪtʃə/
- a **sci**-fi TV **pro**gram / TV **se**ries / **no**vel / **co**mic
- a **wri**ter, a **screen**writer
- a plot = an in**trigue**, a **sto**ry line

Verbs

- be**lie**ve in sth
- hope
- i**ma**gine
- pre**dict** [sth] = fore**tell** [sth]
- **fas**cinate = **mes**merize
- **mar**vel at = be im**pres**sed by

Adjectives

It is...

- ex**ci**ting = **thril**ling /saɪ/
- **fas**cinating = in**tri**guing /eɪ/
- **daz**zling = a**ma**zing, im**pres**sive /æ/ /ə/ /eɪ/

Adverbs

I feel...

- ex**ci**ted = **thril**led
- **fas**cinated = in**tri**gued
- a**ma**zed, im**pres**sed

ISF1574

The impossible?

Nouns

- invisi**bi**lity
- immor**ta**lity
- invinci**bi**lity

Adjectives

- in**vi**sible ≠ **vi**sible
- **im**mortal ≠ **mor**tal
- in**vin**cible ≠ des**truc**tible

- tele**ki**nesis /tɛlɪkɪ'ni:sɪs/ = **mo**ving **ob**jects by the **po**wer of the mind
- te**le**pathy /tɪ'lɛpəθɪ/ = **rea**ding **peo**ple's minds

Verbs

- ap**pear** / disap**pear** / reap**pear** /s/
- walk through walls
- **tra**vel **fas**ter than the speed of light

ISF1575

EXERCISES

❶ What's the word?

Find the words that corresponds to these definitions:

1. The series of events that form the story in a novel, movie, etc.
2. The person whose job is to write the script of a movie or series.
3. Imaginative fiction featuring especially strange settings and grotesque characters (e.g. Game of Thrones).
4. Stories about how people and societies are affected by imaginary scientific developments in the future (e.g. *Independence Day*).
5. To describe something before it happens.

❷ Super powers

Complete each sentence with the missing words:

1. In one of H.G. Wells' most famous novels, the protagonist, an English scientist and inventor, travels into the past and future thanks to a ....
2. In *Harry Potter*, Harry is given an ... as a Christmas present – a piece of clothing that renders him unseeable.
3. *Le passe-muraille* is a short story published by French writer Marcel Aymé in 1941. It is the story of a man who possesses the ability to ...: he can move between different rooms without using the door; he can even escape from prison!

❸ The odd one out

a. Spot the words that don't fit:

1. make up – create – predict – invent
2. foretell – anticipate – recount – predict
3. a plot – an event – an intrigue – a storyline
4. useful – fascinating – practical – convenient

b. Make 5 sentences with the words you have found in order to explain their meanings.

❹ A Unique Experience

Complete this passage, using words from the mind map:

When ***2001, A Space Odyssey*** by Stanley Kubrick, was released in 1968, it absolutely ... spectators, staging a number of ... . The ... shows HAL, the onboard computer, trying to kill the only man left aboard the ....
Kubrick, as a ..., seems to ... the adventure of Man into space, and the danger represented by AI. In any case, the movie is a ... experience.

❺ Appear, disappear, reappear!

• On peut changer le sens d'un mot en lui ajoutant un préfixe. Par exemple le préfixe *re-* : *appear* → *reappear*.
• Les préfixes suivants peuvent facilement être confondus, car ils ont tous un **sens négatif** :

préfixe	sens	exemple
un- *dis-* *im-*	= le contraire	*unthinkable* *disappear* *impossible*
mis-	de manière fausse	*misunderstand*

a. Choose the correct prefix:

1. *Available:* I tried to borrow *The Time Machine* from the library, but it was ....
2. *Likely:* The idea that we might one day travel through time seems very ... to me!
3. *Understand:* I thought this was a science fiction book, but I realize I completely ... the blurb on the back cover!
4. *Predictable:* My friend finds *Game of Thrones* boring but I find it astounding and ... .

b. Write 5 new sentences, using the words you have found.

Pronunciation

PRACTISE ONLINE

❻ Formes faibles IFS1576

Les mots anglais de plus de deux syllabes contiennent presque tous une ou plusieurs syllabes, non accentuées, dont **on entend à peine le son voyelle**, réduit au seul son /ə/. Bien respecter le contraste entre syllabes accentuées et formes faibles est la clef de l'anglais oral.

a. Listen and practise pronouncing these words:

machine /məˈʃiːn/ — literature /ˈlɪtərɪʧə/ — writer /ˈraɪtə/ — appear /əˈpɪə/

b. Now practise saying these sentences:

I would love to be able to suddenly disappear and reappear! Unfortunately, it is only in literature that such things happen.

H.G. Wells, who wrote *The Time Machine*, is also the author of *The Invisible Man*. He is a great writer of science fiction.

GRAMMAR

Dans ce chapitre, on parle d'inventions et on envisage ce qu'elles changeront. Pour cela, on a recours à des **noms composés**, à l'expression de la **possibilité** et à l'évocation de l'**avenir**.

1 Les noms composés

1. I was mesmerized by the possibility of **time travel**, **ray guns** [...] and the like.
2. They began my lifelong **love affair** with the impossible.
3. Today I receive e-mails from **screen writers** [...].

- Les **noms composés** sont formés d'un nom principal *(travel, guns, affair, writers....)* précédé d'un autre mot qui précise le sens de ce nom.
- Les procédés de fabrication sont multiples :

nom + **nom**	adjectif + **nom**	nom + adjectif + **nom**	...
time **travel**	soft**ware**	hands-free **phone**	
ray **guns**	cellular **phone**		
love **affair**	smart**phone**		
science **fiction**			
master**piece**			

2 La possibilité

1. Today 3D printers **can** actually print food.
2. Thanks to the invisibility cloak, you will **be able to** slip out of a boring class without being noticed.

- Le modal ***can*** sert à exprimer la possibilité ❶ (aptitude, capacité, savoir-faire).
- Pour évoquer l'avenir ❷ on le remplace par ***be able + to***. On ne peut en effet avoir deux modaux *(will + can)* à la suite.

Prononciation

*It **can** actually print food.*
/kæn/

***Can** it? It **can't** be true!*
/kæn/ /kɑːnt/

3 L'évocation de l'avenir

1. This gadget **will** be a boon for students with problems memorizing notes.
2. One day, **would** it be possible to walk through walls? [...] Since I was a child, I've always been fascinated by these questions.

- Lorsqu'on envisage un événement à venir comme fortement probable, on emploie ***will***. (❶)
- Lorsque l'événement à venir a été envisagé dans le passé, on emploie ***would***, Prétérit de ***will***. (❷)

EXERCISES

Les noms composés

1 Understanding compound nouns

a. Explain the meanings of these compound nouns:
invisibility cloak – time travel – playground – love affair – bestselling author

→ *An invisibility cloak is a ...*

b. Use these nouns in sentences.

2 Making compound nouns

a. How do you call...
- a machine that allows people to travel in the past or future
- a ship that is used for travel in outer space
- a person who writes screenplays

b. Now go further! How do you call...
- a degree in science
- a device that is worn over or inserted into the ear and is used for listening to music or radio
- a book that you can use when travelling
- a ticket that you use to travel on a plane
- a person who has seen something happen and can give a first-hand description of it.

La possibilité

3 Virtual Reality

Read the definition above.
Imagine what is already possible or will be possible in the future with VR.

Virtual reality (VR) is the term used to describe a three-dimensional, computer generated environment which can be explored and interacted with by a person. That person becomes part of this virtual world or is immersed within this environment and whilst there, is able to manipulate

Think of the following domains:

architecture – medicine – sport – entertainment – travel – the arts

L'évocation de l'avenir

4 Diary of a scientist

Complete this scientist's diary entry, using *WILL* or *WOULD*.

Diary Entry 25
April 20XX
When I was a kid I read sci-fi magazines and thought that in a few years, I ... travel in a rocket ship. Now we are seeing brilliant teenagers training for a trip to Mars! This generation ... indeed travel to space. And who ... have thought, when the first computers were so big that they required a large room to operate, that today a hand-held smartphone ... be just as powerful as those old, massive pieces of hardware? We know that in a few years' time such devices ... be implanted in our bodies. Do we really want that?

Pronunciation

PRACTISE ONLINE

5 Compound nouns IFS1577

L'accentuation est importante, car elle permet de distinguer un nom composé d'un adjectif suivi d'un nom. Ils n'ont pas le même sens !

Nom composé	≠	Adjectif + nom
He is such a big head. He always seems to say 'Look at me.'		*He has such a big head. Most hats won't fit!*

a. In each of the two sentences, say if the underlined element is a compound noun or an adjective + noun.

1. In this text, Michio Kaku describes his love affair with the impossible.
   For years, they had a passionate affair.
2. Do you think this is a good show?
   Michio Kaku has hosted several science shows on TV.
3. Journalists must respond quickly to breaking news.
   Unexpected news bewildered everyone.

b. Practise pronouncing each pair of sentences, then listen and check.

Rhythm & Sounds

Listen then say these sentences out loud, imitating the rhythm of the native speaker. IFS1578

- I'm sure that back in the nineties, nobody could have imagined that phones would become such an essential part of our lives.
- Who could have thought that one day, we would actually be able to print food?
- Wouldn't it be great to be able to travel through time?

HOW TO... write an essay

An essay is a written review of your thoughts and knowledge about a subject.
Always remember that you are writing for someone: be methodical and clear.

An essay is not a novel. Keep focused on the subject!

Introduction

Present the question you are going to answer.

Body

Answer your question through meaningful paragraphs composed of:
- one idea / one argument
- one or several pieces of evidence, examples or anecdotes to illustrate it

To nuance your opinion, always think about what people who disagree with you might say.
e.g. *Although some may think that time travel is impossible, I firmly believe it might become a reality.*

Connectors

They are useful to express changes in:
- time
- reasoning
- point of view

Use them with moderation, though. As you can see here, they are only used in strategic places to make the structure clearer.

Conclusion

Finish strong!
Keep it short and simple.

"One day, would it be possible to walk through walls? To build starships that can travel faster than the speed of light? To read other people's minds? To become invisible? To move objects with the power of our minds? To transport our bodies instantly through outer space?

Since I was a child, I've always been fascinated by these questions. Like many physicists, when I was growing up, I was mesmerized by the possibility of time travel, ray guns, force fields, parallel universes, and the like. Magic, fantasy, science fiction were all a gigantic playground for my imagination. They began my lifelong love affair with the impossible.

I remember watching the old *Flash Gordon* reruns on TV. The program opened up an entirely new world for me. [...]

As I grew older I began to realize that although Flash Gordon was the hero and always got the girl, it was the scientist who actually made the TV series work. Without Dr. Zarkov, there would be no rocket ship, no trips to Mongo, no saving Earth. Heroics aside, without science there is no science fiction. I came to realize that these tales were simply impossible in terms of the science involved, just flights of the imagination [...]

However, I concluded that if I was to continue my fascination with the impossible, the key was through the realm of physics. Without a solid background in advanced physics, I would be forever speculating about futuristic technologies without understanding whether or not they were possible. I realized I needed to immerse myself in advanced mathematics and learn theoretical physics.

So that is what I did. [...]

Today I receive e-mails from science fiction writers and screenwriters asking me to help them sharpen their own tales by exploring the limits of the laws of physics."

Michio Kaku, *Physics of the Impossible*, 2008

YOUR TURN!

Write a similar text, starting from questions about the future you used to ask yourself as a child.

TEST YOUR SKILLS

OBJECTIF BAC

Listening & Writing

Listen to the document three times and report what you have understood. e IFS1579

Write about the same topic, following your teacher's instructions.

AUDIO
Tech as imagined in the not-too-distant future

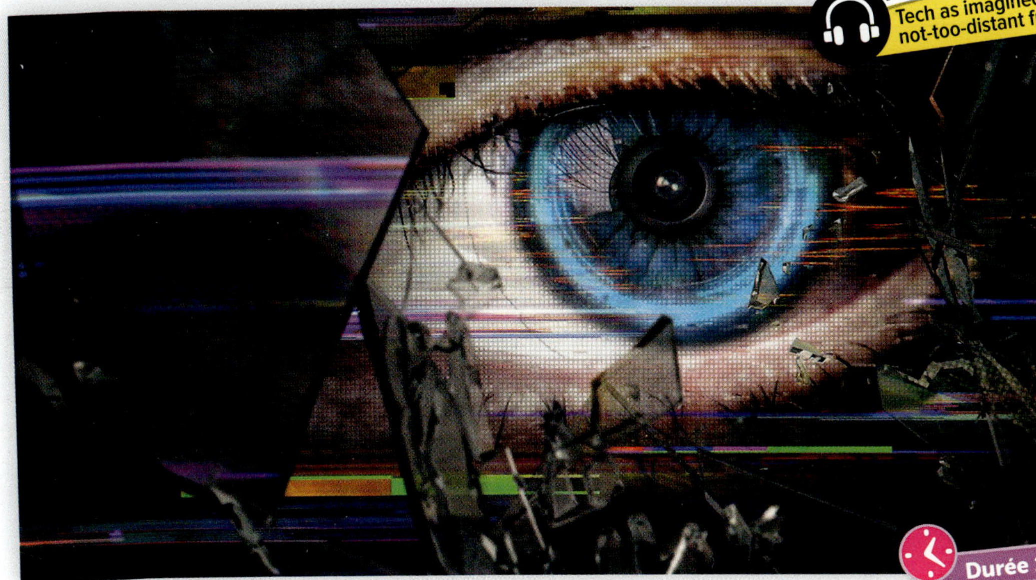

Durée 1'30

Reading & Writing

Your teacher will give you several documents.

- Read them carefully and follow the instructions.

Speaking

React to a document.

- Your teacher will give you a set of two documents.
- In your opinion, which one best illustrates the notion of **FICTION AND REALITY**?
- Explain why.

HOW DOES DETROIT REFLECT THE HISTORY OF THE UNITED STATES?

13

DETROIT MATTERS

REACT

1. **Look at the two pictures.**
What are your impressions? What do you think happened? → **YP 3a, 12a, 21, 25**

2. **Watch the video.** IFS1614
Focus on the young man's feelings and the atmosphere.
What does it say about the city?

VIDEO
Discover another Detroit's landmark

▲ The Michigan Theater now and then

DEBRIEF Do you think these buildings should be destroyed?

1 From Glory Days...

Motown: 1. TRADEMARK. The first black-owned record company in the US was founded in Detroit in 1959. It produced artists such as Aretha Franklin, Stevie Wonder, Temptations and Marvin Gaye;
2. INFORMAL. A name for Detroit *(motor town)*

VIDEO
The Golden Era

▲ The Erie Canal is a partially man-made waterway that connects the Great Lakes with New York's Hudson River, and consequently the Atlantic Ocean.

1 Locate Detroit on the map. → YP 6c, 21
Can you imagine why Detroit's location made it an ideal place for industry?

2 Watch the video. IFS1615

a. Take notes on:
- the development of trade and industry
- the expansion of the city
- the "Great Migration"

b. *IN PAIRS* Compare and complete your notes. Were you right about question 1?

c. Share your notes with the class. How did Detroit become such a successful city?

3 Look at the picture. ▶
Have you heard of Aretha Franklin? What do you know or what can you imagine about Motown music?

4 Listen to one of Aretha Franklin's hits IFS1616
What do you think about the Motown style?

5 a. Watch the video. (1'00→2'24) IFS1617

"It was the same as in the factories."
→ What is the link with Detroit?

"We just had this family of people"
→ What is the link with "The Great Migration"?

b. Explain the Motown recipe for hits!

▼ An homage to Detroit's famous singer Aretha Franklin, a key figure in Motown music, featuring her iconic pink Cadillac

VIDEO
Motown: How it all began

2 ... to hard times

Black Workers Hurt by Detroit's Ills

By MARY M. CHAPMAN, DEC. 29, 2008

DETROIT — Since millions of African-Americans began leaving Southern farms for Northern factories nearly a century ago in what is still known as the Great Migration, the destinies of many of them have been entwined with the auto industry's.

The car companies were hardly multiracial utopias, but they, especially Ford, employed blacks when many industries would not. Through the decades, the automakers and their higher wage scales provided a route to the middle class for many blacks, especially those with limited education, and their children.

Now, with Detroit reeling*, many blacks find their economic well-being threatened.

By last month, nearly 20,000 African-American auto workers had lost jobs, a 13.9 percent decline in employment, [compared] with a 4.4 percent decline for all workers in manufacturing. [...]

In all, blacks made up 14.2 percent of the total automotive work force in 2007, according to the policy institute report, compared with 11.2 percent of the overall American work force. Blacks in the manufacturing and parts sector earned $17.08 an hour, compared with $15.44 an hour for blacks in all industries, the report said.

"Because African-Americans continue to have less education than other groups, the loss of high-paying manufacturing jobs has long been magnified in the black community," said Robert E. Scott of the policy institute.

Blue Collar Worker

Ford and other auto company owners pioneered the hiring of black workers, though many of them were often given the dirtiest jobs. Claudia Perkins, 55, moved north in the 1950s with her parents, who found work in the auto industry. Her earnings helped her buy a home and pay college expenses for her daughter, an Army major who received a teaching degree. Thus far, Ms. Perkins has escaped the job cuts at G.M.

"There was always so much talk down South about the manufacturing jobs up here and how easy you could get a job. People were excited about the pay, and after they'd get a job they would help their families back in the South. They would all the time drive their new cars down and show them off."

*losing balance, falling behind

1. **Look at the photo and read the caption.** Explain how the Perkins family situation changed over three generations.
2. **Focus on the title of the article.** Thinking of Claudia Perkins's experiences, can you imagine why African-Americans would be particularly hurt by Detroit's problems? → YP 26
3. **Read the article and check your ideas.** Consider the following issues:

salaries | education | employment rates

DEBRIEF

How did Detroit's African-American community go from glory days to hard times ?

YOUR TURN

Create a Detroit Motown playlist!

- Explore Motown music on your own. Select one song that represents what you know about Detroit. Get ready to present your choice to the class.
- Discover your classmates' selections and make a class playlist!

3 The beginning of the end

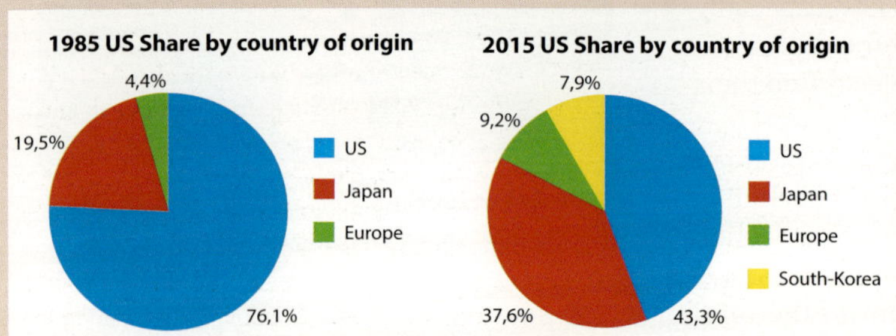

ENERGY CRISIS AIDED JAPANESE IMPORTS

THE CURRENT SKYROCKETING PRICES OF GASOLINE stirred up some powerful memories of 1973 and especially 1979. Those were significant events for a number of reasons, not the least of which was that they solidified Japanese automakers' market share in this country. Prior to the Arab oil embargo of 1973, the "Big Three" US auto producers –General Motors, Ford, and Chrysler– all but had the US market to themselves.

Nat Shulman, WardAuto, May 01, 2000

1 **IN PAIRS** **Read the documents.** List:

- the causes of Detroit's decline
- evidence of Detroit's decline

2 Now place these events on a timeline.

a. Where do they fall compared to what you have already learned?

b. How do they relate?

TIP

- Pick out the dates and figures.
- Try to understand:
  – what events they refer to,
  – how these events are related (cause → consequence).

Detroit is basically broke

Dominic Rushe, *The Guardian,* 2013

Detroit used to be known as "the Paris of the midwest" – a city of wide streets, imposing buildings, and home to the great US auto industry. In 1960, it had the highest per capita income in the nation. But decades of decline, racial tension and corruption have brought the motor city to its knees. [...]

With the city saddled with debts of more than $18bn, Detroit has no choice but to go bust and reorganize its debts in the bankruptcy court [...].

The scale of Detroit's decline is dizzying. The city's population has dropped from 2 million in 1950 to 700,000 today, as Detroiters have become fed up with decades of mismanagement and rising crime and poverty. Detroit's murder rate is at a 40-year high, only a third of its ambulances are in working order, and nearly half its streetlights are broken. [...]

Detroit has 9,700 city employees who all now face pay cuts and worse, close to 20,000 retirees whose pensions and health care benefits are under attack.

4 12th Street Riot

VIDEO The 1967 riots

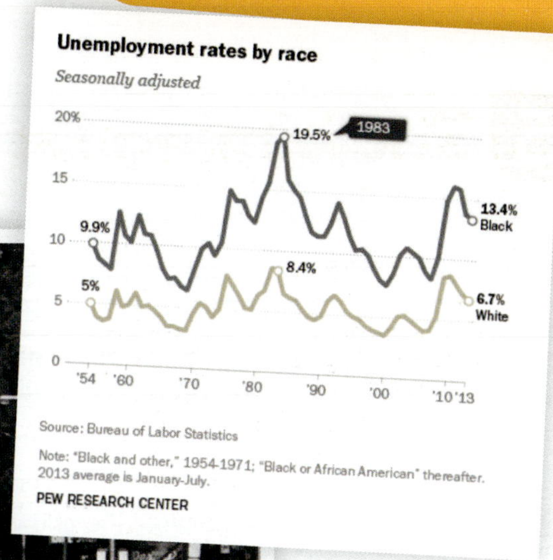

The Civil Rights Movement

It was an organized effort by black Americans to end racial discrimination and gain equal rights under the law. It reached its peak in the late 1960s. Although tumultuous at times, the movement was mostly nonviolent and resulted in laws to protect every American's constitutional rights, regardless of color, race, sex or national origin.
From the beginning, the United Auto Workers union joined the Civil Rights Movement to fight racial bias and open more jobs to black Americans.
Martin Luther King Junior first delivered his "I have a dream" speech to 125,000 people in Detroit during the "Walk to Freedom" in June, 1963.

1 Look at the title, image and graph. ▲
Can you anticipate why there was a riot in Detroit at this moment in history?
→ YP 20, 26

2 Watch the video. e IFS1618

a. Take notes on the following:

cause of Detroit riots | the Detroit riots | consequences

b. *IN PAIRS* Compare and complete your notes. Were you right about question 1?

3 React. Read this definition:

Perfect storm: an especially bad situation caused by a rare combination of negative conditions

How does it apply to the 1967 riots?

DEBRIEF

It has been said that "When America catches a cold, African Americans get the flu." Explain.

YOUR TURN

Create a timeline

- Make a timeline for the American and Detroit history you've learned about so far.

American history events

Detroit-specific events

- What is the correlation?

5 Reclaiming Detroit

IN GROUPS

You are going to discover various current initiatives to revitalize Detroit.

1. **Choose one of the projects presented on these pages.**
Look at the picture. Imagine what the project is about. → YP 20

2. Learn more about it using the documents provided.
a. Is it what you expected?
b. Complete the grid with the information you have found:

Initial problem	People Involved	Project Details	Can this work?

3. **Share with the class.**
Do you think these projects will help rebuild Detroit?

WHOLE CLASS
Let's try this one together, before splitting into groups.

The Detroit Mower Gang

VIDEO The Detroit Mower Gang
IFS1619

The Heildelberg Project

Learn more about the project.
IFS1620

The Dequindre Cut Greenway

Learn more about the project.
IFS1621

Agrihood in Detroit's North End

Learn more about the project.
IFS1622

DEBRIEF How do these projects illustrate Detroit's motto: *"We hope for better things; it shall rise from the ashes."*?

YOUR TURN

VIDEO Tiny houses

Voice over *IN GROUPS*

Dub a video for another initiative in Detroit.

- Watch the video. IFS1623
  - Discuss what the project is about.
  - Decide who will voice Faith, Keith and the journalist.
- Prepare your text and rehearse it.
- Record the sound for the video.

▶ Tiny Houses, developed by Rev. Faith Fowler, help Detroiters become home-owners.

6 Stay up Detroit

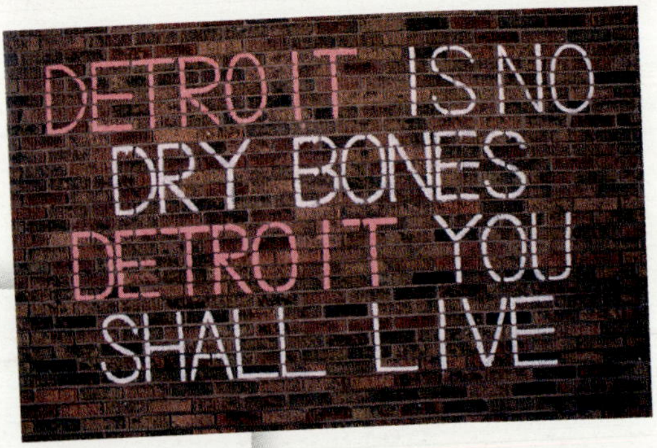

Letter to Detroit

Detroit
There is a resilience that rises from somewhere deep within your streets
You can't define it, but you can feel it
You can feel it overflowing from the people who call you home
From people who are always proud to declare, 'I'm from Detroit'
You took our country from its infancy, into industry
And your name still carries with it the idea of a nation built on steel, muscle and sweat
You became the city that carried a country
The city, like the sport, is built on dreams
People who would arrive here, driven to excel
Who know nothing is accomplished without hard work, without sacrifice
When you hurt, we hurt
Your streets witness our struggle
Your bricks are our rage through the emptiness of each house shuttered, of each factory closed
We've lived through the ups and the downs
But we remain, Detroit
We can never turn our backs on you Detroit, because we are you
My home
The home of Motown, Cadillac and Joe Louis
Through all this, we cannot be defeated, because we've never been defeated
You've built us, you've moved us, you've shaped us
Sometimes down, but never out
Take strength in us, your people

Stay up Detroit.

Eminem, 2009

VIDEO Letter to Detroit

Marshall Bruce Mathers III (born October 17, 1972), known professionally as **Eminem**, is an American rapper, songwriter, record producer, record executive, film producer and actor.

1 **Listen to the song and read the letter.** IFS1624

a. Who do these pronouns refer to throughout the letter?

you / your | we / us / our

b. Lines 2 and 3 are an exception – who is this "you"?

2 **a.** Quote the lines referring to the relationship between Detroit and its inhabitants.

b. What is Eminem's message?

3 **a.** Pick out references to aspects you have explored in the chapter. → YP 26

b. Choose one and explain it. Report your findings to the class.

4 **React.** What do you think of this letter?

DEBRIEF

To what extent does Detroit reflect American history and the American spirit?

FINAL TASK

New opportunities in Detroit

Prepare a presentation to attract new companies to Detroit.

1 Get ready

- Select the advantages you wish to highlight in your presentation.
- Illustrate your arguments with examples taken from the history of the city and its inhabitants.

  Think of: the energy | the competencies | the glorious past | ...

2 Action!

- Prepare your pitch on PowerPoint© or Prezi©.
- Rehearse and present it to the class. Will Detroit attract new business?

Here's what cities are offering Amazon to host its new headquarters

Making Sen$e Nov 30, 2017

Amazon's call for proposals for a second corporate headquarters earlier this year set off a national bidding war between cities from Albuquerque and Detroit to Atlanta and Boston.

or

Letter to a city

Write a letter to a city you feel strongly about.

1 Get ready

- Choose the city you want to write your letter to.

  It can be: Detroit | another American city | a city of your choice (Why not yours?)

- Think of your topics and message.

TIP Have another look at Eminem's *Letter to Detroit*. What are his topics? What is his message?

2 Action!

- Write your letter.

  Why not read it out loud to the class?

WORDS

PRACTISE ONLINE

Cityscape

- **down**town (US) = the **ci**ty **cen**tre (UK)
- **sky**scrapers: *gratte-ciels*
  /eɪ/
- a **re**sidential **a**rea
- **af**fluent **su**burbs = rich suburbs
- **de**velop ≠ ne**glect** an **a**rea, a **dis**trict
- a **neigh**borhood /ˈneɪbərhʊd/
- a street, a road
- a block: *un pâté de maisons*
- **pro**ject **hou**sing (US): *logements sociaux*
- **va**cant lots: *terrains vagues*
  /eɪ/
- **green** space: *les espaces verts*
- a pe**des**trian lane, a **bike** lane
- **knock** down, de**stroy** a **land**mark
  = de**stroy** an i**co**nic place or **mo**nument
  /aɪ/

IFS1625

Views & feelings

☹

- **mi**serable
- sad, de**pres**sing
- **de**solate /ˈdeslət/
- **emp**ty
- run down, di**la**pidated
- **bligh**ted (by **po**verty, war...): *ravagé*
- de**ser**ted, a**ban**doned

☺

- **o**pulent = **com**fortable, lu**xu**rious
  /ʒʊə/
- **weal**thy, **af**fluent = rich
  /θ/
- **re**novated
- re**vi**talized
  /aɪ/
- dy**na**mic, **li**vely
  /aɪ/
- suc**cess**ful

Inhabitants' attitudes

- re**si**lient: *tenace, endurant, resilient*
- dy**na**mic, ener**ge**tic
- cre**a**tive, in**ven**tive
- re**source**ful /rɪˈzɔːsfl/

IFS1626

Story of a city

Failing

- **suf**fer a **cri**sis, go through a **cri**sis
- ex**pe**rience **ra**cial **ten**sion
- go **bank**rupt, file for **bank**ruptcy
- be broke = have no money
  ☝ be broken = need repairs
- **fal**ter: *faiblir, s'essouffler*
  /ˈfɒltə/
  → The economy began to falter
- go **down**hill
- de**cline** fi**nan**cially
- col**lapse**
- make **bud**get cuts
  /ʌ/
- cut **pen**sions = de**ny** re**ti**rement pay
- flee from **ri**sing crime / from **po**verty
- get **fi**red

IFS1627

Fighting back

- rise (from the **a**shes): *renaître de ses cendres*
- **tac**kle a **pro**blem
- strive (to im**prove** a situ**a**tion): *lutter*
  /aɪ/
- perse**vere**, keep trying
  /pɜːsɪˈvɪə/
- im**prove ser**vices
- take the i**ni**tiative
  /ʃ/
- trans**form** sth into sth
- cre**ate** a **bu**siness
- re**vive** an **a**rea
  /aɪ/
- re**claim** a lost **ter**ritory
- rein**vent** sth, **in**novate sth
- build on in**dus**trial ex**pe**rience
- work hard, make **sa**crifices
  /ˈsækrɪfaɪsɪz/
- shape the **fu**ture of a **ci**ty

IFS1628

EXERCISES

1 The odd one out

a. Identify the words that don't fit.

1. wealthy, successful, blighted, affluent
2. neglected, vacant, perseverant, abandoned
3. run down, renovated, desolate, dilapidated
4. resilient, creative, miserable, energetic

b. Use some of the words above to describe Detroit's struggles.

2 What's the word?

Find the words corresponding to the following definitions:

1. a very tall building in a city
2. the main or central part of a city (US)
3. an area where people live near a larger city
4. a piece of land that is not being used
5. community space consisting of land (such as parks) rather than buildings

3 From worst to best

a. Sort the following expressions from worst to best:

go downhill	*keep trying*
persevere	*suffer a crisis*
experience poverty	*rise from the ashes*
revive a city	*collapse*

Worst ☹ ◄·················► Best ☺

b. IN PAIRS Discuss your classifications. If you have differences, justify them. Then use these expressions to explain Detroit's history.

4 Then and now

a. Make a list of words from the mind-map that you could use to describe the split image above.

b. Write a few sentences about this place or any others from the following website. e IFS1632

5 Fill in the blanks

Use the following words to complete the text below:

affluent suburbs – poverty – wealthy – racial – crime – auto industry – crisis – downtown

The 1967 Riots

As the Motor City's famous ... began to fail, ... citizens moved from the city's ... area to its ..., just outside the city. The remaining communities, which were mostly African-American, suffered from rising ... due to unemployment and ... . When ... tensions finally exploded between black residents and a mostly white police force, the city of Detroit suffered a true ... .

Pronunciation

PRACTISE ONLINE

6 Déplacement d'accent

e IFS1629

• À partir d'un mot, on peut construire un nouveau mot en lui ajoutant un suffixe :

happy* → *happiness

• Selon les suffixes, cet ajout peut avoir une incidence sur la place de l'accent dans le mot ; celui-ci est alors déplacé :

***in**dustry* → *in**dus**trious*

↑ accent sur la 1re syllabe — ↑ accent sur la syllabe qui précède le suffixe

a. Écoutez et répétez ces mots du chapitre.

resource - resourceful	*comfort - comfortable*
success - successful	*economy - economic*
power - powerless	*dynamism - dynamic*
misery - miserable	*energy - energetic*

b. Qu'en déduisez-vous ?

• L'ajout des suffixes ... n'affecte pas la place de l'accent tonique.

• L'ajout du suffixe ... affecte la place de l'accent tonique. Il se déplace sur la syllabe qui précède le suffixe.

GRAMMAR

Pour parler des effets de l'histoire sur la ville de Détroit aujourd'hui, on est amené à employer le *Present Perfect* ainsi que le Prétérit.
Et pour situer les événements dans le temps ou indiquer leur durée, on a recours à *for*, *since* ou *ago*.

1 Prétérit vs *Present Perfect*

❶ Claudia Perkins **moved north** in the 1950s with her parents, who **found work** in the auto industry. Her earnings **helped her** buy a home and pay college expenses for her daughter. So far, Ms. Perkins **has escaped** the job cuts at G.M.

❷ In 1960, Detroit **had** the highest per capita income in the nation. But decades of decline, racial tension and corruption **have brought** the motor city to its knees.

❸ Since millions of African-Americans **began** leaving Southern farms for Northern factories nearly a century ago, the destinies of many of them **have been entwined** with the auto industry's.

❹ The scale of Detroit's decline is dizzying. The city's population **has dropped** from 2 million in 1950 to 700,000 today.

- Le **Prétérit** permet de parler d'événements révolus, sans lien avec le moment présent.
  Il est alors **l'outil du récit**, utilisé avec des indications de temps comme *in the 1950s* ❶, *In 1960* ❷ ou *a century ago* ❸ qui situent clairement le récit dans le passé.
- Le ***Present Perfect*** est un temps du présent. Lorsqu'on l'emploie, c'est toujours le moment présent qui est mis en avant.
  Les indications de temps qui l'accompagnent permettent de faire **un bilan au moment de parole** : *so far* ❶, *since* ❸, *in 1950 vs today* ❹.
- On rencontrera fréquemment le *Present Perfect* avec des adverbes tels que *just*, *recently*, *already*, *ever*, *never*, etc. qui permettent de faire le lien avec le moment de parole.

→ Précis 19, 21 p. 239-40

Différence anglais – français !
Comparez ces deux exemples :
Passé composé en français
« Hier, j'ai regardé un documentaire sur Détroit. »
"Yesterday, I watched a documentary about Detroit."
Prétérit en anglais
L'événement est révolu, sans lien avec le moment de parole → l'anglais a donc recours au Prétérit.

2 *For, since, ago*

❶ It is hard to find today the amount of economic activity that was happening in the city 110 years **ago**.

❷ **For** years, Detroit's parks were neglected or abandoned.

❸ **Since** the creation of The Detroit Mower Gang in 2010, children have returned to the playgrounds.

- ***ago*** ❶ fonctionne toujours avec le Prétérit. Il permet de situer un événement par rapport au moment présent : *10 years ago, one month ago, 5 minutes ago,* etc.
- ***for*** ❷ est suivi d'une indication de durée : *for 2 years, for 1 month, for 2 minutes,* etc.
- ***since*** ❸ est suivi d'un repère temporel précis : *since 2010, since you arrived,* etc.

→ Précis 23 p. 242

EXERCISES

Prétérit vs *Present Perfect*

1 Ups and downs

Complete using the verbs provided:

1. The US automobile industry *[suffer]* two oil crises in the 1970s.
2. Since then, this sector of the US economy constantly *[struggle]* to keep up.
3. Claudia Perkins *[move]* to Detroit in the 1950s with her parents, who quickly *[find]* work.
4. 2008 *[be]* the year when the subprime crisis *[hit]* the world economy and *[create]* chaos in many countries.
5. I am impressed at the way Detroit *[rise]* from its ashes since this damaging period.

2 Invest in Detroit

Complete with the appropriate verb forms:

Some say that Detroit's 2013 financial crises ... *(provide)* a shock that the city needed. In 2014, the financial institution JPMorgan Chase ... *(announce)* a $100 million investment in Detroit. Since then, they ... *(give)* money to the city, and effective job training to its residents. They ... *(help)* small businesses get off the ground. Other companies ... *(show)* interest in Detroit, as well. In 2017, Google ... *(say)* it plans to open a Detroit office to help the city's progress.

3 What has changed?

These efforts to revitalize Detroit have improved the city! Explain what has changed.

e.g. Detroit's #movetheworld initiative has brought businesses to Detroit. These businesses have helped the economy.

- Detroit's #movetheworld Initiative
- Detroit Mower Gang
- Heildelberg Project
- Dequindre Cut Greenway
- Agrihood in the North End
- Detroit Tiny Houses

For, since, ago

4 A long time ago

Complete the sentences with *for*, *since* or *ago*.

1. About 30 years ..., the last train left Michigan Central Station.
2. This station had been a functioning building ... around 76 years.
3. ... 2010, the Detroit mower gang has grown to more than 60 volunteers.
4. African Americans began leaving Southern farms for Northern factories nearly a century ...
5. The destructive Detroit riots lasted ... around 2 days.

5 And since then...

1. Since the 1950s, Motown *[shape]* the American music industry.
2. Nearly 100 years ago, the Eerie Canal *[connect]* Detroit with the Atlantic Ocean.
3. Detroit's urban farms *[produce]* food for local people for the last 10 years.
4. Since the 1970s, many Americans *[choose]* to buy fuel-efficient Japanese cars.
5. The Detroit riots *[ravage]* the city about 50 years ago.

Pronunciation

PRACTISE ONLINE

6 Poetry Slam! IFS1624

Eminem's Letter to Detroit is a great example of "Slam Poetry."

- **Listen to his poem again. (p. 150)**
- **Practise saying it.**

Rhythm & Sounds

Listen then say these sentences out loud, imitating the rhythm of the native speaker. IFS1630

- It's part of the Detroit experience.
- Skyscrapers were built and fortunes were made.
- The loss of jobs has been magnified in the black community.
- Detroit used to be known as the Paris of the midwest.
- It was one of the most destructive riots in American history.
- The riots made segregation even worse.
- Motown was the first black-owned record company in the US.

TEST YOUR SKILLS

OBJECTIF BAC

Listening & Writing

AUDIO
Detroit explained by a Detroiter

- **Listen** to the document three times and report what you have understood. IFS1631
- **Write** about the same topic, following your teacher's instructions.

Durée 1'30

Reading & Writing

Your teacher will give you several documents.

- Read them carefully and follow the instructions.

Speaking

React to a document.

- Your teacher will give you a set of two documents.
- In your opinion, which one best illustrates the notion of **TERRITORY AND MEMORY**?
- Explain why.

TRUE OR FALSE?

Two short stories by Peter Medawar

One of these stories happened, and the other did not.
Which one is true, and which one is false?
It's for you to decide...

EINSTEIN'S CHAUFFEUR

I'm a chauffeur, and I'm here to teach Relativity.

I take another drink of water. The audience is getting restless. Can they smell my fear? I see Einstein sitting at the back of the auditorium, wearing my chauffeur's uniform. He sticks his tongue out at me.

He didn't *force* me to do this: he just persuaded me. It's hard to say 'no' to the professor. I remember his calm German accent coming from the back of the car, just last week.

'Harry, did you like the speech I made this evening?'

'Yes, sir.'

'I saw that you were enjoying it.'

I slowed down a little, and glanced up at him in the mirror.

'What do you mean, sir?'

'You were asleep.'

His dark eyes were watching me in the mirror.

'Harry... we have been touring America for some months now, yes? You have heard me explain my theory about twenty times, is that correct?'

'Twenty-three times, sir.'

'Exactly!' He slapped his knees. 'Now, you cannot read a book twenty-three times and stay interested, can you?'

'No, sir.'

I drove on for a few minutes.

'Harry,' he said at last. 'Am I boring?'

'Oh, no, sir.'

'But my speech is boring you, yes?'

'Oh no, Mr Einstein. It's just— I've heard the old Theory of Relativity so many times, I could give your speech myself.'

'*Really*?'

He sounded angry.

'Please, prove it, ' he said.

So I delivered his introduction, word for word. Einstein sat back in the seat, laughing softly.

'You have an *excellent* memory,' he said.

I gave him the rest of the speech in a German accent. I had no idea what it meant.

'Fascinating,' he said when I'd finished. 'I couldn't have said it any better!'

'But it's *important*, Mr Einstein! People listen to every word. One day it could make you famous.'

'Stop the car.'

I pulled over to the side of the road. We sat for a few minutes. I remember the sound of the rain on the roof, like a hundred ticking clocks.

‘I think we can have some fun, yes?’ said Einstein. ‘We have a lecture next week... so, you give the speech, and I rest at the back, yes?’ He smiled in the dark.

I should have said no.

Over the next three days Professor Einstein explained Relativity to me. He drew pictures of a lift in a skyscraper, then trains pulling away from another. Then he gave me a fake moustache and persuaded me to exchange clothes.

So here I am at the front of this great hall, staring at the audience. Einstein’s jacket is too tight. I’m trying to remember what he told me, but all I can see are trains and skyscrapers spinning in a black hole. My boss will fire me if I get discovered.

The audience is excited. I see one young man waiting to write. He looks like a fox. I look at my ‘chauffeur’. He’s sitting at the back of the hall, asleep.

I begin the speech, just as we’d rehearsed it in the hotel. I don’t understand anything I’m saying. I hear Einstein’s voice in my mind: *Don’t think, Harry, don’t think about it all. Just let the words come out.* Soon I’m forgetting myself and just giving a good performance. Before I know it I’m finishing and feeling very clever as I rush down off the stage.

I could do this all week, I’m thinking. *The hell with it: let Einstein drive.*

Albert Einstein is standing at the back, smiling like the proudest uncle in the world. As if in a dream, I go towards him – and the fox-faced student steps in front of me.

‘Excuse me, Professor. I really enjoyed your talk.’

‘Why, thank you,’ I murmur, trying to push past.

‘Can you just elucidate on one point...’

The clapping is dying down. Soon the audience can hear us talking. My knees are starting to tremble.

‘Elucidate...’ I say. *What does **that** mean?*

I look over at Albert Einstein for help. He smiles proudly and says nothing.

‘Yes, sir,’ the student says. ‘You argued that the principle proposed by Newton...’

I have no idea what to say. Soon he will discover who I am. Professor Einstein takes out the car keys and says, ‘Shall I wait outside, sir?’

The student is waiting for me to speak. The other students are all watching us. Einstein sticks out his tongue. Suddenly I hear his voice in my mind, slow and patient and logical.

I look straight at the student.

‘The answer to that is very simple,’ I say. ‘Why, it’s so simple, I’m going to let my chauffeur answer it!’

Peter Medawar

Did Albert Einstein really persuade his chauffeur to deliver a speech on Relativity?

THE INTRUDER

1982

Queen Elizabeth II sits up in bed, terrified.

She clutches her nightdress, thinking,
... it's all right, I am... fine, I am here... it was just a nightmare—someone in my room, an intruder.

The Queen puts her eyepatch on and tries to go back to sleep. She needs the rest: there's a busy week ahead of her, particularly with the visit of the US President. At least she's got her favourite horse race to look forward to on the weekend, but so many people to meet before then...

Something's wrong.

The Queen opens her eyes: something's making her heart race. She sniffs the air. There it is: a smell of Chardonnay. Not just wine: *cheap wine, bad Californian wine.*

Light falls on her bed. Someone pulls the curtain back. Someone sits on the end of her bed. The Queen sits up, startled. There's a man right next to her, a man in a tee shirt and jeans, a man she's never seen before. His eyes seem huge, like an owl's, and his face is soft and round.

He looks as surprised as she is.
'What are you doing here?' she says.
The man smiles shyly.
'You're a lot smaller than I thought you'd be,' he says.
'Get out. Get out!'

The Queen throws back the sheets and jumps to the floor. The marble is cold on her feet. She runs past the man and out into the corridor. *Where's the police officer?* she's thinking. *There's always a police officer outside my door. Is this a coup d'état?*

Hearing a vacuum cleaner, she startles a maid in a nearby room. The Queen's expression is unmistakable; the maid turns off the machine and hurries to the bedchamber. Meanwhile Her Majesty finds the switchboard and calls Security – but no one answers. She tries again – nothing!

The Queen goes back down the corridor, trying to remain calm. There are low voices coming from her bedroom: *it's that man, talking with my maid.*
'... lost my shoes on your roof, I did...'

There's the click of a lighter and smoke comes out of the bedchamber.
'... I've been walking around in my socks, I have...'

The maid bursts out laughing. The Queen stands in the hallway, horrified and fascinated at the same time. *What do people like this talk about? Is it just like on the television?*

She hears footsteps behind her. A large man in an anorak is coming down the corridor: it's the duty footman, who has just been walking her corgis.

He bows his head.

'Good morning, Ma'am.'

When the footman notices the smoke coming from her bedchamber, he goes in. The Queen hears the intruder's voice, getting louder.

'Your security is a disgrace, it is.'

'You look like you need a drink, mate,' says the footman.

'I'll just finish this,' says the intruder.

No one speaks for a while. The Queen imagines the three of them sitting on her bed, waiting for the imposter to finish his cigarette.

'...let me get you a drink, mate...' says the footman. 'Come over here.'

The two men suddenly appear in her doorway; The Queen presses herself against the wall, but her footman leads the invader away from her, down the corridor. The maid comes out of the room, stops to curtsy the Queen, and hurries back to her vacuuming.

When she's gone The Queen puts on a gown and looks for the two men. As she suspected, they are talking in the pantry.

She listens outside.

'This isn't half good, is it?' says the intruder.

'Best whiskey in England, mate— can't beat the booze in the palace.'

'But you can beat the Security, can't you? Second time I done it.' The intruder burps. 'I've been sitting on all your thrones, I have. Great fun. Found some stamps, I did.'

'That's King George V's collection,' says the footman. 'That's worth millions of pounds.'

'Dusty old stamps,' says the intruder. 'This whole place is dusty, squeaky floor-boards, very ordinary. Not how I imagined it all at all. You ask me, it's due a redecoration.'

'Really, sir?'

'I can do the whole place up, make it look like a palace again. But what you *really* need...' He burps again. '... what you *really* need is *toilets*. Couldn't find no toilets.'

There's the *click* of a cigarette being lit.

'What brings you here, sir?' says the footman.

The Queen leans closer, listening.

'... life's getting me down...' says the man. '... wife's got custody of me kids...'

He sounds lost and lonely, just an ordinary man who's good at breaking into Buckingham Palace. The Queen puts her ear to the door. Now she's not alone with him she wants to learn more, but just then there's a quiet voice at her shoulder.

'Ma'am..?'

Two policemen are standing behind her.

'You need to go back to your room, ma'am.'

She feels relieved to see them. But at the same time, she regrets not learning more about this man, this *common* man who climbed a 4.3 meter perimeter wall, avoided spikes and barbed wire and went up a drainpipe like a spider – all without anyone seeing him.

The policemen go into the pantry. One of them says to the intruder, 'Well, well, well... what's your name then, son?'

Next day brings the scandal: the security in Buckingham Palace is a joke. The newspapers report the story in a hundred different ways – the intruder spent ten minutes sitting on the bed... he had a knife... she had a *knife*... they chatted together until she offered him a cigarette and called for help. The Public drinks it up.

Later, much later, The Queen hears the man interviewed on radio, and she remembers his wide eyes in the morning light, like an owl. His voice reminds her of his childish amazement on that strange night:

> '... so The Queen, to me... represents all that is keeping me down. Lack of voice. I just wanted her to know what it feels like to be an ordinary chap, trying to make ends meet. I wanted to make a statement... I am. I am.'

Peter Medawar

Has someone ever broken into the Queen's bedroom?

	TRUE	FALSE
Einstein's Chauffeur	❍	❍
The Intruder	❍	❍

Check your answers e IFS1665

FINAL TASK

Fool your friends!

It's your turn! Write a story and share it with your classmates. Have them guess if it's a true or a false story.

1 Get ready

- **Decide what you want to do:**
  Write about a striking event that really happened *or* make it all up!
- **Think about:** the situation / the place / the time / the characters / their feelings
- **How are you going to start your story?**

TIP
- You want to intrigue and hook your reader right from the beginning. Read again the first sentences of the two short stories:
  I'm a chauffeur, and I'm here to teach Relativity.
  Queen Elizabeth II sits up in bed, terrified.
- What can you say about them? Do they make you want to know more? Why?

- **How are you going to end your story?**

TIP
- Re-read again the endings of the two short stories. What effect is created in each case? Are you... surprised / amused / wondering / ... ?

2 Action!

- **Write your story.**
- **Share it with your classmates.**
  Who managed to fool the greatest number of people?

Yellow Pages

Pour mieux vous exprimer à l'oral et à l'écrit.

Leur classement suit le déroulement du commentaire de document :
description
interprétation
opinion personnelle

Vous y trouverez des exemples concrets et directement utilisables dans lesquels vous pourrez choisir l'expression la mieux adaptée à la nature du document et à ce que vous voulez dire.

Dans les chapitres, les renvois à ces pages sont signalés ainsi : → YP 00

— Aidez-vous de cet index pour choisir la fiche dont vous avez besoin. —

Description

Interpretation

Personal reactions

Les Yellow Pages sont également consultables et téléchargeables sur e IFS1999

1. Planning

Main parts

1. **As an introduction,**
2. **First of all, / Firstly,**
3. **Secondly,**
4. **Thirdly, / Last of all, / Finally,**
5. **To conclude, / As a conclusion,**

→ it can be said / we might say → **that...**

6. **First(ly),** we will
7. **Second(ly),** I will
8. **Third(ly),** I will

→ **focus on** / **examine** / **see** → the way... / to what extent... / how...

Specific arguments

9. **One**
10. **Another**
11. **Yet another**

→ likely / probable / possible / predictable → **cause of** / **consequence of** / **solution to** / **reason for** / **factor explaining** → **this** → is that...

→ interesting / disturbing / exciting / annoying / worrying → **detail** showing / **aspect of** → **this** → is that...

2a. First reactions

1. **What I find (the) most** — striking / incredible / interesting / ironical / ridiculous / impressive / threatening / unpleasant — **about** / **in** — this / this picture / this video / this document — **is that...**

2. **What strikes me (the) most** — **about** / **in** — this / this picture / this video / this document — **is that...**

2b. First impressions

1. This — **looks** / **sounds** / **feels** — bizarre, / strange, — **in that... / because...**

2. This man — **looks** / **sounds** — bizarre, / strange, *(adj.)* — **in that... / because...**
   This man — **looks** / **sounds** — **like** — a journalist, / a preacher, / ... *(noun)* — **in that... / because...**

3. This — **reminds me of** / **sounds like** / **seems to be** — something **being...** / someone **doing...**

4. We are **under the impression** that — someone **is doing...**
5. We **get the feeling** that — someone **is doing...**
6. It **seems** that — someone **is doing...**
7. It **looks as if** — someone **is doing...**

Description

3. Describing a situation

What?

1. **What we have here is** — an article / a video — **about...**

2. **This document** is **about**
3. **This deals with**

— a(n) — essential / crucial / major / topical / controversial — **question. / problem. / issue. / matter.**

Where?

4. **The incident/scene took place**
5. **The attack occurred/occurs**

— **in** a high-speed train, / **on** a beach, / **along** the Irish border, / **outside** a bank in London,

When?

around / **at** approximately / **at** exactly — 10 o'clock **on** Friday.

4a. Announcing an event...

A TV anchor speaking in the studio:

1. **We have news that**
2. **We are told that**
3. **Apparently,**

— there **has been** an accident... / somebody **has been** injured... / a car bomb **has gone** off... / an armed man/group **has invaded** the...

4b. ... Describing the action

A field reporter explaining on the spot:

The way it happened **was** that... — **first,** a car crashed into another,... / **then,** it rolled over,... / **and finally,** it came to a stop against a wall.

5a. Describing habits

In the UK,
In the USA,
In Canada,
In Great Britain,

1. **it is commonplace to do / to avoid doing...**
2. the **tradition / custom / tendency / stereotype / rule** is **to do / to avoid doing...** / **that you should (not) do...**
3. **doing this** is the rule.
4. **you don't...**

The British
The Irish
The Chinese
The French
(The) Americans
(The) Germans
(The) Canadians

5. **will usually do...**
6. **are (not) used to doing...**

Description

5b. Adverbs of frequency

1. (The) Americans — **always / usually / frequently / often / repeatedly** — eat more fat than we do.
2. I am — **periodically / occasionally / sometimes** — late for meals.
3. I have — **seldom / rarely / hardly ever / never** — seen such a great film.
4. I used to go there — **twice a year. / three times a year. / once in a while.**

6a. Describing visuals

Camera angle

1. This is a — **close-up** / **long-distance** / **downward** / **upward** — shot. / view.

2. The **subject** is seen **from** — **below.** / **above.**

3. The horizon is — **close.** / **far away.**

Major lines

4. There are many — **horizontal/vertical/diagonal** lines.

5. We have a — **sense of perspective** / **feeling of movement** — **given by...** / **suggested by...**

6b. Locating elements

At the top,

In the **upper / top left-hand corner** of the picture, we have...

In the **upper / top right-hand corner** of the picture, we have...

On the left, — **In the middle,** — **On the right,**

In the **lower / bottom left-hand corner** of the picture, we have...

In the **lower / bottom right-hand corner** of the picture, we have...

At the bottom,

6c. Locating elements on a map

North of ...,

North-west of ...,

West of ...,

South-west of ...,

North-east of ...,

East of ...,

South-east of ...,

South of ...,

7. Describing sequences

FILM LANGUAGE

1. Framing

1. establishing / panoramic shot
2. medium shot
3. full-length shot
4. close-up
5. extreme close-up

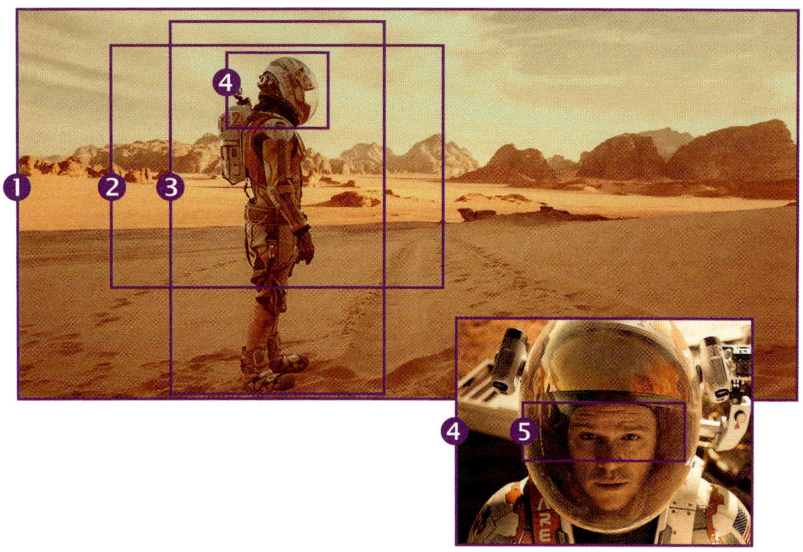

2. Camera movements

- *arrêt sur image* : freeze-frame
- *champ* : shot
- *contre-champ* : reverse shot
- *contre-plongée* : upward shot / low-angle shot / tilt
- *fondu-enchaîné* : cross-fade/dissolve
- *plan* : shot/framing
- *plan long* : long take
- *plongée* : downward shot / high-angle shot / dip
- *retour arrière* : reverse
- *séquence* : sequence
- *travelling* : tracking-shot/travelling-shot
- *voix off* : voice over
- *zoom AV./AR.* : zooming in/out

8. Positioning

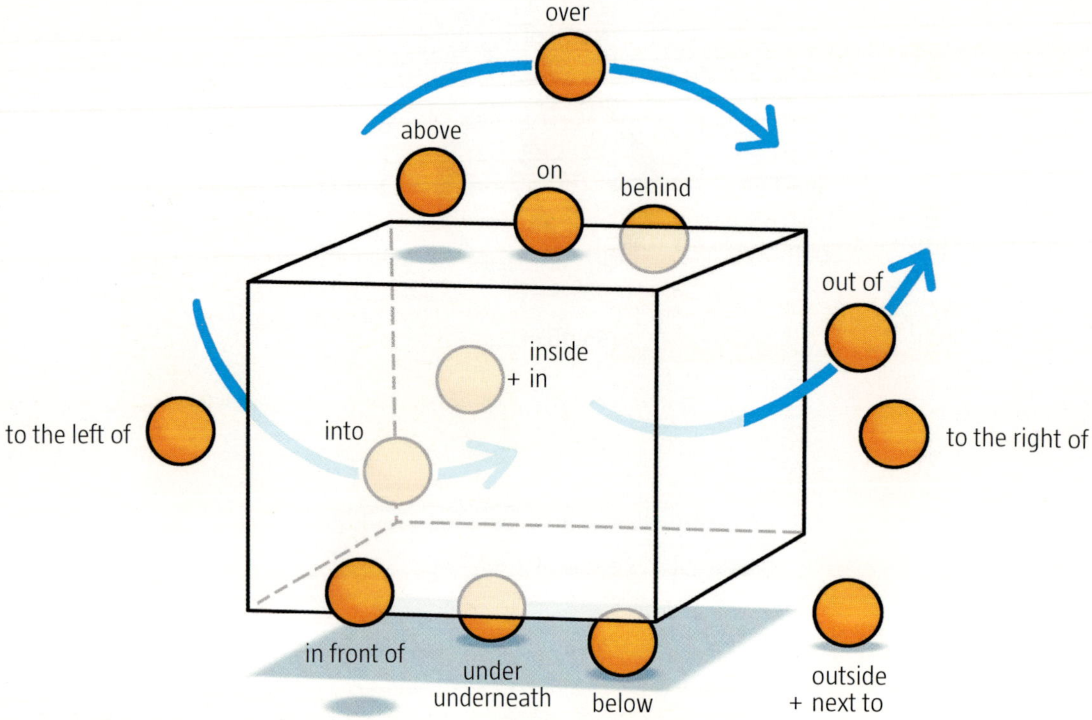

9. Describing charts

1. What we have here is a(n)
2. This here is a(n)

— **chart.**

This is a **3D pie-chart.**

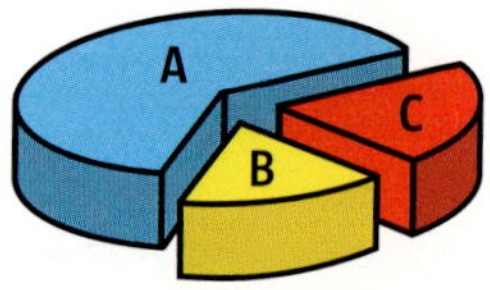

3. **As** is obvious,
4. **As** can be clearly seen,

the **A section** represents **about** 65 per cent of the whole, while **B** and **C** are almost equal, respectively 18 and 17 percent.

A is about **three times as big as** B or C.

10. Commenting on charts/graphs

1. **As** is obvious here in this chart,...
2. **As** can be seen clearly in this chart,...

there has been no significant — **change / increase / decrease / cut / drop / fall** — **in...**

there has been a — huge / tremendous / major / significant / slight / minor — **change / increase / decrease / cut / drop / fall** — **in...**

3. Taxes **have**
4. Stock options **have**

been boosted / increased / augmented / gone up
- **from** 24% / $10,000 **to** 67% / $52,000
- **by** 43% / $42,000

been cut / dropped / gone down / fallen
- **from** 67% / $52,000 **to** 24% / $10,000
- **by** 43% / $42,000

Description

11. Commenting on texts/slides

Texts

1. The — passage / text / poem — is composed of / is divided into — three parts. / three paragraphs.

2. The — first part / second part / third part — is about... / deals with... / is based on...

3. The — issue / problem — raised in the — first part / second part / third part — is...

Slides

1. This here is a(n)
2. What we have here in this
3. This

— image / document / slide / picture / photograph / map

- demonstrating / showing — how...
- is — a number of... / a group of... / a couple of... / a...
- demonstrates / shows — how...

4. In the — **background,** we can see... / **foreground,** clearly visible, we have...

Description

12a. Comparing

1. **Compared** / **In comparison** / **In contrast** — **with** / **to** — her, — he looks fragile.

2. **In comparison,** this appears very **similar,** / **This is similar to...,** / **This is the same situation/idea as in...,** / They **both** convey the **same** idea, — in that...

3. **Similarly,** / **In (much) the same way,** / **In both cases,** — one could say / it could be said — that...

12b. Comparatives

1. This one is
   - **more** — comfortable / appropriate / efficient — **than** — that one.
   - big**ger** / long**er** / **better** / **farther away** / **worse** — **than** — that one.

2. This one is — **as** / **not as** — big / long — **as** — that one.

3. This one is — **less** — comfortable / appropriate / efficient — **than** — that one.

13. Parallel increase

1. **The more** you sell, **the cheaper** you can sell. / **The bigger** the demand, **the higher** the prices.
2. **The fewer** Ferraris they produce, **the more expensive** they will be.
3. **The more** you look at it, **the more difficult** the problem seems to be.
4. The problem gets **more and more** difficult as you look at it. / Prices tend to get **higher and higher.**

14. Superlatives

She is (by far)
- **the most** — intelligent girl — **on** campus. / **in** the group.
- **the more** — brilliant — **of** — the two.
- **the smart**est — kid — **in** — the school.
- **the least** — pleasant person I've ever met.
- **the best** — student I know.
- **the worst** — actress I've ever seen.

15. Contrasting

1. There is a / This is **in** — **sharp contrast with** — the previous document, — **in that...**
2. In the other document, we saw..., — **whereas** / **while** — **here** we have...
3. **Unlike** / **Contrary to** — the document we saw, this one shows...
4. **Instead of** — show**ing**..., this one presents... / a direct message, this one presents a pastiche...

16. Measuring / Counting

Measuring

1. The room **is** — twenty feet **in length / in width / in height.** / twenty feet **long/wide/high.**

2. This motorbike **weighs** — 600 pounds. / 272 kilograms.

3. This **is a** — twenty **foot-long/-wide/-deep** pool. / 600-pound motorbike.

Counting

2.5%	two **point** five **per cent**
2 x 6 = 12	two **times** six **is** twelve
3,000 – 210 = 2,790	three thousand **minus** two hundred and ten **is...**
6÷2 = 3	six **divided by** two **is** three

I have **twice as many** books **as** you.

Sure, but there's **twice as much** information in mine.

This motorcycle **is worth £5,000** (five thousand pounds).

Fractions and powers

1 km = $\frac{5}{8}$ mile	one kilometre is **five eighths of a** mile.
75 cl = $\frac{3}{4}$ litre	seventy-five centilitres is **three quarters of a** litre.
10^4	ten **to the fourth**

Statistics

1. The birth rate in Britain is **18 per thousand.**
2. In the music industry, total UK single sales **increased 6 per cent to 188.6 million.**

Description

17. Reporting speech

1. He said: "I'm tired." / "I was here yesterday." / "We will be here tomorrow." → He said (**that**) he **was** tired. / he **had been there** the day before. / they **would** be **there** the day after.

2. He said to him: "Take your car and come over." → He **told** him **to** take his car and come over.

3. He asked her: "Will you come over?" → He asked her **if** / **whether** she **would** come over.

18. Quoting a document

In this **passage, paragraph, sentence, line, sequence,**

- we are **told** that...
- the **writer** / the **editor** / the **adman** / the **film director** — insists **on** / emphasizes — phrases such as / like "..." / words such as / like "..."

19. Making hypotheses

Adverbs of eventuality

Do you think this happened?
Do you think this is happening?
Do you think this will happen?

→

No doubt. (+)
Most probably.
Probably.
Possibly.
Maybe.
Perhaps. (–)

Modals of eventuality

Past

She/He/They — **must / might / may / can't** — **have done** this.

Present

She/He/They — **must / might / may / can't** — **be doing** this.

Future

She/He/They —
- **is / are sure to**
  is / are bound to
  is / are likely to
- **may**
  might
  is / are unlikely to

— **do** this.

20. Anticipating

1. **From**
2. **Judging from**
3. **Given**

— **what we already know** of the document,
the information available so far,
the way things are going,
the elements contained in this paragraph, **such as** "..." **or/and** "...",

we can — **predict** / **infer** / **presume** / **suppose** / **expect** — that...

Interpretation

21. Observing, deducing

1. **Obviously,**
2. **Apparently,**
3. **We can observe that**

→ the man / the character / the journalist / the writer → does... / is doing... / uses...

4. **This might**
5. **This may**
6. **This could**
7. **This tends to**

→ **result from** / **result in** → the fact that...

→ **indicate** / **suggest** / **imply** / **show** / **prove** → that...

→ **explain why...**

22. Analysing impressions

1. The → writer / film director / journalist / character → **manages** / **attempts** / **tries** → **to** → **create** / **convey** / **put across** / **give us**

→ **the impression that...**

→ **an impression** / **a feeling / a sense** / **an atmosphere** → **of** → danger. / suspense. / threat. / beauty. / peace.

2. **And he obtains this** → **by** / **through** → do**ing...** / us**ing...** / **the use of...**

23. Inferring meaning

1. When reading/hearing the word/phrase "...",
   - we **can infer** / we **can assume** — **that** — **it means "...".** / **it is equivalent to "...".**

2. The word/phrase "..."
   - seems **to be explained by** — the **previous/following** word/phrase "...", which means "...".

24. Describing allusions

1. What we have here / What we can see here — is
   - **an allusion** / **a comparison** / **a reference** — **to...**
   - **a parallel** — **with...**

2. This is a — distorted **image** — **of...**

3. This is a — **parody** / **pastiche** — **of...**

25. Expressing intentions

1. **By** — show**ing** this, / choos**ing** this character, / us**ing** this word,

2. **With** — this commercial, / this character, / this word,

→ the adman / the company / the film director / the journalist / the author

- **wants to** / **intends to** — **show** / **demonstrate** / **prove** / **suggest** / **indicate** — **that...**
- **makes** — the audience / the readers / the public / the clients / the viewers — **ø** — **realize** / **believe** / **understand** / **feel** — **that...**
- **wants** — the audience / the readers / the public / the clients / the viewers — **to** — **realize** / **believe** / **understand** / **feel** — **that...**

26. Expressing causality

Event or action → **As a result**, ... / **So**, ... → **Consequence**

Expressing cause

- This is **due to...**
- This **results from...**
- This is **caused by**
- Another **reason/cause** is...
- This is **explained by the fact that...**

Expressing consequence

- This **leads to...**
- This **results in...**
- This **causes** a...
- This is **one reason why...**
- This **explains why...**

27. Targeting (adverts)

1. Obviously, 2. Presumably, 3. It seems that 4. It looks as if	the **target** of this **advert** is this **commercial is aimed at** this **ad is directed to/toward(s)** this **campaign is meant to** reach	teenage girls. the élite. men and women. all walks of life.

28. Expressing purpose

Action → **Effect**

1.

The journalist The adman The company	**used** **chose**	this strategy this approach this image	**so as to** **in order to** **to**	obtain this effect. convey the idea that... create an impression of...

2.

The purpose of	this this movie this advert	**is to make**	you people viewers the audience	**believe** **feel** **think** **understand**	that...

3.

This This movie This advert	**is meant to make**	you people viewers the audience	**believe** **feel** **think** **understand**	that...

Interpretation

29. Appearance / Reality

From appearance...

1. **At first sight,** —
   - we are **under the impression** that...
   - it **seems** that...
   - it **looks as if...**
   - we **take it for granted** that...
   - we are **led to think** that...

...to reality

2. **But in fact, / actually,** —
   - we **realize** that...
   - we are **made to understand** that...
   - the writer / film director **takes great care to show** that...
   - we gradually **become aware** that...

30. Expressing paradox

1. **Although** / 2. **Even though** — this animal — looks small and fragile, it is an efficient predator.

3. **Despite** / 4. **In spite of** — **the fact that** — it looks small and fragile, this animal is an efficient predator.

5. It looks small and fragile. — **And yet,** / **However,** — this animal is an efficient predator.

6. **Granted,** this animal looks small and fragile. — **But still,** — it is an efficient predator.

31. Analysing symbols

What we have here is a(n)
This is a(n)

metaphor,
allegory,

— **in that** we have —

an object
a character

— **representing** / **symbolizing** — a concept.

The painting / The image / This detail / This montage / This photo / This animal	**represents** / **symbolizes** / **is a symbol of** / **stands for**	**ø**	beauty. / majesty/power. / wisdom. / peace.
		the	conflict between... / birth of... / death of... / development of...

Interpretation

32. Preventing / Enabling

Preventing

1. Security personnel — **prevented** — the journalists **from entering** the building.

Enabling

2. This — software / technology / equipment / strategy —
   - **enables to/allows** you **to** create all sorts of things.
   - **allows for** better performance and creativity.

33. Persuading

		Action	→	Effect	
1.	He	**made**	her	**leave**	the company. *(he forced her)*
2.	She	**got**	him	**to stop**	working for them. *(she persuaded him)*
3.	She	**talked**	him	**out of** / **into**	tak**ing** the job.
4.	He	**had**	his car	**repaired.**	*(by a garage mechanic)*
5.	Do not	**let**	them	**enter.**	
6.	Do not	**keep**	them	**waiting.**	

34. Concluding

As a conclusion,
To conclude,
Overall,

we can say that it seems that I would say that	the document this chapter this sequence this video this article	is **based on** **revolves around**	the **fact** the **notion** the **idea**	**that...**

35. Interacting

Asking for information

1. Er, excuse me, **could you tell me**
2. Excuse me, sir, **do you know**
3. Hey pal! **Any idea***

→

where you found this information?
how heavy the file is?
who's calling?
if there is...?
what...?

Making suggestions

1. **I suggest** tak**ing** the video first.
   I suggest that we take...
2. **Let's** check it out, **OK?***
3. **Why don't we**
4. **Why not**
5. **Shall we**

→ get out now?

6. **How about** leav**ing** now?
7. **Care for***
8. **Would you like**

→ a coke?

Accepting / Refusing

Fine with me.
I don't feel like it.

OK.
No, thanks.

Sounds great!*
I'd rather stay in.
No way!*

Good idea.
I don't think it's such a good idea.

A coke it is, then*.
I'm not too keen on the stuff*, I'm afraid.

Gaining time

1. **Er..., well, you see,... / you know,...**
2. **Well, it's like..., / it's sort of.../ it's kinda** strange, **but...***
3. **I'll tell you what...**
4. **Now that's a tricky question...**
5. **Now please bear with me** a second / a minute...
6. **Hold on now, let me put it in another way...** *(trying to reformulate)*
7. **Anyway, let's get back to** our subject now please...
8. **Mind you, / Actually, / As a matter of fact,...**
9. **What I'm trying to get at,** you see, is that...
10. **What I mean to say** is that... **/ in other words,...**

*(*This is oral language to be avoided in writing)*

36. Opinions

Stating opinions

1. **I can't help thinking**
2. **My belief is**
3. **Personally, I'd tend to think**
4. **Well, obviously, there's no doubt**
5. **As has been said, I think**
6. **Contrary to what has been said, I believe**

→ **that...**

7. **To my knowledge,** there is no such thing → **as...**

Modifying opinions

1. **Having said that,** → **I do believe that...** / **I also think that...**

2. **This depends on**
3. **This is a matter of**

→ **how you look at it.** / **how much... / how many...** / **who... / what... / where...** / **whether...**

4. **No matter** →
what you think, I'll keep saying that...
whose opinion it is, I think it's absurd.
how hard you try, you can't prove your point.
which way you look at it,...

37. Agreeing / Disagreeing

1. **Yes,** → **I agree,** / **I think this is true,**

2. **No,** → **I disagree,** / **I don't agree,** / **I don't think it's true,** / **I think this is wrong,** / **I think this is biased/unobjective,**

→ **in that** → when you read the text, / when you look at the picture, / when you watch the video closely, → you find that... / you observe that... / you understand that...

Personal reactions

38. Criticizing

1. I'm afraid I don't like it at all, / It really is a failure / a flop, — in that... / because...

2. I find this / I think it is — worrying, / disturbing, / distressing, / troubling, / risky, — in that... / because...

3. I find this is / I think it is — not — clear — enough.
   I find this is / I think it is — too — dangerous — .

4. I find there are — too few / too many — cases / examples / uncertainties — to be able to...

5. I find there is — too little / too much — information / opacity / transparency — in this to...

39. Praising

1. I like it a lot, — in that... / because...

2. I think it's — good, / great, / clear, / fine, / well done, — in that... / because...

3. I find there is — just the right amount of — examples. / evidence. / details. / anecdotes.

Personal reactions

40. Expressing preference

1. I **like** play**ing** **better than** work**ing**.
2. I **prefer** play**ing** **to** work**ing**.
3. I'**d rather** play **than** work.
4. I'**d rather** he **paid** cash.

41. Judging / Advising

Judging a particular event

1. He was / They were / We have been — **wrong** / **right** — to do this.

2. **Instead,** / **Instead of** do**ing** this, / **Rather than** do this, — he / they / we — **should have** done that.

Advising about any future actions

3. **Instead,** / **Instead of** do**ing** this, / **Rather than** do**ing** this, — he / they / you — **should** do that.

42. Accusing

Clearly, / To my mind, / My view is that,

1. they should **be blamed**
2. they **are to blame**
3. they should feel **responsible**

— **for** — do**ing**... / what happened.

4. they **were guilty**
5. he is **accused**
6. he **accused** them

— **of** — do**ing**...

7. he **felt guilty** — **about** — do**ing**...

43. If...

(The hypothesis is quite probable.)

1. **If** the boy — **does** this, — he — **will** / **may** — **get** into trouble.

(The hypothesis is not really envisaged.)

2. **If** the boy — **did** this, — he — **would** / **might** — **get** into trouble.

(In the end, the hypothesis has not come true.)

3. **If** the boy — **had done** this, — he — **would** / **might** — **have got** into trouble.

44. Remembering

Past

In those days,
In those times,
At that time,

1. we **used to** do...
2. we **would** do...
3. we **would** spend our time do**ing**...

Present

But now,
These days,
Nowadays,

4. we **no longer** do it.
5. we do**n't** do it **any more.**
6. it's **no longer** the case.
7. it's **not** that way **any more.**

45. Imagining

These days, we are **used to** doing...

But...

one day,
sooner or later,
within a decade or so,
in the near future,
in the short/long term,
tomorrow,
any time now,

we will **no longer** do it.
we wo**n't** do it **any more.**
it will **no longer** be possible.
it will **no longer** be that way.

46. Wishing / Regretting

Present

I wish / If only

1. she **came** more often.
2. she **played** the guitar.

(but she doesn't)

Future

I wish / If only

3. she **would play** the guitar. *(she knows how to but I don't think she will)*
4. I **could** go. *(but I'm not allowed to)*

Past

5. He **regrets having** done that.

I wish / If only

6. I **had** never **done** that.
7. she **had called** me.
8. I **could have left.**

(but it's too late now anyway)

Personal reactions

Précis grammatical

I. Le groupe nominal

I. Le groupe nominal

Les types de noms

1 Dénombrables et indénombrables

Noms dénombrables	• Peuvent se mettre au pluriel • Peuvent être précédés au singulier de ***a(n)*** et ***one*** et au pluriel de numéraux comme ***two, three...***, et de ***(how) many, (a) few...***	*a computer, two computers* *a car, one book, two tables* *how many flowers?* *(a) few cats*
Noms indénombrables singuliers	• Ne peuvent être précédés ni de ***a(n)***, ni de ***one***. • Sont suivis d'un verbe qui s'accorde au singulier. • Ne se mettent pas directement au pluriel : recours à un « dénombreur » comme ***piece(s) of***. • S'emploient avec ***(how) much, (a) little***.	*Ø advice* (des conseils) *Ø hair* (les cheveux) *My advice **is** good.* (Mes conseils sont bons.) *He gave me three **pieces of** advice.* (Il m'a donné trois conseils.) *You did not buy **much** fruit.* (Tu n'as pas acheté beaucoup de fruits.)
Noms indénombrables pluriels	• Sont suivis d'un verbe qui s'accorde au pluriel. • Ne peuvent pas être précédés directement ni de ***a(n)***, ni des numéraux ***one, two*** etc. • Sont souvent des objets doubles qui peuvent être comptés grâce à ***a pair of***.	*These stairs **are** dangerous.* (Cet escalier est dangereux.) *How many **pairs of** trousers do you have?* (Combien de pantalons as-tu ?) *I have four **pairs of** trousers.* (J'ai quatre pantalons.)

Les déterminants et les pronoms

2 L'article Ø

Ø + nom dénombrable au singulier	*Ø man / Ø woman* (l'homme / la femme en général)
Ø + nom dénombrable au pluriel	*Ø Schools are closed on Ø Sundays.*
Ø + nom indénombrable singulier	*We must protect Ø nature.*
Ø + nom indénombrable pluriel	*She has bought Ø trousers, not Ø dresses.*

3 L'article indéfini *a/an*

• ***a*** + nom dénombrable au singulier commençant par un son consonne :
a window / a university
/juː/

- *an* + nom dénombrable au singulier commençant par un son voyelle : *an airport / an hour* (le son <h> ne se prononce pas dans ce mot)
- *a(n)* correspond à peu près aux mêmes types d'emplois que l'article indéfini en français.

> ⚠ On utilise *a(n)* avant les noms de profession : *I am **a** teacher* (Je suis Ø professeur.)

4 L'article défini *the*

Prononciation

the = /ðə/ devant un son consonne, /ðiː/ devant un son voyelle.

Pour parler de notions connues, qui font partie de notre culture	*the* + nom au singulier	*the sun, the moon, the earth, the sky, the past, the present, the future...*
Pour parler de quelque chose en général	*the* + nom dénombrable au singulier	*the environment*
Pour parler de quelque chose de spécifique, connu de l'interlocuteur	*the* + nom au singulier ou au pluriel	*Where is the cat?* (= nous savons que nous avons un chat)

5 Les déterminants possessifs et le génitif déterminatif

Déterminants possessifs		
• mon/ma/mes	*my*	*my phone, my house, my cats*
• ton/ta/tes	*your*	*your phone, your house, your cats*
• son/sa/ses	*her* (possesseur féminin) *his* (possesseur masculin) *its* (possesseur neutre)	*her phone, her phones* *his phone, his phones* *its phone, its phones*
• notre/nos	*our*	*our phone, our house, our cats*
• votre/vos	*your*	*your phone, your house, your cats*
• leur/leurs	*their*	*their phone, their house, their cats*

Le génitif déterminatif	
Forme	Emplois (les mêmes qu'un déterminant possessif)
's	Après un nom au singulier : *The pupil's parents* (les parents de l'élève) *The pupil's* détermine le nom *parents* = *his parents* *Mary's parents* (les parents de Mary) *Mary's* détermine le nom *parents* = *her parents*
	Après un nom qui a un pluriel irrégulier, sans **s** : *The children's dog* (le chien des enfants) *The children's* détermine le nom *dog* = *their dog*
' (apostrophe seule)	Après un nom qui a un pluriel régulier : *My parents' car* (la voiture de mes parents) *My parents'* détermine le nom *car* = *their car*

6 Les pronoms possessifs

• le mien/la mienne/les miens /les miennes	*mine*
• le tien/la tienne/les tiens/les tiennes	*yours*
• le sien/la sienne/ les siens/les siennes	*hers* (possesseur féminin) *his* (possesseur masculin) *its* (possesseur neutre)
• le nôtre/la nôtre/les nôtres	*ours*
• le vôtre/la vôtre/les vôtres	*yours*
• le leur/la leur/les leurs	*theirs*

⚠ • leurs voitures → *their cars* (pas de *-s* au déterminant possessif *their)*
• les leurs → *theirs* (*-s* quand il s'agit du pronom possessif)

7 Les pronoms personnels

Un pronom personnel remplace un groupe nominal et permet d'éviter une répétition :
–> *The president and the Prime Minister arrived an hour ago,*
but they haven't said anything yet. Our reporter wants to meet them.

⚠ Soyez attentif à l'ordre des mots, différent du français :
*meet **them*** = **les** rencontrer (le pronom complément du verbe se place après le verbe, en anglais)

	Pronom personnel sujet	Pronom personnel complément
• 1re pers. du singulier	*I*	*me*
• 2e pers. du singulier	*you*	*you*
• 3e pers. du singulier	*she* (féminin) *he* (masculin) *it* (neutre)	*her* *him* *it*
• 1re pers. du pluriel	*we*	*us*
• 2e pers. du pluriel	*you*	*you*
• 3e pers. du pluriel	*they*	*them*

8 Les pronoms réfléchis, les pronoms réciproques

	Pronoms réfléchis	
	Singulier	Pluriel
• 1re personne	*myself*	*ourselves*
• 2e personne	*yourself*	*yourselves*
• 3e personne	*herself / himself / itself*	*themselves*

- Un pronom réfléchi renvoie à une personne déjà mentionnée.
- Le pronom réfléchi permet souvent de traduire les verbes pronominaux du français :

–> *Damn, I've cut **myself**.* (Zut, je **me** suis coupé !)

Mais de nombreux verbes pronominaux français se traduisent par un simple verbe, sans pronom réfléchi en anglais :

–> *He woke up early and dressed quickly.* (Il s'est réveillé tôt et il **s'**est habillé rapidement.)

- Ne confondez pas les pronoms réfléchis avec les pronoms réciproques *each other* et *one another* :

–> *Ron and Harry looked at **themselves** in the mirror.*
(= Ron regarde son propre reflet dans le miroir tandis que Harry regarde le sien à lui)

–> *Ron and Harry looked at **each other**.* (= Ron regarde Harry et réciproquement, Harry regarde Ron)

–> *The pupils were looking at **one another**.*
(= les élèves ne regardent pas leur propre reflet, ils se regardent les uns les autres, mutuellement)

9 Les déterminants et pronoms démonstratifs *(this/that)*

Pour parler de quelque chose de proche de l'énonciateur (physiquement ou mentalement)	*this* /ðɪs/ (singulier) *these* /ðiːz/ (pluriel)
Pour parler de quelque chose d'éloigné de l'énonciateur (physiquement ou mentalement)	*that* /ðæt/ (singulier) *those* /ðəʊz/ (pluriel)

10 Les déterminants et pronoms quantifieurs

Déterminants quantifieurs français	Déterminants quantifieurs anglais + noms dénombrables	Déterminants quantifieurs anglais + noms indénombrables	Pronoms quantifieurs
aucun / pas du tout de	*no books*	*no money*	*none* (pas du tout)
pas de	*not any books*	*not any money*	*not any* (pas du tout, pas un seul)
peu de	*few books*	*little money*	*little/few* (peu)
un peu de / quelques	*a few books*	*a little money*	*a little/a few* (un peu)
des / une certaine quantité de	*some books*	*some money*	*some* (quelques-uns)
beaucoup	*many books* *a lot of books*	*much money* *a lot of money*	*many/much/a lot* (beaucoup)
tout/tous/toutes	*all the books*	*all the money*	*all* (tous/tout/toutes)
chaque	*every book* *each book*	*every / each amount of money*	*each* (chaque, chacun)

Some

Some /səm/ s'emploie dans les phrases affirmatives *(a)* et dans les offres polies *(b)* pour renvoyer à une quantité indéfinie:

a. *I have **some** apples in my bag.*

b. *Would you like **some** tea?*

Prononciation

Some est accentué et se prononce /sʌm/ quand il est employé comme pronom *(c)* ou quand il renvoie à quelque chose ou quelqu'un qui n'est pas nommé précisément *(d)* :

c. *I have bought oranges. Would you like **some**?*

d. ***Some** teacher told her to stay there.*

Any

Any /ənɪ/ s'emploie dans les phrases négatives *(e)* et interrogatives *(f)* :

e. *There aren't **any** socks under my bed.*

f. *Did you buy **any** stamps yesterday?*

Prononciation

Any se prononce /enɪ/ quand il est utilisé comme pronom *(g)* et quand il signifie « n'importe lequel » *(h)*.

g. *"You should wear gloves."*
"I haven't got any"

h. *Any teacher knows that!*

All

⚠ Ne confondez pas *all* et *whole* :
He bought all the books (Il a acheté tous les livres.)
He read the whole book. (Il a lu tout le livre. = le livre en entier).

Most

- *Most* + nom au pluriel = la plupart de + groupe général.
  ***Most** children like Harry Potter.*
- *Most* + *of* + déterminant + nom au pluriel = la plupart de + groupe particulier.
  ***Most of** my pupils can speak three languages.*

Les adjectifs

En anglais les adjectifs sont invariables : ils ne s'accordent ni en genre ni en nombre.

11 Place et ordre des adjectifs

- Les adjectifs épithètes se placent entre le déterminant et le nom : *a blue car* (une voiture bleue)
- Dans un groupe nominal, quand il y a plusieurs adjectifs épithètes entre un déterminant et un nom, on place les adjectifs qui dépendent du point de vue du locuteur près du déterminant, et les adjectifs les plus objectifs près du nom. Pour retenir cet ordre, mémorisez le mot ATACOM.

Déterminant	Adjectif(s)						Nom
	Appréciation	Taille	Âge	Couleur	Origine	Matière	
a	*flashy*			*pink*	*American*		*car*
a	*handsome*	*tall*	*young*				*man*

12 Adjectifs de nationalité

- Les adjectifs de nationalité s'écrivent avec une majuscule en anglais, contrairement au français.
  -> *a French car* (une voiture française) -> *an English book* (un livre anglais)

- Les adjectifs de nationalité peuvent être employés comme noms pour désigner toute une nation :

Adjectif	Nom singulier	Nom pluriel
English (anglais) *British* (britannique)	*an Englishman* (un Anglais) *a Britishman* (un Britannique)	*the English* (les Anglais) *the British* (les Britanniques)

13 Adjectifs en *-ing* / *-ed*

⚠ Ne confondez pas les adjectifs en ***-ing*** et les adjectifs en ***-ed***.

*interest**ing*** (intéressant) — *interest**ed*** (intéressé)
*frighten**ing*** (effrayant) — *frighten**ed*** (effrayé)

14 Le comparatif

Comparatif de supériorité	***more*** + adj. long + ***than***	*Harry Potter is **more** famous **than** Heidi.*
	Adj. court + ***-er*** + ***than***	*Hermione is bright**er** **than** Ron.*
Comparatif d'égalité	***as... as***	*The film is **as** interesting **as** the book.*
Comparatif d'infériorité	*less... than*	*This detective story is **less** thrilling **than** I thought.* OR : *This detective story is not **as** thrilling **as** I thought.* (comparatif d'inégalité)

⚠
- Adjectifs courts = adjectifs d'une syllabe (***tall*** → ***taller***) ou de deux syllabes finissant par ***-er***, ***-y***, ***-le***, ***-ow*** (***narrow*** → ***narrower***)
- Les adjectifs finissant par une consonne + ***-y*** font leur comparatif en ***-ier*** : ***silly*** → ***sillier***.
- Les adjectifs d'une syllabe doublent leur consonne finale si elle est précédée d'une seule voyelle : ***big*** → ***bigger***

15 Le superlatif

Superlatif de supériorité	• ***the most*** + adj. long	*Hermione is the **most** intelligent pupil in the class.*
	• ***the*** + adj. court + ***-est***	*Hermione is the bright**est** pupil in the class.*
Superlatif d'infériorité	***the least*** + adj.	*Coyle is the **least** intelligent pupil.*

⚠
- Les adjectifs en ***-y*** font leur superlatif en ***-iest*** : *dirty* → *the dirt**iest***.
- Les adjectifs d'une syllabe doublent leur consonne finale si elle est précédée d'une seule voyelle : *big* → *the biggest*
- Les adjectifs *good* et *bad* ont des formes irrégulières au comparatif et au superlatif, de même que les adjectifs bon et mauvais en français :
  – *good, better* (meilleur), *the best* (le meilleur)
  – *bad, worse* (pire), *the worse* (le pire)

II. Le groupe verbal

Les auxiliaires

16 Be, have, do

Formation

	Be		*Have*		*Do*	
	présent	prétérit	présent	prétérit	présent	prétérit
I	*am / 'm*	*was*	*have*	*had / 'd*	*do*	*did*
you	*are / 're*	*were*	*have*	*had / 'd*	*do*	*did*
she / he / it	*is / 's*	*was*	*has*	*had / 'd*	*does*	*did*
we / you / they	*are / 're*	*were*	*have*	*had / 'd*	*do*	*did*
Participes passés	***been***		***had***		***done***	

Emplois

	Emploi comme verbe lexical	Emploi comme auxiliaire, pour aider à conjuguer un autre verbe
Be	*Harry Potter* ***is*** *a wizard.* *I* ***am*** *hungry.* (J'ai faim.) *He* ***is*** *thirty (years old).* (Il a trente ans.)	*What* ***were*** *you doing when he called you?*
Have	*Spiderman* ***has*** *very useful powers.*	***Have*** *you seen the new Star Wars?*
Do	*I* ***did*** *my best yesterday.*	*Where* ***did*** *you go last summer?*

Les temps et les aspects

17 Le présent simple

Formation

Forme affirmative	
I / you / we / they	***know***
she / he / it	***knows***

Phrase négative		
I / you / we / they	***do not / don't*** /dəʊnt/	***know***
she / he / it	***does not / doesn't***	***know***

Phrase interrogative		
Do	*I / you / we / they*	***know*** *that?*
Does /dəz/	*she / he / it*	***know*** *that?*

Emploi

Le présent simple s'emploie lorsqu'on veut simplement donner une information.

He usually gets up very early and works a lot.
(Il se lève généralement tôt et travaille beaucoup.)

18 Le présent en *BE + -ING*

Formation

	Phrase affirmative	
	Be au présent	+ V-*ING*
I	*am*	*waiting*
she / he / it	*is*	
we / you / they	*are*	

	Phrase négative	
	Be au présent + not	+ V-*ING*
I	*am not*	*waiting*
she / he / it	*is not / isn't*	
we / you / they	*are not / aren't* /ɑːnt/	

Emploi

Le présent en *BE + -ING* s'emploie lorsqu'on veut non pas simplement informer (ou demander une information) mais expliquer ou commenter **un fait présent** :

–> *"What the hell are you doing under the car?"* (« Mais que fais-tu donc sous la voiture ? »)
–> *"I'm looking for one of my earrings!"* (« Je cherche l'une de mes boucles d'oreille ! »)

19 Le prétérit simple

Formation

Phrases affirmatives	*I / you / she / he / it / we / they*	*succeeded* (verbe régulier) *fell asleep* (verbe irrégulier)	
Phrases négatives	*I / you / she / he / it / we / they*	*did not / didn't*	*succeed / fall asleep*
Phrases interrogatives	*Did*	*I / you / she / he / it / we / they*	*succeed / fall asleep*

⚠ *stay* + *-ED* = *stayed* pour les verbes réguliers.

Y + *-ED* = *IED* quand *Y* est précédé d'une **consonne** :
marry + *-ED* = *married*

Prononciation

-ED se prononce :

/t/ après *f*, *k*, *s*, *p*, et *sh*, *ch*, *th*, *gh* *(laughed)*

/id/ après *t* et *d* *(printed)*

/d/ dans les autres cas *(explained)*

Emplois

Pour parler du passé	On parle d'événements ou d'états passés, en rupture avec le moment présent. Le prétérit est le temps du récit, il est utilisé avec des circonstants de temps comme ***yesterday, last week, two years ago, in July.***	*Tim Berners-Lee **invented** the World Wide Web in 1989.* (Tim Berners-Lee **a inventé / inventa** le Web en 1989.) ⚠ Le prétérit traduit dans ce cas le passé composé français : a inventé = *invented* (et non ~~*has invented*~~ : il ne faut pas utiliser le présent en *HAVE -EN* pour parler d'événements datés, clairement situés dans le passé) *He **worked** in Switzerland at that time.* 
Pour parler de faits imaginaires	On parle de faits en rupture avec le réel.	• après ***if*** : *If I **had** a driving licence...* • après ***wish*** : *I wish I **lived** in London...* (Si seulement j'**habitais** à Londres...)

20 Le prétérit en *BE + -ING*

Formation

BE au prétérit + V-*ING*

Phrases affirmatives	*I / she / he / it*	*was*	*working*
	we / you / they	*were*	

Emplois

Le prétérit en *BE + -ING* est utilisé pour expliquer une action située dans le passé :
*–> Suddenly she started out. The phone **was ringing.***
(Le fait que le téléphone sonne explique son sursaut de surprise.)

21 Le *present perfect*

Formation

	Forme affirmative	
	Present perfect	*Present perfect* en ***BE + -ING***
	HAVE au présent + V au part. passé	*HAVE* au présent + *BE* au part. passé + V + *-ING*
I	*have / 've worked*	*have / 've been working*
she/he/it	***has / 's** worked*	***has / 's** been working*
we/you/they	*have / 've worked*	*have / 've been working*

Emplois

- Le ***present perfect*** (*HAVE* au présent + *V-EN*) est un temps du présent et il est utilisé pour parler d'un événement passé qui a des conséquences observables au moment présent.

–> *Look! He's been to the hairdresser's. I like his new haircut.*
(Regarde, il est allé chez le coiffeur. J'aime bien sa nouvelle coupe.)

On observe que ***He*** a une nouvelle coupe de cheveux : l'énonciateur voit au moment présent le résultat *(new cut)* d'une action passée *(go to the hairdresser's)*.

Passé ……………… Présent ………►

> ⚠
> - Le *present perfect* se traduit souvent par du passé composé en français.
> - Mais le passé composé se traduit par du *present perfect* seulement s'il y a un résultat observable au présent.
> - Dans tous les autres cas, il faut utiliser le prétérit pour traduire le passé composé :
>
> Il est allé chez le coiffeur. Ensuite, il a fait des courses et il a joué avec ses enfants.
> (passé composé)
> *He went to the hairdresser's. Then he did some shopping and played with his children.*
> (prétérit)

- Le ***present perfect*** en *BE* + *-ING* est principalement utilisé avec les prépositions ***since*** et ***for*** (voir **23**).

22 Le *past perfect*

Formation

	Forme affirmative	
	Past perfect	*Past perfect* en ***BE*** + ***-ING***
	HAVE au prétérit + V au part. passé	*HAVE* au prétérit + *BE* au part. passé + V + *-ING*
I *she/he/it* *we/you/they*	*had worked* Forme contractée : *'d worked*	*had been working* Forme contractée : *'d been working*

Emplois

- Le ***past perfect*** (*HAD* + *V-EN*) est utilisé pour marquer l'antériorité d'une action par rapport à un moment situé dans le passé.

–> *When the police arrived, the murderer* ***had already killed Tom***.

The murderer killed Tom. ……… The police arrived. ……… X Moment de parole ►

- Le ***past perfect*** en *BE* + *-ING* est principalement utilisé avec les prépositions ***since*** et ***for*** (voir **23**).

Les prépositions

23 *For / since / ago* : depuis / il y a

depuis	+ date ou événement passé	*since*	• Si on parle du présent : *He has known Mr Hill **since 1989**.* (caractéristique) (Il connaît M. Hill **depuis 1989**.) *She has been waiting for her son **since midnight**.* (activité) (Elle attend son fils **depuis minuit**.) • Si on parle du passé : *He had known Mr Hill **since 1989**.* (caractéristique) (Il connaissait M. Hill **depuis 1989**.) *She had been waiting for her son **since midnight**.* (activité) (Elle attendait son fils **depuis minuit**.)
depuis	+ durée	*for*	• Si on parle du présent : *He has known Mr. Hill **for two weeks**.* (caractéristique) (Elle connaît M. Hill **depuis deux semaines**.) *She has been waiting for her son **for ten minutes*** (activité) (Elle attend son fils **depuis dix minutes**). • Si on parle du passé : *He had known Mr. Hill **for two weeks**.* (Il connaissait M. Hill **depuis deux semaines**.) *She had been waiting for her son **for ten minutes**.* (Elle attendait son fils **depuis dix minutes**.)
Il y a	+ durée	*ago*	*He met her **three years ago**.* (Il l'a rencontrée **il y a trois ans**.)

⚠ Avec *for* et *since* dans le sens de « depuis », le verbe est obligatoirement :
- au présent ou au *past perfect* si on parle d'une caractéristique du sujet,
- au présent ou au *past perfect* en *BE* + *-ING* si on parle d'une activité du sujet.

24 *For et during* : pendant

pendant	*for* + durée plus ou moins quantifiable	*She stayed in the USA **for two months**.* (Elle a séjourné aux Etats-Unis **pendant deux mois**.)
	during + période de temps	*You will be able to talk **during the break**.* (Tu pourras parler **pendant la pause**.)

Les modaux et leurs substituts

Il existe principalement cinq auxiliaires modaux en anglais, qui permettent d'exprimer l'avis de l'énonciateur (= la personne qui parle) : ***can***, ***may***, ***must***, ***will*** et ***shall***.

Présent	*can*	*may*	*must*	*will*	*shall*
Prétérit	*could*	*might*		*would*	*should*

> ⚠ • Les auxiliaires modaux ont une forme identique à toutes les personnes du présent : pas de *-s* à la 3e personne du singulier !

- Les auxiliaires modaux sont suivis de la base verbale du verbe et jamais de l'infinitif :

–> *I* ***can speak*** *English.*

- On remplace dans certains cas les auxiliaires modaux ***can***, ***may***, ***must***, ***shall***, ***will*** par ***be able to***, ***have to***, ***be going to*** car il est impossible en anglais d'avoir deux auxiliaires modaux dans un même groupe verbal. On remplace donc l'un d'eux par son substitut :

–> *I* ***will be able to go*** *to the swimming-pool tomorrow.* (et non : *I ~~will can~~ go*)
(Je **pourrai aller** à la piscine demain.)

25 Must / Have to

Must	Forte probabilité, du point de vue de l'énonciateur	*He isn't in. He* ***must be shopping.*** (Il n'est pas chez lui. Il **doit être en train de faire des courses.**)
	Nécessité, du point de vue de l'énonciateur	*You* ***must work*** *more.* (**Il faut que tu travailles** plus./ Tu **dois travailler** plus.)
Have to	Obligation extérieure, objective	*He missed his bus and* ***had to call*** *a taxi.* (Il a raté son bus et **a dû (= a été obligé d') appeler** un taxi.) *I* ***have to get up*** *early tomorrow. I have an important appointment.* (Il **faut que je me lève** tôt. / Je **dois me lever** tôt.)

26 May / Might

May	Éventualité, possibilité	*It* ***may rain*** *tomorrow.* (Il **se peut qu'il pleuve** demain.)
	Permission	***May*** *I* ***borrow*** *your car tonight?* (**Puis**-je **emprunter** ta voiture ce soir ?) *You* ***may not smoke*** *in her house.* (Vous **n'avez pas la permission** de fumer dans sa maison.)
Might	Incertitude plus grande qu'avec *may*	*It* ***might rain*** *soon.* (Il **se pourrait qu'il pleuve** bientôt.)
	Possibilité, permission dans un contexte passé	*I asked her if I* ***might smoke*** *in her car.* (Je lui ai demandé si je **pouvais fumer** dans sa voiture.)

27 Can / Could / Be able to

Can	Possibilité / capacité présentes	***Can** you **drive** me to the station?* (**Peux**-tu me **conduire** à la gare? *I **can see** you! Stop hiding!* (verbe de perception) (Je te **vois.** Arrête de te cacher!)
Could	Possibilité, capacité hypothétiques	***Could** you **drive** me to the station?* (**Pourrais**-tu me **conduire** à la gare?)
	Possibilité / capacité passées	*He **couldn't help** you, he didn't know you were ill.* (Il **ne pouvait pas** t'aider, il ne savait pas que tu étais malade.) *I **couldn't see** a thing.* (verbe de perception) (Je **n'y voyais** rien.)
Be able to	Capacité	*The inspector **was able to find** the thief quickly.* (L'inspecteur **a pu / a réussi à trouver** le voleur rapidement.)

28 Will / Would / Be going to

Will	Pour parler de ce qui arrivera probablement dans le futur	*He **will go** to London next week.* (Il **ira** / Il **va aller** à Londres la semaine prochaine.)
	Pour exprimer la volonté du sujet	*He **won't go** to his sister's wedding.* (Il **refuse** d'aller au mariage de sa sœur.)
Would	Dans le discours indirect, pour rapporter des paroles parlant du futur ou de la volonté de quelqu'un	*He said he **would not go** to his sister's wedding.* (Il a dit qu'il **n'irait pas** au mariage de sa sœur.)
	Pour parler d'un futur hypothétique	*If I worked more, I **would have** better results.* (Si je travaillais plus, **j'aurais** de meilleurs résultats.)
	Pour parler d'une caractéristique du sujet	*When I was young, I **would play** football on Sundays.* (Quand j'étais jeune, je **jouais** au football le dimanche.)
Be going to	Pour annoncer un événement futur déjà en cours de préparation	*"Look at those big clouds! It's **going to rain**!."* (Regarde ces gros nuages! Il **va pleuvoir**.)

29 *Shall / Should / Ought to*

Shall	Pour prendre un engagement formel	*I* ***shall*** *do it.* (Je le **ferai.**) = Je m'y engage
	Pour demander un avis sur une action future	***Shall*** *I buy this DVD for David?* (**Est-ce que j'achète** ce DVD pour David ?) = qu'en penses-tu ?
Should	Pour donner des conseils	*He* ***should*** *call her.* (Il **devrait l'appeler.**)
	Pour faire des reproches	*You* ***should have*** *called me.* (Tu **aurais dû** m'**appeler.**)
Ought to	Pour indiquer, de manière objective, ce qu'il convient de faire	*You* ***ought to see*** *a doctor.* (Tu **devrais consulter** un médecin.) = C'est ce qu'il faut faire dans cette situation.

30 *Used to / Be used to*

used to + V	Permet de parler d'un état ou d'une habitude appartenant au passé et n'existant plus au moment présent	*There* ***used to*** *be a library here.* (**Autrefois**, ici, il y **avait** une bibliothèque.)
be ***used to*** + V *-ING*	Signifie « avoir l'habitude de »	*I am* ***used to getting*** *up early.* (J'ai l'habitude de me lever tôt.)

31 *Be likely to*

be likely to permet d'exprimer la probabilité : *He is likely to become our new president.*
(Il est vraisemblable / probable qu'il va devenir notre nouveau président.)

Les adverbes

L'adverbe permet de nuancer le sens d'un adjectif, d'un adverbe ou d'un verbe.

32 Règles et fonctions

Les adverbes de fréquence *always*, *never*, *sometimes*, *rarely*, *often* et *usually* se placent…	juste avant le verbe s'il est au présent ou au prétérit simple	*I **usually** go to bed at 10 pm.*
	après le premier auxiliaire	*She had **never** been to London!*
	après le verbe ***be*** quand il est suivi d'un adjectif attribut	*He is **often** sad.*
Les adverbes de modalité *certainly*, *perhaps*, *probably*, *clearly*, *obviously* se placent…	comme les adverbes de fréquence ou bien en tête de phrase	*I'll **probably / certainly** go to London tomorrow.* ***Perhaps** I'll go to London tomorrow.*
Les adverbes de manière *carefully*, *slowly*, *quietly* se placent…	comme les adverbes de fréquence ou bien après le verbe + son complément obligatoire	*He **carefully** opened the door.* *He opened the door **carefully**.*
Les adverbes de lieu et de temps *yesterday*, *tomorrow*, *today*, *here*, *there* se placent…	souvent en fin de phrase ou parfois en début	*How long have you been waiting **here**?* ***Tomorrow**, we'll go to London.*
Les adverbes de degré se placent…	juste avant l'adjectif ou l'adverbe qu'ils nuancent	*He was **very** sad.* *She spoke **too** quickly.*

Les types d'énoncés

33 Les énoncés affirmatifs, négatifs, interrogatifs et exclamatifs

Énoncés affirmatifs	Énoncés négatifs
He is German.	*He is not / isn't English.*
I like tea.	*I do not / don't like coffee.*
He called the police.	*He did not / didn't call his lawyer.*
She was playing football.	*She was not / wasn't playing the piano.*
The police have arrested the murderer.	*The police have not / haven't arrested the thief.*
You can warn the police.	*You cannot / can't warn the police.*

Énoncés interrogatifs	
Questions fermées (réponse par *yes* ou *no*) auxiliaire au présent ou au passé + sujet + verbe + complément(s)	**Questions ouvertes** **mot interrogatif** + auxiliaire au présent ou au passé + sujet + verbe + complément(s)
Do you like tea?	***What** do you drink in the morning?*
Did he call the police?	***Why** did he call the police?*
Was she playing football?	***Where** was she playing football?*
Have the police arrested the murderer?	***Who** have they arrested?*
Can they warn the police?	***How** can they warn the police?*

Dans les questions ouvertes portant sur l'identité du sujet, l'ordre des mots est :
mot interrogatif + verbe + complément(s)
***Who** called you at 3 a.m. last night?* (Qui t'a appelé la nuit dernière ?)

Principaux mots interrogatifs	
Who	***Who** are you?* (Qui êtes-vous ?)
What	***What** are you doing?* (Que fais-tu ?)
Which	***Which** do you prefer? The blue car or the red car?* (Laquelle préfères-tu ?)
Whose	***Whose** are those keys? / **Whose** keys are those?* (À qui sont ces clefs ?)
When	***When** are you leaving?* (Quand partez-vous ?)
Where	***Where** did he go last summer?* (Où est-il allé l'été dernier ?)
How	***How** did you find her address?* (Comment as-tu trouvé son adresse ?)
Why	***Why** are you crying?* (Pourquoi pleures-tu ?)
How far	***How far** is it from here?* (C'est à quelle distance d'ici ?)
How often	***How often** do you go to the dentist's?* (À quelle fréquence allez-vous chez le dentiste ?)

Énoncés exclamatifs		
What	***What*** + ***a***/***an*** + (adjectif) + nom dénombrable singulier	***What** an idiot!* ***What** a nice umbrella!*
	What + **Ø** + (adjectif) + nom dénombrable au pluriel	***What Ø** beautiful houses!*
	What + **Ø** + (adjectif) + nom indénombrable	***What Ø** awful weather!*
	Expressions figées	***What** a pity!* ***What** a shame!*
How	***How*** + adjectif	***How** cold it is today!*
	How + adverbe	***How** fast she was driving!*
	How + énoncé	***How** he missed her!*

So	*So* + adjectif ou adverbe	*Her dog is* ***so*** *intelligent! She speaks* ***so*** *fast!*
	So + quantifieur + nom	*She has* ***so much*** *money! He has* ***so many*** *cars!*
Such	*Such* + déterminant *a/an* + nom dénombrable singulier	*He is* ***such*** *a good doctor!*
	Such + déterminant *Ø* + nom dénombrable pluriel	*They're* ***such Ø*** *pleasant neighbours!*

34 Les énoncés au passif

Actif	Passif
L'actif est utilisé quand on s'intéresse à l'agent qui fait l'action.	Le passif est utilisé quand on s'intéresse plus à l'action en elle-même qu'à l'agent de cette action. Le passif est formé de l'auxiliaire *Be* conjugué et du participe passé du verbe. L'agent apparaît parfois sous la forme d'un complément d'agent introduit par la préposition *by*.
Prétérit simple *David Bowie released his new album 'Blackstar' in January 2016.*	Prétérit simple *'Blackstar' was released two days before David Bowie's death.*
Présent en *BE + ING* *Forecasters are warning motorists of the risk of frost and ice on roads.*	Présent en *BE + ING* *Motorists are being warned of the risk of frost and ice on roads.*
Prétérit en *BE + ING* *Forecasters were warning motorists of the risk of frost and ice on roads.*	Prétérit en *BE + ING* *Motorists were being warned of the risk of frost and ice on roads.*
Present perfect (en *HAVE -EN*) *A veterinarian has identified a new case of bird flu at a farm.*	*Present perfect* (en *HAVE -EN*) *A new case of bird flu has been identified at a farm (by a veterinarian).*
Past perfect (en *HAVE -EN*) *The police had made no arrests at that stage.*	*Past perfect* (en *HAVE -EN*) *No arrests had been made at that stage.*
Auxiliaire modal + BV *They may find something.*	Auxiliaire modal + BV *Something may be found.*

Les constructions verbales complexes

35 Les *phrasal verbs* (verbes + particule adverbiale)

- La particule adverbiale se met avant ou après le groupe nominal complément.
- La particule adverbiale se met toujours après le pronom complément.

get up	se lever	*I **get up** at 7.*
give up	abandonner	*She **gave up** her job last year. / She **gave** it **up**.*
put on	mettre	***Put on** your coat! / **Put** your coat **on**. / **Put** it **on**!*
throw away	jeter	*They **threw away** all the letters. / They **threw** them **away**.*
turn on	allumer	*She **turned on** the radio. / She **turned** the radio **on**. / She **turned** it **on**.*

36 Les verbes à construction prépositionnelle

Préposition en anglais	Autre préposition en français
*depend **on** something*	dépendre **de** quelque chose
*succeed **in** something*	réussir **à** quelque chose
*suffer **from** something*	souffrir **de** quelque chose
*think **about** something*	penser **à** quelque chose

Présence d'une préposition en anglais	Absence de préposition en français
*look **at** something*	regarder quelque chose
*listen **to** something*	écouter quelque chose
*ask **for** something*	demander quelque chose
*pay **for** something*	payer quelque chose

Absence de préposition en anglais	Présence d'une préposition en français
answer a question	répondre **à** une question
remember something/somebody	se souvenir **de** quelque chose / **de** quelqu'un
enter a room	entrer **dans** une pièce
lack something	manquer **de** quelque chose
play football	jouer **au** football
ask somebody something	demander quelque chose **à** quelqu'un

37 Les verbes suivis de l'infinitif ou du gérondif

Verbe + (GN) + *to V*	
want	*I **want** to read this book.* (Je veux lire ce livre.) *She **wants** me to work more.* (Elle veut que je travaille plus.)
need	*I **need** to talk to my father.* (J'ai besoin de parler à mon père.)
forget	*He **forgot** to wash the dish.* (Il a oublié de laver le plat.)
tell	*She **told** him to leave.* (Elle lui a dit de partir.)
ask	*He **asked** his brother to help him.* (Il a demandé à son frère de l'aider.)
advise	*She **advised** him to go abroad.* (Elle lui a conseillé de partir à l'étranger.)
decide	*He **decided** to stay at home.* (Il a décidé de rester chez lui.)
allow	*They **allowed** her to go to the cinema.* (Ils l'ont autorisée à aller au cinéma.)
encourage	*I **encouraged** her to call you.* (Je l'ai encouragée à t'appeler.)
agree	*He **agreed** to buy a new car.* (Il a consenti à acheter une nouvelle voiture.)
hope	*I **hoped** to see him today.* (J'espérais le voir aujourd'hui.)
fail	*We **failed** to meet yesterday.* (Nous n'avons pas réussi à nous voir hier.)
manage	*He **managed** to warn her in the evening.* (Il a réussi à la prévenir dans la soirée.)

Verbe + *V-ING* (= gérondif)	
avoid (éviter de)	*Our company should avoid doing business with that firm.* (Notre société devrait éviter de faire des affaires avec cette entreprise.)
consider (envisager de)	*I am considering buying a dog.* (J'envisage d'acheter un chien.)
enjoy (prendre plaisir à)	*She enjoys repairing cars.* (Elle aime beaucoup réparer les voitures.)
give up (cesser de)	*My mother gave up smoking three months ago.* (Ma mère a cessé de fumer il y a trois mois.)
like (aimer)	*They like skiiing.* (Ils aiment skier.)
love (adorer)	*I love eating chocolate.* (J'adore manger du chocolat.)
stop (arrêter de)	*Stop crying!* (Arrête de pleurer !)
suggest (suggérer de)	*He suggested meeting at the restaurant.* (Il a suggéré de se rencontrer au restaurant.)

38 Les traductions de « faire faire »

→ Relisez la YP 33 p. 224.

Les propositions subordonnées

39 Le discours indirect : rapporter les paroles de quelqu'un

Discours direct	Discours indirect
She said: "The president is waiting for Mr. Hill."	*She said that the president **was waiting** for Mr. Hill.*
"Where do you live?", he asked her.	*He asked her where she **lived**.*
"Are you Mr. Brown?", I asked him.	*I asked her if /whether he **was** Mr. Brown.*

Quand le verbe introducteur (*say*, *ask*...) est au passé, les verbes du discours rapporté doivent tous être mis au passé. Les pronoms *I* et *you*, utilisés au discours direct, deviennent, selon le cas, ***he*** ou ***she***, voire ***they***.

40 Le choix du pronom relatif

Relatives en *that*, *Ø*, *which*, *who(m)*		
That	antécédent animé ou inanimé	*The young man **that** Peter met at the station is Mr Hill's son.* (*that* est le complément du verbe *meet*) *The young man **that** talked to you at the party is Mr Hill's son.* (*that* est le sujet du verbe *talk*) *The vase **that** you broke yesterday was very expensive.* (*that* est le complément du verbe *break*) *The television **that** exploded last month was very old.* (*that* est le sujet du verbe *explode*)
Ø	antécédent animé ou inanimé	*The young man **Ø** Peter met at the station is Mr Hill's son.* (*Ø* est le complément du verbe *meet*) *The vase **Ø** you broke yesterday was very expensive.* (*that* est le complément du verbe *break*) Attention : *Ø* ne peut pas occuper la fonction de sujet
Which	antécédent inanimé	*This vase, **which** I bought in London, is very heavy.* (*which* est le complément du verbe *buy.*) *The bus, **which** was late, was driven by a very strange man.* (*which* est le sujet du verbe *be*)
Who / Whom	antécédent animé	*His brother, **whom** you met yesterday, is very pleasant.* (*whom* est le complément du verbe *meet*) *His brother, **who** spent two years in England, speaks English fluently.* (*who* est le sujet du verbe *spend*)

Traduire **ce que, ce qui, ce dont**		
What	***What** surprised her was the heat.* (**Ce qui** l'a surprise, c'est la chaleur.) ***What** I'm telling you about is a brand new system.* (**Ce dont** je te parle, c'est d'un tout nouveau système.)	***What*** renvoie à un élément visible dans la suite de la phrase.
Which	*She began shouting, **which** frightened him.* (Elle se mit à crier, **ce qui** l'effraya.) *Her son works in London, **which** she is very proud of.* (Son fils travaille à Londres, **ce dont** elle est très fière.)	***Which*** reprend ce qui précède dans la phrase.
All (that)	***All (that)** I want is a cup of tea.* (**Tout ce que** je veux c'est une tasse de thé !)	***All*** ou ***All that*** permet de traduire **tout ce que**

41 Les circonstancielles

Propositions circonstancielles	conjonctions	exemples
de but	***(in order) to*** pour	*He broke the window-pane **(in order) to** get into the room.* (Il a cassé la vitre pour entrer dans la pièce.)
	so that afin de	*He often left work early **so that** he could watch his favourite American series.* (Il finissait souvent son travail tôt afin de regarder sa série américaine préférée.)
	so as to pour, afin de	*He turned the radio off **so as to** listen to the birds.* (Il éteignit la radio pour écouter les oiseaux.)
de cause	***because*** parce que	*She took the bus **because** she was late.* (Elle a pris le bus parce qu'elle était en retard.)
	since puisque	***Since** you are so intelligent, find a solution!* (Puisque tu es si intelligent, trouve une solution !)
de concession	***(al)though*** bien que	***(Al)though** winter's coming, it is still warm.* (Bien que l'hiver approche, il fait encore chaud.)
de condition	***if*** si	***If** you had told me that before, I could have helped you.* (Si tu m'avais dit ça plus tôt, j'aurais pu t'aider.)
	unless à moins que si… ne… pas	*They will kill the child **unless** the parents give them money.* (Ils tueront l'enfant si les parents ne leur donnent pas d'argent.)
	provided à condition que	***Provided** you work hard, you'll pass your exam.* (Si tu travailles dur, tu réussiras ton examen.)
	as long as tant que	***As long as** he abides by the law, he won't get into trouble.* (Tant qu'il respectera la loi, il n'aura pas d'ennuis.)
de contraste	***whereas / while*** tandis que, alors que	*Kate is a Princess, **while/whereas** Elizabeth is the Queen.* (Kate est une princesse, tandis qu'Elizabeth est la Reine.)
de résultat	***so… that*** si… que	*He was **so** disappointed **that** he resigned.* (Il fut si déçu qu'il démissionna.)

de temps	***when*** quand	*He was cooking dinner **when** she arrived.* (Il préparait le diner quand elle est arrivée.)
	as soon as dès que	***As soon as** you arrive in London, give me a call.* (Dès que tu arriveras à Londres, appelle-moi.)
	before avant de / avant que	***Before** you buy a new car, check you have enough money!* (Avant d'acheter une nouvelle voiture, vérifie que tu as assez d'argent !)
	after après que	***After** he had met her, he understood why she was famous.* (Après qu'il l'eut rencontrée, il comprit pourquoi elle était célèbre.)
	while pendant que	*He woke up **while** she was watching television.* (Il s'est réveillé pendant qu'elle regardait la télévision.)
	till, until jusqu'à ce que	*They will wait **until/till** the elections are over.* (Ils attendront que les élections soient finies.)
	since depuis que	*I haven't seen her **since** she got married.* (Je ne l'ai pas vue depuis qu'elle s'est mariée.)

⚠ Dans les propositions subordonnées circonstancielles de temps (introduites par *when*, *as soon as*...), il est impossible d'employer l'auxiliaire modal *will* / *would* :

*When she **goes** to Paris, she will send you a postcard.*
(Quand elle ira à Paris, elle t'enverra une carte postale.)

Les dates

année	*in 1874 –> in eighteen seventy-four* *in 1915 –> in nineteen fifteen* *in 2000 –> in the year two thousand* *in 2001 –> in two thousand **and** one* *in 2013 –> in two thousand **and** thirteen / in twenty thirteen*
mois	*in January 2013* *in May*
jour	***on** June 19, 2007* • **En anglais britannique** - on écrit : jour/mois/année *19/06/07* ou *19(th) June 2007* ou *June 19, 2007* - on lit : *June the nineteenth, two thousand and seven* ou bien *The nineteenth of June, two thousand and seven* • **En anglais américain** - on écrit : mois/jour/année : *06/19/07* - on lit : *June nineteenth, two thousand and seven*

Les verbes irréguliers

Base verbale, Prétérit et participe passé sont identiques

Base verbale	Prétérit	Participe passé	Sens en français
bet	*bet*	*bet*	parier
cost	*cost*	*cost*	coûter, valoir
cut	*cut*	*cut*	couper
hit	*hit*	*hit*	frapper
hurt	*hurt*	*hurt*	blesser, vexer, faire mal
let	*let*	*let*	laisser, permettre / louer
put	*put*	*put*	mettre, poser
quit	*quit*	*quit*	quitter, abandonner
shut	*shut*	*shut*	fermer
split	*split*	*split*	séparer, se séparer
spread	*spread*	*spread*	étaler, étendre / se répandre
upset	*upset*	*upset*	bouleverser / renverser

Prétérit et participe passé sont identiques

bend	*bent*	*bent*	plier, se pencher
bring	*brought*	*brought*	apporter
build	*built*	*built*	construire, bâtir
burn	*burnt*	*burnt*	brûler
buy	*bought*	*bought*	acheter
catch	*caught*	*caught*	attraper, saisir
dream	*dreamt*	*dreamt*	rêver
feed	*fed*	*fed*	nourrir
feel	*felt*	*felt*	sentir, ressentir, se sentir / toucher
fight	*fought*	*fought*	se battre, combattre
find	*found*	*found*	trouver
get	*got*	*got*	obtenir / devenir
hang	*hung*	*hung*	pendre, suspendre
have	*had*	*had*	avoir, posséder
hear	*heard*	*heard*	entendre
hold	*held*	*held*	tenir
keep	*kept*	*kept*	garder
lay	*laid*	*laid*	poser, mettre
lead	*led*	*led*	mener
learn	*learnt*	*learnt*	apprendre
leave	*left*	*left*	partir / quitter
lend	*lent*	*lent*	prêter
light	*lit*	*lit*	éclairer, allumer
lose	*lost*	*lost*	perdre
make	*made*	*made*	faire, fabriquer
mean	*meant*	*meant*	signifier
meet	*met*	*met*	rencontrer
pay	*paid*	*paid*	payer
read	*read* /red/	*read* /red/	lire
say	*said* /sed/	*said* /sed/	dire
sell	*sold*	*sold*	vendre
send	*sent*	*sent*	envoyer
shine	*shone*	*shone*	briller
shoot	*shot*	*shot*	tirer un projectile
sit	*sat*	*sat*	être assis
sleep	*slept*	*slept*	dormir
smell	*smelt*	*smelt*	sentir (odeur)
spell	*spelt*	*spelt*	épeler
spend	*spent*	*spent*	dépenser / passer du temps
spoil	*spoilt*	*spoilt*	gâcher / gâter (enfant)
stand	*stood*	*stood*	se tenir debout
stick	*stuck*	*stuck*	coller
sweep	*swept*	*swept*	balayer

Base verbale	Prétérit	Participe passé	Sens en français
teach	*taught*	*taught*	enseigner
tell	*told*	*told*	dire, raconter
think	*thought*	*thought*	penser, réfléchir, croire
understand	*understood*	*understood*	comprendre
win	*won*	*won*	gagner

Base verbale, Prétérit et participe passé sont différents

awake	*awoke*	*awaken*	se réveiller
be	*was, were*	*been*	être
bear	*bore*	*borne*	porter, supporter
begin	*began*	*begun*	commencer
drink	*drank*	*drunk*	boire
bite	*bit*	*bitten*	mordre
blow	*blew*	*blown*	souffler
break	*broke*	*broken*	casser, briser, rompre
choose	*chose*	*chosen*	choisir
do	*did*	*done*	faire
draw	*drew*	*drawn*	dessiner / tirer
drive	*drove*	*driven*	conduire
eat	*ate*	*eaten*	manger
fall	*fell*	*fallen*	tomber
fly	*flew*	*flown*	voler
forbid	*forbade*	*forbidden*	interdire
forget	*forgot*	*forgotten*	oublier
forgive	*forgave*	*forgiven*	pardonner
freeze	*froze*	*frozen*	geler
give	*gave*	*given*	donner
go	*went*	*gone*	aller
grow	*grew*	*grown*	grandir, croître / faire pousser
hide	*hid*	*hidden*	cacher / se cacher
know	*knew*	*known*	savoir, connaître
lie	*lay*	*lain*	être allongé / être couché
ride	*rode*	*ridden*	monter à cheval, moto, vélo
ring	*rang*	*rung*	sonner
rise	*rose*	*risen*	s'élever / se lever
see	*saw*	*seen*	voir
shake	*shook*	*shaken*	secouer / trembler
show	*showed*	*shown*	montrer
sing	*sang*	*sung*	chanter
sink	*sank*	*sunk*	couler, sombrer / s'enfoncer
speak	*spoke*	*spoken*	parler
steal	*stole*	*stolen*	voler, dérober
swear	*swore*	*sworn*	jurer
swim	*swam*	*swum*	nager
take	*took*	*taken*	prendre
throw	*threw*	*thrown*	lancer, jeter
wake	*woke*	*woken*	réveiller
wear	*wore*	*worn*	porter (sur soi)
write	*wrote*	*written*	écrire

Base verbale et participe passé sont identiques

become	*became*	*become*	devenir
come	*came*	*come*	venir
run	*ran*	*run*	courir

Base verbale et Prétérit sont identiques

beat	*beat*	*beaten*	battre

Références iconographiques. Couv Jessica He ; **Couv** WE THE PEOPLE – Shepard Fairey “Defend Dignity” ; **3, 6, 91, 98** Collection Christophel © DNA Films / Film4 ; **3, 8, 10, 151, 167** Entertainment Pictures / Alamy Stock Photo ; **4, 13** Fer Gregory / Shutterstock ; **4, 33** TASOS KATOPODIS / GETTY IMAGES NORTH AMERICA / AFP ; **6, 49** Collection Christophel © Elizabeth Meriwether Pictures / American Nitwits ; **6, 63** Peter Hapak ; **6, 75** Julie Jacobson / ASSOCIATED PRESS ; **8, 125** Collection ChristopheL © Les films du fleuve / Why not Productions / Wild bunch ; **8, 135** Jewel SAMAD / AFP ; **8, 109** RODINA OLENA / Shutterstock ; **8, 109** Kuchina / Shutterstock ; **8, 109** Radek Sturgolewski / Shutterstock ; **8, 109** Victoria Chudinova / Shutterstock ; **10, 183** Manning Brothers ; **10, 183** Marchand Meffre ; **14, 139** CBW / Alamy Stock Photo ; **14 (b)** ROGERS ©2014 Reprinted by permission of ANDREWS MCMEEL SYNDICATION. All rights reserved. ; **14, 35, 97, 107, 112** deagreez / Adobe Stock ; **14 (h)** Felipe Sanchez / Adobe Stock ; **15 (c)** Andrew Twort / Alamy Stock Photo ; **15 (h)** theartofphoto / Adobe Stock ; **15 (b)** jes2uphoto / Adobe Stock ; **17 (d)** Photoshot / Getty Images ; **17, 121, 153** Pictorial Press Ltd / Alamy Stock Photo ; **18 (4)** © 2019 H.J. Heinz Foods UK Limited. All rights reserved. ; **18 (1)** “Think Different” is a trademark of Apple Inc. ; **18 (2)** McDonald’s France, Agences DDB Paris et TBWA Paris / EYEDEA ILLUSTRATION, Passerelles Productions, Guillaume Lebrun. ; **18 (3)** © 2019 Kentucky Fried Chicken. All rights reserved. ; **18 (5)** © 2019 Nike. All rights reserved. ; **18 (c)** Rose Carson / Shutterstock ; **19** focal point / Shutterstock ; **21 (h)** tharun15 / 123RF ; **21 (b)** Georgiy Pashin / Adobe Stock ; **21 (c)** WavebreakmediaMicro / Adobe Stock ; **23** © McHumor, Theresa McCracken ; **26** DR ; **27** Doug Chayka ; **28** Tom Curry Studio ; **29** Ian Bottle / Alamy Stock Photo ; **29** Tom Bachtell / Cartoon Collections ; **29** age fotostock / Alamy Stock Photo ; **31 (h)** WENN Rights Ltd / Alamy Stock Photo ; **31 (c)** Tom Toles ; **31 (b)** Kevin Siers ; **34 (1)** Museum of Hoaxes ; **34 (2)** Patti McConville / Alamy Stock Photo ; **34 (3)** Mayank Yadav / Alamy Stock Photo ; **35 (b)** 2019, FactCheck.org ; **35 (h)** 2019, CBS Group / CBS2 ; **35 (c)** 2019, CNN ; **36 (h)** 2019, Thinkthevote.com ; **36 (c)** naurisart ; **36 (b)** “Free Speech Conditions Apply” by FUKT. Newtown Grafitti ; **37** Artepics / Alamy Stock Photo ; **38 (h)** The Financial Times Limited 2019. All rights reserved. ; **38 (b)** Signe Wilkinson ; **38 (c)** Do Ra / Adobe Stock ; **39 (b)** International Federation of Library Associations and Institutions, 2019 ; **39 (h)** “How to teach kids to spot fake news”, Quartz, 03/01/2018 ; **41** Romolo Tavani / ShutterStock ; **43 (d)** Weekly World News, 05/03/1991 ; **43 (g)** saquizeta / Adobe Stock ; **45** Mark Lynch / Cartoonstock ; **46** Martin Shields / Alamy Stock Photo ; **47 (b)** Ian Dagnall / Alamy Stock Photo ; **47 (h)** Charles Beyl / Cartoon Stock ; **50** Collection Christophel © Zeppotron : NETFLIX ; **50 (c)** Jim Spellman / Getty Images ; **51** Essena O’Neill, DR ; **52 (h)** “This is Us”, Twentieth Century Fox, 2016. All rights reserved. ; **52 (bg)** Khosrork / Istock ; **52 (bd)** GlobalP / Istock ; **53 (h)** Previously TV ; **53, 70** Brad Pict / Adobe Stock ; **53 (3)** macrovector / 123RF ; **53 (2)** aurielaki / 123RF ; **53 (1)** Evgenii Naumov / 123RF ; **54, 55** Collection Christophel © Universal Pictures ; **54 (b)** Reproduced by permission of Historic England / English Heritage ; **55 (b)** Popperfoto / Gettyimages ; **56, 59** Collection ChristopheL © Left Bank Pictures / Netflix ; **56 (d)** © J.D. Dallet / AGE Fotostock ; **57 (b)** Vadym Drobot / Alamy Stock Photo ; **57, 76, 102** AF archive / Alamy Stock Photo ; **59 (d)** COLLECTION CHRISTOPHEL © HBO / Television 360 / Generator Entertainment / Bighead littlehead ; **59, 181** Collection Christophel © Zeppotron / Netflix ; **60** pantid123 / ShutterStock ; **61** Collection ChristpheL / Productions 20th Century Fox Television ; **62 (b)** NadinaS / ShutterStock ; **62 (h)** “In dystopian ‘Handmaid’s Tale,’ a warning for a new generation not to take rights for granted”, PBS NewsHour, 25/04/2017 ; **64** Joe Raedle / Getty Images ; **65** RHONA WISE / AFP ; **66** Gabriella Demczuk for TIME Magazine, 2019 ; **67** CNN, Cameron Kasky & Marco Rubio, 2019 ; **68** Win McNamee / Getty Images / AFP ; **69** Tribune Content Agency LLC / Alamy Stock Photo ; **70 (b)** Win McNamee/Getty Images/AFP ; **70 (h)** DR ; **71 (h)** Cover of the book GLIMMER OF HOPE by The March for our Lives Founders, copyright © 2018. Used by permission of Random House LLC. All rights reserved. ; **71 (b)** TARIK KIZILKAYA / Getty Images ; **73** Larry French / GETTY IMAGES NORTH AMERICA / AFP ; **76 (g)** Lakeshore entertainment / Screen gems / Sketch films ; **77 (1)** The Washington Post / Getty Images ; **77 (2)** MARIO TAMA / GETTY IMAGES NORTH AMERICA / AFP ; **79 (h)** Cover of the book GUN LOVE by Jennifer Clement, copyright © 2019 by Jennifer Clement. Vintage, an imprint of Random House LLC. All rights reserved. ; **79 (bg)** Cover of the book GUN LOVE by Jennifer Clement, copyright © 2018 by Jennifer Clement. Hogarth, an imprint of Random House LLC. All rights reserved. ; **79 (bd)** Cover of the book GUN LOVE by Jennifer Clement, copyright © 2018, published by Suhrkamp Verlag, Germany. All rights reserved. ; **80 (h)** Lambert / Getty Images ; **80 (b)** The Granger Collection / Alamy Stock Photo ; **80, 81** sirius_star / Adobe Stock ; **81 (h)** World History Archive / Alamy Stock Photo ; **81, 139** grzegorz knec / Alamy Stock Photo ; **81 (b)** Niday Picture Library / Alamy Stock Photo ; **82** “Trump Vows to Protect 2nd Amendment at NRA Conference”, NBC News, 20/05/2016 ; **83 (h)** Brazil Photo Press / Alamy Stock Photo ; **83 (b)** Stephanie Frey / Adobe Stock ; **85** Walt Handelsman ; **87 (b)** “Guns” by John Fewings, 2016 ; **87 (h)** © Rob Rogers, 2014 ; **88** Oleksiy Maksymenko Photography / Alamy Stock Photo ; **89 (h)** Cameron Cardow ; **89 (b)** COLLECTION CHRISTOPHEL © Rafran Cinematografica / Paramount ; **92, 101** “Next Generation Robots - Boston Dynamics, Asimo, Da Vinci, SoFi”, ColdFusion, 07/04/2018 ; **92 (h)** MicroSure ; **92 (h)** Matt Young / Stanford University ; **93 (1)** Frederic Osada and Teddy Seguin / Drassm ; **93 (3)** Kim Kulish / Getty Images ; **93 (2)** KIM DONG-JOO / AFP ; **94** “Virtual Assistant - powered by Artificial Intelligence”, Servion Global Solutions, 06/02/2017 ; **95 (h)** Collection Christophel © Annapurna Pictures ; **95 (d)** PictureLux / The Hollywood Archive / Alamy Stock Photo ; **95 (b)** Vasily Merkushev / Adobe Stock ; **96** Bantam Doubleday Dell, 1973 ; **97** Charles Brutlag / Shutterstock ; **99 (h)** DEA / G. NIMATALLAH / Getty Images ; **99, 101** Anton Gvozdikov / Alamy Stock Photo ; **99 (bd)** Maksim Grebeshkov / Alamy Stock Vector ; **101 (h)** Moviestore collection Ltd / Alamy Stock Photo ; **102 (h)** Timo Elliott ; **105** alluregraphicdesign / Pixabay ; **106, 164** pikselstock / Adobe Stock ; **107** COLLECTION CHRISTOPHEL © Kudos film and television / Endemol shine group / Matador film ; **110 (b)** Andy Watt ; **110 (h)** “Class” from THE FROST REPORT, BBC. ; **112 (h)** “From Middle Class Problems” by Benjamin Lee published by Square Peg. Reproduced by permission of The Random House Group Ltd. © 2014 ; **112 (b)** The Mash Report, BBC Two, 08/02/2018 ; **113 (b)** Collection ChristopheL © BBC / Little Britain Productions ; **113, 119** “The Catherine Tate Show” © 2006, Tiger Aspect Production ; **114 (bd)** Stills Press / Alamy Stock Photo ; **114 (bg)** Peter Nicholson / Cagle Cartoons ; **114 (h)** “‘Accentism’: New classism determines social status in UK”, Russia Today, 12/10/2014 ; **117 (h)** Tim P. Whitby / Getty Images ; **117 (b)** Glasshouse Images / Alamy Stock Photo ; **118** geogphotos / Alamy Stock Photo ; **119 (h)** DGLimages / Shutterstock ; **121 (b)** Collection Christophel © BBC 2011 ; **124 (h)** Kathy deWitt / Alamy Stock Photo ; **124 (b)** Charles Griffin ; **126 (g)** Anterovium / Adobe Stock ; **126 (c)** Ingo Friedrich / Adobe Stock ; **126** Sixteen films/Joss Barratt ; **127** Destina / Adobe Stock ; **127 (bd)** Tony Farrugia / Alamy Stock Photo ; **128 (b)** REUTERS/Roy Letkey ; **128 (h)** Martin Jenkinson / Alamy Stock Photo ; **129 (d)** nigel james / Alamy Stock Photo ; **129 (g)** “I, Daniel Blake wins Outstanding British Film | BAFTA Film Awards 2017”, BAFTA, 12/02/2017 ; **129 (b)** Benjamin LEFEBVRE / Adobe Stock ; **130 (b1)** Photocreo Bednarek / Adobe Stock ; **130 (h)** EnVogue_Photo / Alamy Stock Photo ; **130 (b2)** © AFP ; **130 (b3)** “PM asked about 17,000 patients in ambulances”, BBC News, 10/01/2018 ; **131 (b)** Nicky J Sims / Getty Images ; **133** ALBERTO PIZZOLI / AFP ; **136 (h)** Lightspring / Shutterstock ; **136 (b2)** R. Gino Santa Maria / Adobe Stock ; **136 (b4)** pixelrobot / Adobe Stock ; **136 (b1)** Public Domain. ; **136 (b3)** DR ; **137 (h)** “Documented: A film by an undocumented American”, Jose Antonio Vargas, CNN Films, 2014 ; **137, 187** ZUMA Press, Inc. / Alamy Stock Photo ; **138 (h)** CPC Collection / Alamy Stock Photo ; **138 (b)** UbjsP / Adobe Stock ; **139 (1)** Michael Zagaris / Getty Images ; **139 (5)** dehooks / IStock ; **139 (3)** RapidEye / IStock ; **140 (h)** Katie Hayes Luke for NPR. ; **140 (bc)** usa.gov, public domain. ; **140 (bg)** Robyn Beck / AFP ; **140 (b)** ALEX WONG / GETTY IMAGES NORTH AMERICA / AFP ; **141 (h)** Susan Walsh / Associated Press ; **141 (b)** GRANGER / GRANGER — All rights reserved. ; **141 (c)** Scott J. Ferrell / Congressional Quarterly / Alamy Stock Photo ; **142** Illustration by Arthur Hochstein for The Time Magazine, April 10 2006 ; **142** Marvin E. Newman / Getty Images ; **143 (h)** John W. Tomac for The New Yorker n°201707, February 19-20, 2017 ; **143 (b)** Vitezslav Valka / 123RF ; **143** White House Photo / Alamy Stock Photo ; **145, 165** Bob Daemmrich / Alamy Stock Photo ; **145 (d)** Collection Christophel © 2015 Disney Pixar ; **149 (b)** Lucas Jackson / Reuters ; **149 (b)** Image courtesy of Tereza Lee ; **152** bekkersara / Adobe Stock ; **154** New York Daily News Archive / Alamy Stock Photo ; **155 (b3)** gotpap/Bauer-Griffin / Getty Images ; **155 (b4)** Hyperstar / Alamy Stock Photo ; **155 (b5)** INTERFOTO / Alamy Stock Photo ; **155 (h)** Tim Mosenfelder / Getty Images ; **155 (b1)** Stanisic Vladimir / Adobe Stock ; **155 (b2)** Todd Buchanan ; **156** Glenn CHAPMAN / AFP ; **157 (b)** imageBROKER / Alamy Stock Photo ; **157 (h)** Lauren Fritschi, 2016 ; **158 (1)** realstockvector / Adobe Stock ; **158 (3)** MicroOne / Adobe Stock ; **158 (4)** T.Sander / Adobe Stock ; **158 (2)** Monkey Business / Adobe Stock ; **159 (b)** GMint / Istock ; **161** BFA / Alamy Stock Photo ; **161** Nate Beeler ; **163** Xuejun li / Adobe Stock ; **164, 24, 46, 88, 148, 180** Rohappy / IStock ; **168** Hulton Archive / Getty Images ; **169 (h)** “Flash Gordon”, serie TV 1955, Collection ChristopheL ; **169 (b)** Evan Agostini / AP / Sipa ; **170** COLLECTION CHRISTOPHEL © Paramount Television ; **171** White House Photo / Alamy ; **172 (h)** Wonderland Records ; **172 (b)** Reginald Haines / Getty Image ; **173 (h)** Front cover image from PHYSICS OF THE IMPOSSIBLE by Michio Kaku (Penguin Books, 2009). Copyright © Penguin Books, 2009. ; **173 (b)** N-Photo Magazine / Getty Images ; **174 (2)** ITAR-TASS News Agency / Alamy Stock Photo ; **174, 196** dpa picture alliance / Alamy Stock Photo ; **174 (4)** Liu Bolin Studio ; **175 (b)** Rido / Adobe Stock ; **175 (h)** edel-fotograffe / Istock ; **179** Sergey Nivens / Adobe Stock ; **181 (b)** mode_list / Adobe Stock ; **184 (b)** Danny Whitfield ; **184 (h)** Pure Michigan ; **185** Stephen McGee ; **186 (d)** Oldtimer / Alamy Stock Photo ; **186 (g)** PNC Collection / Alamy Stock Photo ; **186 (b)** Paul Fleet / Adobe Stock ; **187 (b)** “King : de Montgomery à Memphis”, Sydney Lumet, 1970 ; **187 (g)** “What Started the 1967 Detroit Riots? | History”, HISTORY, 26/02/2018 ; **188, 189 (b)** Jim West / Alamy Stock Photo ; **189 (c)** 2019, The Michigan Urban Farming Initiative (MUFI) ; **190 (b)** Jeff Kravitz / Getty Images ; **190 (h)** Camila José Vergara ; **191 (b)** pixelrobot / 123RF ; **191 (h)** Peter Mocsonoky / 123RF ; **193** © Detroit Urbex ; **195** Kristoffer Tripplaar / Alamy Stock Photo ; **196 (b)** Susan Montgomery / ShutterStock.

Références textes. 4, 25 Baloo -Rex May- / CartoonStock ; **16** “These Boots are Made for Walkin’”, written by Lee Hazelwood, arranged by Billy Strange, perfomed by Nancy Sinatra. 1965 © Hal Leonard Corporation ; **19** “‘The Real Thing’? The language of advertising slogans” by Charles Doyle, oxforddictionaries.com, 20/10/2011 ; **20** “Verbing” by Brian Bilston © 2016. Published by Picador, an imprint of Pan Macmillan. All rights reserved ; **26** Nineteen Eighty-Four by George Orwell (Copyright © George Orwell, 1949). Reproduced by permission of Bill Hamilton as the Literary Executor of the Estate of the Late Sonia Brownell Orwell. ; **27** “Trump’s Trashy “77-Word” Vocabulary Exemplifies Sly Intelligence” by Sarah Sloat, Inverse, 07/02/2017 ; **28** Shooting an Elephant and Other Essays by George Orwell (Copyright © George Orwell, 1946). Reproduced by permission of Bill Hamilton as the Literary Executor of the Estate of the Late Sonia Brownell Orwell. ; **40** “From The Encyclopedia of Alternative Facts” by Brian Bilston, 2017 ; **51 (b)** “Tripadvisor why did you ruin my life”, tripadvisor-warning.com, 06/03/2011 ; **51 (h)** “An 18-Year-Old Instagram Star Says Her “Perfect Life” Was Actually Making Her Miserable” by Stephanie McNeal, Buzzfeed.com, 02/11/2015 ; **52** “Why We Get Emotionally Attached To TV Shows” by Elizabeth Rodriguez, The Odyssey, 27/07/2015 ; **55** “The real life Downton Abbey: The true story of servants” by Adrian Lee, Express.co.uk, 25/09/2012 ; **64-69** Excerpt from the book GLIMMER OF HOPE by The March for our Lives Founders, copyright © 2018. Random House LLC. All rights reserved. ; **78** Excerpt from the book GUN LOVE by Jennifer Clement, copyright © 2018. Random House LLC. All rights reserved. ; **82** Extrait du discours de Donald Trump à la NRA Convention, mai 2018. ; **93 (h)** “The world’s first robot ‘super-microsurgery” was successful” by Mike Wehner, New York Post, 04/10/2017 ; **93 (b)** “Deep learning algorithm does as well as dermatologists in identifying skin cancer” by Taylor Kubota, Stanford News, 25/01/2017 ; **96** “Demon Seed” by Dean Koontz, 1973 ; **98** Alex Garland, NBC Universal, 2015 ; **100** “Alexa, What Is There to Know about Love?” by Brian Bilston, 22/07/2018 ; **110** “Britain now has 7 social classes - and working class is a dwindling breed” by Liam O’Brien, The Independent, 03/042013 ; **111** “No such thing as the British class system any more? That’s rich” by Paul Routledge, mirror.co.uk, 05/04/2013 ; **116** “Common People’”, produced by Chris Thomas, perfomed by PULP. 1995 © Universal Music © Bertelsmann Music Group © Kobalt Music Group ; **118** “Educating Rita” by Willy Russel, 1980. ; **128** “How Margaret Thatcher accidentally revived British cinema” by Jaime Weinman, Maclean’s, 09/04/2013 ; **137** “My Life as an Undocumented Immigrant” by Jose Antonio Vargas, The New York Times Magazine, 22/06/2011 ; **141** “Attorney General Jeff Sessions”, 05/09/2017, US Department of Justice, public domain. ; **142** “Refugees” by Brian Bilston, from “You Took The Last Bus Home” © Unbound, 2016 ; **152** “The Scarlet Letter”, Nathaniel Hawthorne, 1850 ; **154** “Analysis: More Apology, Mr. President, And Less Politics, Please” by Kathleen Hayden, AllPolitics (CNN), 18/08/1998 ; **156** “Dirty Laundry” written by Danny Kortchmar, written and performed by Don Henley, 1982. © Universal Music © Warner Music Group / Chappell Music ; **156 (d)** “Police Need Warrants for Driveway Searches, Supreme Court Rules” by Adam Liptak, The New York Times, 29/05/2018 ; **156 (g)** “Reality Check: Who’s right about constitutionality of stop-and-frisk?” by Steven A. Holmes, CNN Politics, 01/10/2016 ; **157** “A Message to our customers”, Apple Corps Ltd., 16/02/2016 ; **168, 169, 173** Excerpt from PHYSICS OF THE IMPOSSIBLE by Michio Kaku, copyright © 2008. Random House LLC. All rights reserved. ; **172** “The invisible Man” by H.G. Wells, 1897 ; **185** “Black Workers Hurt by Detroit’s Ills” by Mary M. Chapman, The New York Times, 29/12/2008 ; **186 (b)** “‘Detroit is basically broke’: cuts, cuts and cuts to follow bankruptcy filing” by Dominic Rushe, The Guardian, 19/07/2013 ; **186 (h)** “ENERGY CRISIS AIDED JAPANESE IMPORTS” by Nat Shulman, Wards Auto, 01/05/2000 ; **190** “Letter to Detroit” written and performed by Eminem, 2009.

Références vidéos. 15 Excerpt from “Birth of a Language”, The Adventure of English created by Melvyn Bragg, 2003, ITV. ; **31** “The Language of Politics” from Fry’s Planet Word, created by Stephen Fry © 2011, BBC Two / BBC HD ; **33** “‘Unpresidented’: Fake edition of Washington Post claims Trump resigned”, Washington Post, 16/01/2019 ; **39** “How to teach kids to spot fake news”, Quartz, 03/01/2018. ; **50** “Creator Charlie Brooker Explains… | Black Mirror: White Christmas”, Channel 4, 16/12/2014 ; **52** “This is Us” created by Dan Fogelman, Season 1, Episodes 1, 2 and 3. 2016 © Twentieth Century Fox. All rights reserved. ; **61** “What TV shows do you watch?”, Mark, ELLLO.org ; **63** “Alex Wind: ‘When Joan of Arc fought back English forces she was 17’”, CBS News, 24/03/2018 ; **92, 93** “Next Generation Robots - Boston Dynamics, Asimo, Da Vinci, SoFi”, ColdFusion, 07/04/2018 ; **93** “Say Hello to Waymo”, Waymo, 13/12/2016 ; **94** “Virtual Assistant - powered by Artificial Intelligence”, Servion Global Solutions, 06/02/2017 ; **97** “Amazon Echo shared Oregon family’s private audio Amazon confirms (CNET News)”, CNET, 25/05/2018 ; **110** “Class” from THE FROST REPORT, BBC. ; **112** “Posh People in Lidl - The Mash Report”, BBC Two, 26/09/2017 ; **113** “The Catherine Tate Show” © 2006, Tiger Aspect Production ; **114 (h)** “‘Accentism’: New classism determines social status in UK”, Russia Today, 12/10/2014 ; **114 (b)** “James McAvoy Addresses The ‘Class Ceiling’” from THE LATE SHOW WITH STEPHEN COLBERT, 26/05/2016 ; **126** Sixteen films ; **129** “I, Daniel Blake wins Outstanding British Film | BAFTA Film Awards 2017”, BAFTA, 12/02/2017 ; **130** “PMQs: Corbyn tells May to watch I Daniel Blake film”, BBC News, 02/11/2016 ; **138** Courtesy Barack Obama Presidential Library. ; **140** “What is DACA?”, CNN Business, 30/08/2017 ; **156** “White House Summit on Cybersecurity and Consumer Protection”, The White House, 13/02/2015, public domain. ; **167** Footage supplied by British Pathé. ; **183** Extrait de “Detroit, Ville sauvage” de Florent Tillon, 2010, Ego Productions. ; **184 (h)** “How Detroit Went From A Booming Metropolis To A Shrinking City | NBC Nightly News”, NBC NEWS, 19/12/2018 ; **184 (b)** “Motown: How It All Began | Oprah’s Master Class | Oprah Winfrey Network”, OWN, 16/06/2013 ; **187** “What Started the 1967 Detroit Riots? | History”, History, 26/02/2018 ; **188** “Detroit Matters | Craftsman & The Detroit Mower Gang” ; **189** “Can tiny houses save Detroit?”, Curbed, 01/03/2018.

Références audios. 18 “How To Create Amazing Slogans”, VIEW VAST, 17/04/2014 ; **23** “Watch Your Mouth” hosted by Shankar Vedantam for HIDDEN BRAIN, 12/07/2018 © 2018 NPR. All rights reserved. ; **36** “Censorship On Social Media” hosted by Lakshmi Singh for “All Things Considered”, 11/02/2018. Copyright © 2018 NPR. All rights reserved. ; **47** “Fact Checkers” hosted by Sandra Kanthal for The Why Factor © 13/11/2018 BBC World Service ; **62** “In dystopian ‘Handmaid’s Tale,’ a warning for a new generation not to take rights for granted”, PBS News Hour, 25/04/2017 ; **89** “Carrying Guns” hosted by Aasmah Mir, BBC World Service, 30/04/2018, ; **93** “Inside DARPA, The Pentagon Agency Whose Technology Has ‘Changed the World’” hosted by Terry Gross for “Fresh Air”, 28/03/2017. © 2017 WHYY. All rights reserved. ; **93** “Tech Experts Warn Of Artificial Intelligence Arms Race In Open Letter” hosted by Audie Cornish for “All Things Considered”, 28/07/2015. © 2015 NPR. All rights reserved ; **103** “Audrey Shafer: Why Frankenstein still holds a mirror to modern science”, Stanford Radio, 28/10/2017 ; **107** “Does Artificial Intelligence Need A Code Of Ethics?” hosted by Ray Suarez, WBUR, 09/01/2018 ; **124** “The Class Ceiling” Episode 1, hosted by Polly Toynbee, BBC Radio 4, 01/09/2011 ; **133** “I, Daniel Blake”, Film 2016, BBC, 27/10/2016 ; **140** “Nearly 9,000 DACA Teachers Face An Uncertain Future” by Claudio Sanchez, NPR, 29/01/2018 ; **147** “What is DACA?”, CNN Business, 30/08/2017 ; **149** “The Original DREAMer Recalls ‘All Pervasive’ Fear As An Undocumented Child” by Mary Louise Kelly © 2018 NPR. All rights reserved. ; **165** “Who’s Using The Data Mined From Students?” hosted by Melissa Block © 2014 NPR. All rights reserved. ; **181** “The Father Of The Internet Sees His Invention Reflected Back Through A ‘Black Mirror’” hosted by Steve Inskeep for All Tech Considered © 2018 NPR. All rights reserved. ; **196** “David Maraniss: ‘Once in a Great City: A Detroit Story’”, David Maraniss, 04/06/2015.

DR : malgré nos efforts, il nous a été impossible de joindre certains photographes ou leurs ayants droit, ainsi que les éditeurs ou leurs ayants droit pour certains documents, afin de sollciter l’autorisation de reproduction, mais nous avons naturellement réservé en notre comptabilité des droits usuels.